# THE AIR WAR
## THROUGH
## GERMAN EYES

*To all those who fought and suffered in the war in the skies over central Europe and specifically the men and women of RAF Bomber Command, whose sacrifice and courage I have come to greatly admire through the course of researching and writing this book.*

# THE AIR WAR THROUGH GERMAN EYES

## HOW THE LUFTWAFFE LOST THE SKIES OVER THE THIRD REICH

JONATHAN TRIGG

AMBERLEY

*Half-title page*: A twin-barrelled 128mm flak gun. These gigantic weapons sat atop concrete flak towers across Nazi Germany, including Hamburg and Berlin. (Author's collection)

*Title page*: B-17 'Blue Streak' goes down in flames over 'Murderous Merseburg'. There were no survivors. (Courtesy USAAF)

First published 2024

Amberley Publishing
The Hill, Stroud
Gloucestershire, GL5 4EP

www.amberley-books.com

Copyright © Jonathan Trigg, 2024

The right of Jonathan Trigg to be identified as the Author of this work has been asserted in accordance with the Copyright, Designs and Patents Act 1988.

ISBN 978 1 3981 1650 4 (hardback)
ISBN 978 1 3981 1651 1 (ebook)

British Library Cataloguing in Publication Data. A catalogue record for this book is available from the British Library.

1 2 3 4 5 6 7 8 9 10

Typesetting by SJmagic DESIGN SERVICES, India.
Printed in the UK.

# CONTENTS

# INTRODUCTION

The third of August 1914. Kaiser Wilhelm's Germany declares war on France. Across Europe hundreds of thousands of men report to their mustering depots and swap their best walking-out suits for military serge. The continent's railway systems surge into life; platforms are packed with men and equipment, lines are jammed with trains puffing and hissing their way to destinations chosen by the military mobilisation planners. In cities, towns and villages people gather to read the latest editions of the newspapers and swap rumours with friends and neighbours. Everywhere the talk is the same: WAR, WAR, WAR. The summer is hot, very hot, and if anyone does bother to look skywards, they see only a blazing sun in cloudless skies, beating down on baked cobbles and fields, especially in *la belle France*. That is until Sunday 30 August. On that day, high above Paris, a tiny machine less than ten metres long and made of little more than tubular steel and stretched canvas was about to change warfare – and history with it – forever.

There were no anti-aircraft batteries with serried rows of gun barrels pointed skywards, no fighter aircraft scrambling from nearby airfields, indeed the intruder's translucent wings made it almost invisible to the naked eye. Inside the weird contraption a begoggled pilot kept his wraith-like charge flying steady and straight, while the observer sitting behind him reached down into the footwell and picked up a 3 kg bomblet. Ensuring it was primed, the leather-clad crewman held it over the side, fins uppermost, and let it go. Plunging downwards, the bomblet sped to the ground, detonating as its nose hit the street below. The explosion shattered the peace on the Rue des Récollets, a few hundred metres south of the Gare de L'Est, startling Parisian passers-by and shattering windows. This first bomblet was swiftly followed by two more, one hitting the nearby Quai de Valmy and the third the adjoining Rue des Vinaigriers. The last one was the deadliest, wounding three civilians and killing an elderly lady.

The city authorities, already overwhelmed by the advent of war, banned any mention of the casualties in the press. The Germans, however, came back the following day, only this time the same aircraft dropped hundreds of rapidly printed news sheets proclaiming German victory at the front and calling on Paris to surrender! Without waiting for a formal response, the raider appeared the next day, switching back to bomblets and killing another Parisian and injuring sixteen more. A new era had begun. From now on, the bombing of an enemy's towns and cities, far from the frontline, was to become a feature of modern war.

Contrary to the once almost universally accepted view of 'lions led by donkeys', the speed with which both French and British generals reacted to this revolution in warfare was breathtaking. Only a matter of days after the latest bomblets fell on Paris the French formed a strategic bombing unit of their own – the *Groupe de Bombardment No. 1* – while Britain went one step further, its Royal Naval Air Service launching bombing missions against Germany a mere three weeks after the Paris raids. With admirable foresight, the Naval airmen were sent to attack the German Zeppelin bases at Cologne and Düsseldorf, in an attempt to forestall any possible airship attacks on Britain. Their endeavours were more successful than was hoped, with at least one giant Zeppelin completely destroyed and several others damaged. Two months later the British returned to Germany, bombing the Zeppelin factories in Friedrichshafen and Ludwigshafen.

For their part, the French were more reticent about bombing German towns, the vulnerability of so many of their own to reprisal raids being an understandable brake on their actions. So, on direct orders from Paris, French aircrews were restricted to hitting tactical targets: supply routes, ammunition dumps and German troop concentrations. Whether or not this self-imposed restriction worked or not is moot, the fact was that it was Britain that bore the brunt of German bombing during the war, suffering over a hundred raids that killed 1,414 people and wounded 3,416 more, prompting the then Prime Minister, David Lloyd George, to promise to repay Germany "with compound interest". True to his word, Lloyd George sanctioned the creation of the Independent Bombing Force in June 1918, hot on the heels of the establishment of the Royal Air Force two months earlier. By war's end, British aircraft had dropped 660 tons of bombs on Germany, more than twice the amount Berlin dropped on England.

Thereafter, the stipulations of the Versailles Treaty forbade Germany's new Weimar Republic from possessing any kind of air force, a situation which the German high command seemed to take as a personal challenge. Under a secret deal with the Soviet Union – another international outcast – a way round the treaty was found whereby a relatively small number of eager young men were sent to Lipetsk, deep in Soviet Russia on the banks of the River Voronezh, to train as pilots on modern aircraft and lay the groundwork for a future German military air force. One such pilot was Wolfgang Falck:

> Everything was done in civilian clothing ... we flew Dutch aircraft, with all the writing on the plane in Spanish ... All the flight mechanics were Russian, but the supervisor was German. We were kept separate from the Russians, we had our own barracks, our own officers' club and our own hangar. The Russians were very friendly, we had civilian friends and girlfriends too, but they weren't supposed to speak to us because we were evil capitalists!

Secrecy became less of an issue with Adolf Hitler's accession to the German chancellorship on 30 January 1933, as the Nazi leader began to re-order society along national socialist lines and prepare the Third Reich for the war he planned to start. A host of measures were brought in as a precaution against possible enemy air raids, including the replacement of the hitherto decentralized German fire service with a new, national service, run from Berlin and kitted out with standardized fire-fighting equipment. Civilian gliding clubs – already popular across the country – were brought under State control and Nazi propaganda encouraged thousands of young men to take to the skies. One such eager volunteer was the Silesian, Norbert Hannig, thrilled at the adventure of it all: "The launch crew disappeared beneath me as I soared over their heads. The bracing wires sang like a finely tuned violin … I was flying!" Hitler's motives weren't simply philanthropic though, as the 21-year-old Helmut-Peter Rix explained. "As soon as I was old enough I took up gliding, and with a C Class Glider Pilot's Licence I then joined the Luftwaffe," The Luftwaffe – Nazi Germany's *illegal* air force – was itself a shadow organisation, hiding in plain sight, until it was publicly acknowledged by Berlin on 26 February 1935.

From then on, this new branch of the German armed forces – the *Wehrmacht* – grew at an incredible rate, its expansion a much-heralded advert for the Third Reich's rearmament and Nazi Germany's drive to modernise. First blooded in the Spanish Civil War under its cover name of the Condor Legion, by the autumn of 1939 the Luftwaffe was regarded – and feared – as one of the most powerful aerial forces in the world. Over the next nine months or so, its performance in Poland, Scandinavia, France and the Low Countries seemed not only to confirm but enhance that view. In particular, its bombing of major cities such as Warsaw and Rotterdam – understandably denounced as *terror raids* – caused widespread horror and panic. However, even as the Luftwaffe rained down high explosive on cities across Europe, Berlin didn't consider Germany immune to retaliation and invested heavily in air defences, primarily by manufacturing a mass of anti-aircraft guns, *fliegerabwehrkanonen*, shortened and adopted around the world as *flak*. Before a single German soldier marched into Poland in September 1939 almost one thousand flak guns were positioned across Germany, and that number had almost doubled by the end of spring 1940. In truth, many of the Nazi hierarchy – and Hitler especially – were hugely fearful of enemy air raids on German cities leading to a collapse in civilian morale, and the subsequent evaporation of support for the Nazi regime.

To help allay fear of air attack among the populace, Hermann Goering – the Luftwaffe's supreme commander and the Third Reich's Minister for Air – went so far as declaring on 9 August 1939 that "We [the Nazis] will not expose the Ruhr to a single bomb dropped by enemy aircraft." Such a declaration was always going to be a hostage to fortune, although Berlin's worries regarding the supposed power of the French air force proved misplaced, as the diminutive French Chief of Air Staff, General Joseph Vuillemin, admitted in 1939 in a confidential letter to his boss at the Air Ministry, stating baldly that "the poor performance of our bombers will make it necessary to be cautious in our operations," although characteristically he laid the blame for the situation elsewhere. "The modern types [of bombers] built in France or expected from overseas have not yet been delivered to the units." Britain's Royal Air Force, however, was a different matter.

Separated from the Continent by the sea, Britain considered a capability to launch bombing raids on possible hostile nations as an essential part of its military armoury, and as Hitler plunged Europe into war London had almost 200 modern bombers – Hampdens and Wellingtons – ready to go. It also had around eighty or so Whitley bombers, although the ageing Whitley was rather acidly described by one RAF pilot as "not the sort of vehicle in which to pursue the King's enemies". Notwithstanding, all three types were capable of reaching Germany from their airfields in Britain, and RAF Bomber Command fully expected them to be deployed as such. However, political sensibilities initially restricted the bombers to attacking German shipping and naval bases, with German cities out of bounds. Then, a raid on 18 December 1939 on Germany's Heligoland Bight went badly wrong and convinced the RAF to abandon daylight bombing altogether and switch to night raids – a shift in policy that dictated Britain's bombing campaign for the rest of the war. However, Britain didn't possess the aircraft, infrastructure or trained manpower to carry out a night-time campaign, and subsequently spent the following two years making good these deficiencies, while at the same time keeping up some sort of offensive against Germany. The move to night operations also presaged an inevitable shift towards the area bombing of German cities, as the technology simply didn't exist to accurately hit military industrial targets in the dark.

The German reaction to Britain's determination to send bombers into its skies was two-fold; firstly, German society had to adjust to life under threat from the air. Early warning systems were put in place to send citizens scurrying into cellars, newly built shelters, or wherever else was deemed safe, and a nationwide civil defence programme was established to protect life and property as the Nazi Party increasingly took over every facet of German life. Secondly, the German military was forced to add home defence to its roster of duties, with the Luftwaffe taking the lead in creating a defensive umbrella that spread across Germany and right up to the North Sea coast of occupied Europe. While that meant a huge increase in the country's flak capability, it also included brand new radar chains and the establishment of a night fighter force. The Luftwaffe's fighter arm – the *Jagdwaffe* – had to learn on the job, as Johannes 'Macky' Steinhoff recalled in horror: "We tried flying our Bf 109s [Messerschmitt fighters] after dark, and when I say dark, I mean pitch-black – all German cities had black-outs ... it was a miracle that we survived at all."

By the beginning of 1942 the battle over Germany was finely balanced, only for two seismic events to irrevocably tip the scales. The first came in February when Arthur Harris took over as head of RAF Bomber Command. Eccentric and extremely affable in his personal life, at work he was determined and focused to the point of obsession. 'Butch', as he became known to his adoring crews, was messianic in his belief that Bomber Command could win the war by turning Germany into one gigantic battlefield. True to his word, he launched the first ever 1,000-bomber raid against Cologne in May that same year, reducing much of the city to ashes. Then, in early July, the first American-crewed Boeing B-17 bomber landed at RAF Polebrook in Northamptonshire. That first 'Flying Fortress' was followed by thousands more bombers and fighters, as President Roosevelt lived up to the agreement he had struck with Winston Churchill and Joseph Stalin to prioritize the defeat of Nazi Germany above that of Imperial Japan. This 'Germany First' policy precipitated a military build-up in Britain by the American Air Force of truly breathtaking scale. It also necessitated a strategic shift in German military priorities as the American entry to the air war over Germany meant the Reich would soon be subjected to a 24-hour a day struggle as the British bombed at night and the newcomers by day.

Wedded to the theory of precision daylight bombing, the Americans began a campaign designed to throttle vital German war industries, by turns hitting strategically important ball bearing factories, followed by any and every facet of German aircraft production. The sheer numbers of aircraft involved turned the skies over the Third Reich into the largest aerial battlefield the world has ever seen. Air armadas over a thousand strong collided head on as the Luftwaffe flung itself at the massive US bomber formations. Darkness brought no respite for the Germans as the RAF would then appear, pulverising city after city.

In three distinct battles, Harris waged war on Germany's industrial heartland in the Ruhr, on its capital, and on its second city, Hamburg. By the end of 1943 the German Luftwaffe was fighting for its life against the Anglo-American air forces, even as exhausted German civilians stumbled down into their air raid shelters night after night, normal life disintegrating around them. German civil society was transformed; women, traditionally circumscribed by Nazi policies that focused on their roles as mothers of the nation, were increasingly drafted into air defence roles, joining their children, who now manned anti-aircraft batteries where their teachers taught them makeshift lessons in between raids.

Germany wasn't helpless, though. Her previously underperforming aircraft industry was revolutionised by the Minister for Armaments Production, Albert Speer, and his sidekick in the Air Ministry Erhard Milch, leading to an all-time high in production. This enabled the head of the Luftwaffe's fighter force, Adolf 'Dolfo' Galland, to land a series of heavy blows on the Allied bombers, especially over the skies of Schweinfurt, and gave the Luftwaffe a desperately needed breathing space. At the same time, Allied high command dictated a change in strategy, with the bombers redirected in the spring of

1944 away from Germany to occupied France's transport system in preparation for the planned D-Day landings. But for the Luftwaffe the respite was a false dawn, the writing was already on the wall. A new aircraft had joined the US arsenal – the P-51 Mustang. Its arrival as a day fighter in the European Theatre of Operations (ETO) was akin in military terms to the arrival of the breech-loading rifle on a battlefield hitherto dominated by muzzle-loaders. Not only capable of escorting US bombers deep into Germany and back, the aircraft and its pilots were also a match in combat for anything the Germans could put in the sky.

With the bombers now free of their D-Day duties they turned back to Germany with a vengeance. After searching in vain for Nazi Germany's Achilles heel for the best part of eighteen months, the 'Bomber Barons', as the Anglo-American senior officers were nicknamed, had finally hit upon a new strategy – it was called the *Oil Plan*. It was based on the supposition that the Third Reich's lack of access to meaningful amounts of oil would necessitate the fanatical defence of any it did have. In an unconscious echo of the Luftwaffe's tactic in the early days of the Battle of Britain of forcing RAF Fighter Command into the air by attacking the country's vital radar stations and airfields, massed daylight American attacks on petroleum facilities effectively forced the Luftwaffe to do the same.

German day fighter losses were staggering, with an increasingly desperate Berlin forced to resort to emergency measures including the deployment of highly trained and technologically unsuitable night fighters into futile day defence sorties, thereby freeing the RAF to wreak ever more havoc on German cities. The Germans were now locked into a death spiral of their own making, as attrition among the day fighter force in particular ground the once-arrogant Luftwaffe into dust. For the mass of Nazi Germany's weary populace, the terror grew in tandem with resignation and apathy as the bombs continued to rain down. The twice-weekly newspaper the *Berliner Börsen-Zeitung* opined in late March 1944 that 'even the greatest terror gradually wears off or corresponding countermeasures are found.'

The final months of the war in 1945 were a world away from the early years of 1940, '41 and '42, with the Luftwaffe a spent force and the Anglo-Americans everywhere triumphant. However, Germany fought on, and young men continued to die in the skies and at the front, giving the Allies no choice but to carry on hitting her with everything they had until she finally yielded.

Many campaigns and battles of the Second World War have been the source of controversy ever since, few more so than the Allied bombing offensive against Nazi Germany. Almost uniquely, however, the campaign was a matter of fierce debate at the time, with British politicians and theologians questioning the morality of bombing civilians. Notably, there was no such outcry in the United States, the American policy of precision daylight bombing popularly viewed as meaning there was little, if any, 'collateral damage', to use the modern euphemism. The fact that this was untrue was conveniently disregarded. The counters to such criticism of Allied bombing strategy are many, not least that it was a bit rich to be condemned as *terrorflieger* (terror flyers) by a Nazi State that deliberately targeted civilians with massed aerial attacks when it suited them, as the citizens of Guernica, Warsaw, Rotterdam and Belgrade could attest, not forgetting the likes of Liverpool, Coventry and London. However, it is not the aim of this book to discuss the rights and wrongs of the policy of bombing, but rather to describe and explain how the Luftwaffe – the most powerful air force in the world at the advent of war in 1939-1940 – had been comprehensively defeated months before the war was actually over and, specifically, to do so through the medium of the human reality of the campaign from the German perspective.

At war's end, Germany was a country shattered; much of it a wasteland. For years the war had been mainly fought out of sight, its images broadcast on the weekly *Wochenshau* newsreel in cinemas, in newspapers and on the 'People's Receiver' radio – the *Volksempfänger*, but always *elsewhere* – not so the war in the air. By day, a German only had to look up to see the war, and by night they could hear the drone of the aircraft, the blaring of the air raid sirens and the thud of the bombs. Unlike every other battle Hitler's war forced on the world, the battle in Germany's skies was every German's war, and not a single man, woman or child could avoid it. This is their story.

# NOTES ON THE TEXT

Two seminal events in the air war over Germany during the Second World War were the bombing of Hamburg in July/August 1943, and the attacks on Dresden in February 1945. In writing about them I have relied extensively on Martin Middlebrook and Sinclair McKay's works respectively. Both have produced exceptional books on the topics and I would encourage those who would like to know more to read them. On a point of detail – and one I have been picked up on previously – I have used the designation 'Bf 109' throughout the book to describe the German Messerschmitt 109 fighter plane, except where an individual quoted uses the alternative 'Me 109' term. For those interested enough to want to understand more as to why the two different nomenclatures exist I can recommend pages 12-13 of Martin Caidin's excellent 1973 book, *Me 109*, written as part of the Pan/Ballantine Illustrated History of World War II series. Also, as is usual in this *Through German Eyes* series, I have used German ranks throughout, so *Captain* is *Hauptmann*, *Colonel* is *Oberst* etc. There is a table of comparative German and British/American air force ranks in Appendix A.

Luftwaffe unit sizes did not correspond to their British or American equivalents, hence a German *Staffel* was not the same size as an RAF squadron. A table of German tactical unit sizes is provided in Appendix B to help readers understand the overall establishments, although it should be remembered that due to losses etc, these numbers were fluid. Individual unit designations were a mixture of Arabic and Roman numerals, hence the third *Gruppe* of *Jagdgeschwader* 3 would be designated III./JG 3; however, I have chosen not to use that system except where a quoted individual has used it themselves. I apologise to any readers who think this is a 'dumbing down', but I feel the flow of the narrative is better without them. One more point where I may again have purists cursing is my use of the German unit term 'gruppe' and the English word 'group' as interchangeable depending on the context. As with the previous point on designation I have opted to do so to aid the narrative.

# ACKNOWLEDGEMENTS

I would like to thank my editor, Shaun Barrington at Amberley, for all his support and counsel, not just with this book, but over the many years we've worked together, and also Amberley's Managing Editor, Nikki Embery, who has always been a staunch supporter of my work – thank you.

As ever, my deepest gratitude goes to everyone who agreed to be interviewed in the preparation of this book, their courage in fighting a war several miles up in the air in what is a uniquely hostile environment for human beings has been humbling. As the late RAF officer Patrick Foss once wrote: "The bravest men, I found, were those who conquered their fear by facing it, not those who had no idea of the danger of what they did."

# I

## 1939–1940

# ROUND ONE TO GERMANY

Adolf Hitler was a worried man. In the summer of 1939, he believed Germany – *his* Germany – was surrounded by enemies determined to crush him and his National Socialist revolution. In particular, he feared an attack on the ground from the French Army – still regarded as the most powerful in Europe – and in the air from Great Britain's Royal Air Force. After all, the French had marched unopposed into the Ruhr in 1923, occupying Germany's industrial heartland and inflicting national humiliation. As for the British, they'd had an air force for twenty years, while Germany's own version – the *Luftwaffe* – had barely existed for four. The thought of British bombers raining down fire and destruction onto German cities gave the Nazi dictator sleepless nights – not from any sense of altruism, but rather from fear of an enraged population taking to the streets and ejecting Hitler and his acolytes in a bloody revolution.

Only ever really interested in land warfare, Hitler nevertheless wanted the defence of Germany from air attack to be given the highest priority. Signalling the importance he placed on the project, the Führer gave the task to none other than his own deputy and designated successor, Hermann Goering – "When I talk with Goering it's like a bath in steel for me, I feel fresh afterwards." Hitler admired the former First World War flying ace, particularly his ruthlessness and lack of scruples, facets of his character he was at pains to hide from most, preferring instead to present a picture of affability, as Marianne Hoppe, the wife of the Superintendent of the Prussian State theatre, recalled: "He was the kind of man who always picks up the cheque … a very jovial man, friendly." He was also renowned for the common touch, as the young German naval officer, Rolf Johannesson, saw for himself during Goering's visit to his ship in the Mediterranean in early 1939, when Goering disappeared one night to hand out handfuls of fresh strawberries to the sweating sailors below decks. Johannesson was taken aback, describing Goering as "impressive; big blue eyes, a round but pleasant face … he definitely possessed charisma."

The new appointment as air defence chief suited him very well indeed. A collector by nature, he was never happier than when garnering more titles and powers, continually seeking to add to his ever-growing portfolio. Already head of the Reich Air Protection League – the *Reichsluftschutzbund* or simply the RLB – in charge of air raid precautions across residential areas and for small businesses, Goering was now able to grant the RLB a much-coveted semi-autonomous status – the so-called *Körperschaft des öffentlichen Rechts* (literally Public Corporation) – and expand its remit considerably. By 1939, the RLB could boast 15 million members – it was 22 million by 1942, a quarter of the population – organised into individual *Blocke* (Blocks); described by Leipzig's police chief Wilhelm von Grolman as "the smallest and, at the same time, the most important unit in civil air defence".

Each Block comprised a single apartment building or several houses, with its own *Blockwächter* – block warden, along with designated fire fighters, messengers and so on. Uwe Köster, a teenaged member of the Hitler Youth and one such RLB messenger in Hamburg, explained his role: "When an alarm sounded, we had to be there and open the bunker with the *Blockwächter* … we had to then care for the children, give them milk and so on, if the alarm lasted a long time … and I also ran messages from one bunker to another if the telephones went dead."

While preparing the civilian population for the possibility of air raids, Goering was clear that the best way of combating the threat was to keep Germany's skies free from British bombers, and that job was to be done primarily by the men and guns of the flak force. German military thinking had long viewed anti-aircraft artillery as the best way of destroying enemy bombers, and heavy investment in the service meant that by the summer of 1939 there were already 197 heavy and 48 light flak batteries deployed across the country, each typically composed of four guns. A boost in production during the year would rapidly increase this number, with some 450 heavy batteries available by the summer of 1940. It was this mass of firepower that prompted Goering's declaration in August 1939 that the Ruhr wouldn't be exposed "to a single bomb dropped by enemy aircraft", although the showman in him meant he couldn't resist going further, and the following month he boasted that "Germany will not be subjected to a single bomb. If an enemy bomber reaches German soil, my name is not Hermann Goering; you can call me Meier!"

The Nazi invasion of Poland at the beginning of that same month did not result in the anticipated bombing offensive against German soil. In fact, the skies stayed serenely empty as Germany's *blitzkrieg* in the east was matched in the west by a *sitzkrieg*, as both France and Britain sat on their hands and waited to see what Berlin would do after defeating the gallant Poles.

At this stage in the war, both sides feared air raids against their civilian populations and were at pains not to provoke each other, even as German bombers pulverised Warsaw. The result was a self-imposed bombing embargo, with the Luftwaffe not launching any raids across the North Sea, and the RAF restricting itself to targeting German shipping and naval installations, such as the home of the *Kriegsmarine* (German navy) in Wilhelmshaven. Beginning only a few days after war was declared on 3 September, RAF Bomber Command began to send unescorted bombers on daytime patrols along the German coast, relying on its fleet of Vickers Wellingtons to do the heavy lifting.

The 'Wimpy' as it was affectionately nicknamed by its crews, was a firm favourite in the RAF's frontline squadrons: "It was an aircraft that took an enormous amount of punishment and came back … very forgiving."[1] This wasn't a sentiment shared across all Bomber Command's inventory, with the Fairey Battle light bomber viewed as "obsolete ... inclined to be temperamental ... underpowered", the Armstrong Whitworth Whitley medium bomber adjudged "as slow as a funeral",[2] and the Handley Page Hampden seen as "almost obsolescent ... very cramped". Indeed, so unpopular was the Hampden the crews dubbed it the "flying coffin".[3] With British bombers on the scene, the Luftwaffe had no option but to take to the air, but with little in the way of early warning systems the first clashes between the two air forces were hit and miss affairs. Hamstrung by the rudimentary bomb aiming technology of the time, British dogma dictated their aircraft attack during daylight and fly as low as possible in order to achieve accuracy, but this played right into the hands of a German defence based on anti-aircraft guns, which were visually aimed and therefore most effective during the day and at relatively low altitude.

Indeed, Berlin's emphasis on guns, rather than aircraft, as the primary means of tackling the bomber threat, seemed to be justified less than three months later on 14 December, when a force of Wellingtons tried to attack the German cruisers *Leipzig* and *Nürnberg* in the bay of their homeport at Wilhelmshaven. The two ships had already been damaged by torpedoes from the Royal Navy submarine HMS *Salmon*, but they had managed to limp home for repairs. Now the bombers went in to finish the job. The weather that day was filthy, forcing the Wellingtons to fly low under the cloud, exposing them to concentrated flak fire that broke up their formation and spoiled their aim. No hits were scored on the cruisers, and the sortie went from bad to worse when German Bf 109 fighters pounced on the homeward-bound bombers, shooting down six of them – half the force. The fighter commander *Oberstleutnant* Carl-Alfred Schumacher was delighted by his men's performance, explaining their success was because "[most of the] pilots were ex-naval men ... in that weather any normal unit would have made a mess of it and come home empty-handed." RAF Bomber Command, however, was undeterred.

The following Monday dawned bright and cold. The sea was covered by mist, but above it the sky was blue without a cloud in sight. Around noon, 24 Wimpys took off from their base in eastern England, climbed to their cruising height, and headed northeast towards Wilhelmshaven. There was nothing special about the mission, the crews had been briefed to patrol the coastline around the Heligoland Bight, the southern part of the bay near the mouth of the River Elbe, where German shipping tended to gather, and to attack any targets of opportunity. As usual, they had no fighter escort, Bomber Command firmly believing that being armed with six machine-guns arranged in three twin turrets was enough to protect each aircraft. As the bombers neared the German coast, two had to turn back with mechanical problems, leaving the remaining 22 to fly on "shoulder to shoulder like Cromwell's Ironsides", as an RAF report said later. A few minutes before two in the afternoon the Wellingtons were picked up by German naval radar, who then tried to alert their Luftwaffe brethren and get their fighters in the air. But there was a problem. The Navy's reporting chain was upwards within the Kriegsmarine, it wasn't sideways to a wholly different service arm, so the radar crew had no quick way of contacting the Luftwaffe.

The minutes ticked by, until a certain *Leutnant* Hermann Diehl in the radar station took it upon himself to call the nearby Jever fighter base on the telephone. The Luftwaffe response was dismissive: "You're plotting seagulls or there's interference on your set." The airmen simply refused to believe that the RAF would be so stupid as to fly unescorted in such perfect weather. Diehl tried again, calling another airfield, but the commanding officer there was away from the base at the time and nothing could be done in his absence. At this point, an official report did finally get through from the radar teams to the Luftwaffe, but it inaccurately claimed there were 44 bombers, and not just twenty-two.

Spurred into action at last, the Germans managed to get the grand total of six Bf 109s off the ground, led by *Oberleutnant* Johannes 'Macky' Steinhoff. Steinhoff had originally enlisted in the Kriegsmarine, before transferring to the newly created Luftwaffe to become one of the service's first 176 pilots, a cohort that would be forever known as 'Goering's cadets'. Believing they were going to be outnumbered by almost eight to one, Steinhoff and his men nevertheless tore straight into the Wellingtons, shrugging off the bombers' defensive fire and raking them with machine-gun and cannon fire. *Unteroffizier* Heilmayr was the first of the Bf 109 pilots to down a bomber, closely followed by Steinhoff himself who had already made one pass when he attacked again from the beam, firing into his chosen victim until it turned over and went down in flames. By now the German defences were fully alert, and more and more aircraft were speeding towards the battle. Eventually, no fewer than 44 Bf 109s and 110s would be involved in the fight.

To the disbelief of many of the German fighter pilots, the British crews seemed determined to stay on station, regardless of the by-now swarm of attackers. Those attackers – almost all in their first combat – tried out all manner of assaults on the loitering bombers; flying in from above, from a beam, head on, standing off and firing their cannon at maximum range, or getting in terrifyingly close and letting loose with everything they had. At last, the British seemed to understand the danger, with two Wellingtons breaking away and heading out to sea, hoping to escape their tormentors, only to be spotted by *Leutnant* Gustav Uellenbeck in his twin-engine Bf 110 heavy fighter. Warning his radio operator – *Unteroffizier* Dombrowski who was sitting behind with his back to him – Uellenbeck sped after the would-be escapees. Swiftly closing with the first, he "attacked the leader from the side and it caught fire. Then I opened fire on the second one from the left and above." This second bomber didn't catch fire and flew on, so Uellenbeck went in again and "opened up with everything. The bomber's nose fell off and it dived towards the sea." The German pilot had scored his first two successes, but had been over-eager, and for that there was a price to pay. "I was hit by a bullet between my neck and shoulder, the round went clean through me and hit my radio operator on the left wrist." Bleeding profusely, Uellenbeck managed to land safely back at base.

That same base had earlier seen its own drama as Bf 110 pilot Helmut Lent sat helpless in his cockpit as his armourer, Paul Mahle, crouched on the wing and struggled to fit a new ammunition drum. Screaming with frustration that he would miss the unfolding action in the sky, Lent refused to wait any longer and opened the throttles of his twin engine fighter and set off down the runway. Mahle had no option but to slide off the wing and hurl himself away from the trailing tail unit. Finally in the air, Lent desperately sought to gain height as he headed towards the Bight.

Approaching the bay, his radio operator, Walter Kubisch, spotted a pair of Wellingtons that had left the main formation and were heading west over the sandbanks. Diving to gain speed, Lent got close enough to loose off a burst at the lead aircraft, but it seemed to have no effect, so he tried again, this time attacking from behind. His 20mm nose cannons far outranged the Wellington tail gunner's .303-inch machine-guns and he was killed where he sat. Lent then switched his aim to one of the bomber's wings and thick black smoke began to belch out from the stricken aircraft. With the first bomber swiftly losing height, Lent swung away and went after the remaining Wellington, which had dropped down to wave height and was running for home. The German pilot mimicked his first success and attacked from astern. "Both the enemy's engines began burning brightly" and, with no room to manoeuvre, "the plane hit the water, the impact broke it apart and it sank." Meanwhile, Lent's first victim had ploughed into nearby Borkum island. A single crewman managed to get out before the aircraft burst into flames.

Unbelievably, Lent then attacked a third Wellington and shot it down. However, this one had already been badly damaged by *Oberstleutnant* Carl-Alfred Schumacher's Bf 109, and the bomber was credited to him rather than Lent. Later, Lent would write to his parents about the battle, describing how on viewing the last Wellington belly-land in the water and seeing the crew safely scramble out, his instinct was to drop them his own survival dinghy. "War is nonsensical, first you shoot them down and then you want to help them."

By now the British formation had splintered as the pilots desperately sought safety. Outnumbered more than two to one, the bombers fought back bravely, but their defensive armament was simply not enough to keep the fighters at bay, and Wellington after Wellington was shot from the sky. Macky Steinhoff attacked another one – which he claimed but was later disallowed – and then it was the turn of Gordon Gollob, an Austrian named for his American-Scottish godfather. Having already fought in Poland,

Gollob knew exactly what to do and got in close to his chosen target before opening up: "… my fire was accurate … after the attack I climbed to port and saw the Wellington pouring out smoke from its stern, curve off to the left and disappear downwards."

The battle had now been going on for more than twenty minutes and was finally coming to a close as the last Wellingtons made good their escape. But it hadn't finished quite yet. Late on the scene was Gustav Uellenbeck's commanding officer, *Hauptmann* Wolfgang Falck, who had been on patrol with his wingman – *katschmarek* was the Luftwaffe term – and now happened on the battle in its final stages. Chasing the remaining Wellingtons out over the sea, Falck managed to shoot one down, while his wingman – *Unteroffizier* Fresia – got two. Closing in on his second, Falck misjudged his attack and was hit by a full burst from the bomber's tail gunner. "My starboard engine jerked to a standstill. Petrol streamed out from the wing, and it was a miracle the plane didn't catch fire. As it was *Feldwebel* Waltz [his radio operator] and I were hard put to prevent our ammo going up. The whole cabin was full of smoke." Falck turned for home, praying to get back safely. Losing height and with smoke pouring out from his smashed starboard engine, his greatest fear was fire, and so he opened his tanks to dump fuel and fired off his remaining ammunition.

Running out of time, he decided to go for the airfield on the nearby island of Wangerooge, but when he tried to lower the landing gear it was stuck. The two crewmen desperately cranked a hand pump to lower the undercarriage even as the second engine failed. Remarkably, Falck somehow managed to land the fighter, bringing it to a screeching halt just yards from the control tower. Both men walked away, shaken but alive.

The battle was a bloody nose for RAF Bomber Command. Only ten of the 22 Wellingtons returned, and three of those made forced landings back in England and were subsequently written off. Fifty-seven aircrew lost their lives. The Germans didn't get off scot-free, no Bf 110s were destroyed, although several were badly damaged, but three Bf 109s were lost, and one pilot, *Oberleutnant* Johann Fuhrmann, died. Attacking a Wellington from astern, he was hit by return fire from the tail gunner. Seriously wounded, he crash landed in the sea, managed to get out of his cockpit but was unable to swim the hundred yards to the shore of nearby Spiekeroog island. He drowned.

By the standards of later battles in the skies over Europe, the fight at Heligoland Bight was a small skirmish, but its impact was far-reaching. Hitherto, Bomber Command was a firm believer that its aircraft could only accurately hit their targets by bombing during daylight, and that those same aircraft could operate without the need for fighter escorts. Heligoland Bight proved this was not the case, and that gave Bomber Command a dilemma; the RAF didn't have any fighters with the range to escort the bombers to Germany and back. At that stage in the war that meant Bomber Command would have to base its bombers – and fighter escorts - on French airfields close enough to the German border so they could be protected from fighter attack. This was unacceptable, and in any case the fall of France the following summer removed it as an option anyway. The outcome was a complete volte face by Bomber Command. Unescorted daylight bombing was abandoned. From now on, Britain's war over Germany would be prosecuted under the cover of darkness.

That decision was to have momentous consequences. For Britain it meant a complete rethink of its bombing strategy, and a total reorganisation of Bomber Command itself. For Germany it meant much the same regarding its fighter arm. In Britain's case Bomber Command didn't have the aircraft, the crews or the infrastructure to fight en masse at night, and it would take at least a year to put in place enough of each to start really taking the war to Germany. In the meantime, it would have to work with what it had.

In May 1940, Nazi Germany turned west and invaded France and the Low Countries. On the 14th the Luftwaffe bombed the Dutch city of Rotterdam, mangling its historic centre and killing 711 people. The following day the British War Cabinet authorised Bomber Command to cross the Rhine and attack industrial targets in the Ruhr. One hundred and eight bombers were involved – the highest number in the war so far – and as the bombs fell it was clear to the civilians below that Goering's idle boast back in September was exactly that – he was now rechristened 'Meier'.

Anti-aircraft fire was heavy though, as the co-pilot of an RAF Hampden acknowledged: "In the beginning one would hear distant bangs, and then you immediately saw a great explosion like a star exploding, some way away ... it was extremely good on the whole from the German point of view, very often quite accurate, nasty stuff." Direct attacks on cities, however, were still off limits, with both sides fearing the consequences.

That didn't mean the RAF's bombers sat idle, far from it, but their frailties were obvious and casualties mounted. Wolfgang Falck – the same Wolfgang Falck who had narrowly survived the Heligoland Bight battle – was baffled by British tactics: "We were surprised ... they didn't fly in a closed group. The majority of the British flew in an open formation and we were able to penetrate very easily and attack them from behind without being shot at by the others." However, not all the blame lay with the way the bombers operated. "The other major handicap for the RAF was that the aeroplanes were old." Regardless of tactics or the aircraft themselves, as losses increased the impact on crew morale was devastating. "We were drinking brandy for breakfast in the Sergeant's Mess ... half of us probably wouldn't have gone in the air if we'd been cold sober."[4]

The bomber might not have been winning in the air, but it was winning in Whitehall, with the new Prime Minister, Winston Churchill, declaring on 29 June that "overwhelming air attack on Germany [is] the sole decisive weapon in our hands." Two months later when German bombers mistakenly hit London, Churchill sent 81 RAF bombers out on the night of 25 August to drop their payloads on and around Tempelhof airport in Berlin in their first ever raid on the German capital. Another five attacks swiftly followed, but damage was minimal and there was little disruption to normal life. The real impact was on the Luftwaffe's ongoing *Luftschlacht um England*, the Battle of Britain, where a furious Adolf Hitler famously ordered a switch of focus from the RAF's vital airfields to the bombing of London instead. The change in strategy was decisive.

Before the war the accepted thinking was that the biplane was still the dominant design in terms of fighters – just as it was in the First World War – as it was far nimbler than a monoplane and, crucially, could turn inside a single-winged aircraft, get into a firing position and shoot down its opponent. However, down in Bavaria in southern Germany, a young aircraft designer called Wilhelm Messerschmitt was working with his colleague Walter Rethel on turning that orthodoxy on its head. What Messerschmitt and Rethel came up with in 1934 was an aircraft that would come to define Nazi Germany's fighter arm and become the second most-produced warplane in history – the Messerschmitt Bf 109. The 109 was a monoplane and freakishly quick for its day, reaching speeds of over 290 miles per hour in test flights the following year, when one of the pilots involved – Adolf Galland – made a note of "this fabulous but still highly secret Me 109 monoplane". Showcased to the Nazis, it was kept away from prying eyes until its big debut in July 1937 at the International Flying Meeting in Zurich, Switzerland. Revealed to the world, it was a phenomenon, with the media dubbing it simply 'sensational'.

A hawk among pigeons, the 109 made its fighting debut that same year, when Nazi Germany's contribution to General Francisco Franco's Nationalist rebellion in Spain – the so-called Condor Legion – used them to great effect against the Republican government's own biplanes. As the future German fighter ace, Günther Rall, commented: "The 109 was a dream, the *non plus ultra*. Of course, everyone wanted to fly it as soon as possible." Sleek, fast, and well-armed, the new fighter was used as the basis for a revolution in aerial tactics led by pilots such as the young Werner Mölders and his compatriot Adolf Galland. What they came up with was described by one British fighter pilot as

> … the perfect fighter formation … based on what they called the *Rotte* … some 200 yards separated a pair of fighters and the main responsibility of the number two or wingman, was to guard his leader from a quarter or an astern attack. Meanwhile the leader navigated his force and covered his wingman. The *Schwarme*, four fighters, simply consisted of two pairs … three *Schwarme* made up the *Staffel*.

The whole thing was flexible and manoeuvrable at a time when all other air forces employed rigid formations with pilots forever struggling to stay tight together. The Luftwaffe went all in with the 109, beginning the war in 1939 with around a thousand and using them as the mainstay of their fighter arm. As the RAF's Asher Lee said, "It was the 109 that was the aerial juggernaut, the spearhead of the Luftwaffe." However, no aircraft is perfect, and neither was the 109. Galland himself described it as "an aircraft with a distinct character which did not forgive many pilot errors," although at the same time he called it "the best fighter plane in the world". His main regret was that "it was put into mass production far too late. Had this stage been reached during the first two years of the war it would have given the Germans absolute supremacy in the air." This error was to cost Germany dear in the years to follow.

The Luftwaffe, then, was a service designed to fight in daylight, and, as such, wasn't equipped with any sort of specialist night fighting capability. However, the switch from day to night bombing by the British did not catch the Germans entirely unprepared. Senior figures in Luftwaffe high command – the *Oberkommando der Luftwaffe* (OKL) – believed it inevitable that German superiority in daylight operations would eventually force their opponents to turn to night attacks, and so a limited amount of effort had been put into preparing for such an outcome. A staffel equipped with Bf 109s was nominated for night operations and based at Greifswald in western Pomerania on the north German coast. Its first commander was none other than Macky Steinhoff. "I had been tasked with setting up Germany's first night fighter unit. I didn't have the slightest idea how to hunt down enemy aircraft in the dark."

The outbreak of war had signalled a major change in German nightlife, one which Steinhoff saw for himself, wincing at the recollection of his first attempt at night flight. "We tried flying our Bf 109s after dark, when I say dark, I mean pitch-black – all German cities had black outs ... it was a miracle that we survived at all."[5] Steinhoff wasn't alone in finding night flying extremely hazardous and the unit lost several aircraft and pilots to accidents, especially on landing and take-off when the risk was at its greatest.

However, the biggest issue for the new unit was how to find the enemy in the night-time sky. Without any radar to guide them, the pilots were limited to their own eyesight to find the enemy, a task that was incredibly difficult and led to huge frustration as they endured sortie after sortie without making any contact with the elusive bombers.

Knowing such efforts were fruitless, the staffel changed its tactics, flying in the evening twilight and just before dawn to use the ambient light as an aid. The switch brought a small change in fortune, with *Oberfeldwebel* Willi Schmale credited with the unit's first score – and the Luftwaffe's first night victory – when he shot down a British Fairey Battle flying a reconnaissance mission north of Crailsheim in southern Germany on 21 April 1940. Five days later, his fellow flier Hermann Förster followed suit, shooting down a Hampden bomber laying sea mines off the island of Sylt in the Baltic Sea.

OKL, however, wasn't hugely enamoured with Steinhoff's lack of success and he was called to a high-level meeting in Berlin with Goering and some of his cronies. Steinhoff remembered the absurdity of it all: "Everything in the room seemed to be of oversized medieval dimensions, the huge chandelier was made out of a wagon wheel, the chairs were covered in thick yellow leather." The centrepiece was Goering himself, "smoking a Virginia cigar" and lecturing them all "for at least half an hour" about what it was like as a pilot in World War One, "biplanes looping ... flying so close you could see the whites of the enemy's eyes". Steinhoff thought it ridiculous. "I simply said everything had changed, we flew at much higher altitudes and wore oxygen masks." Jaws dropped. No-one told the chief he was wrong, but Steinhoff wasn't finished, and he went on to tell Goering that night flying was impossible, as "we had no navigational aids and the cities were blacked out. The only way we could see the enemy was if he happened to be picked up by a searchlight." Goering – who had infamously prophesied before the war, "Night fighting! It will never come to that!" – waved away the young pilot's arguments and told him to "sit back down on your little rear end." Steinhoff fumed: "At that moment I realised he was obviously an amateur and I began to hate him." The meeting concluded with Steinhoff dismissed from night flying and sent back to his previous unit; an outcome he was more than happy with.

That wasn't the end of the Luftwaffe's infant night-fighting experiment, far from it. With British aircraft seemingly flying into Germany at will during the hours of darkness, Goering was acutely aware that not only was his personal prestige on the line, but that of his beloved air force too. The problem was not a simple one, as the Luftwaffe fighter controller Walter Knickmeier[6] summarised: "In the spring of 1940 when the first English bombers penetrated the north German coastal area [at night] … there were neither aircrews specially trained for night fighting, nor a ground organisation capable of giving the night fighters the navigational assistance to find the enemy." He was equally clear as to what he believed lay behind it all. "The Luftwaffe leadership was caught entirely unprepared and confusion was absolute."

Others also recognised the lack of leadership regarding Luftwaffe night operations. At Aalborg airbase in occupied Denmark, Wolfgang Falck had become so frustrated by the repeated RAF attacks on his unit that he had organised night-time patrols to protect the base from incoming bomber raids, and interceptor missions to follow the intruders out to sea and shoot them down on their way home. He even wrote a paper on his operations and circulated it within the senior ranks of the Luftwaffe.

Falck's initiative didn't go unnoticed, and in May he was summoned to a hotel in Wassenaar, near the Hague in the Netherlands, to a conference of Luftwaffe top brass presided over by Goering himself. Once there, Goering not only announced the creation of a new night fighter arm within the Luftwaffe – the *Nachtjagd* (Night hunters) – but to Falck's astonishment, he was proclaimed as the commander of said unit. The only problem was that the Nachtjagd didn't actually exist at the time. However, following his sudden elevation, he was introduced in late June to his new boss, *Oberst* Josef Kammhuber, who had just been released from a French prisoner-of-war camp, and together the two men set about making their appointments a reality. Their new unit, *Nachtjagdgeschwader* 1 – NJG 1, Night Fighter Geschwader 1, was operational by the end of July 1940. The new *geschwader* – a geschwader being the basic Luftwaffe unit large enough to operate independently and composed of three or four *Gruppen* (Groups), each usually containing three Staffeln – was ad hoc to say the least.

Falck brought his own Bf 110 staffel with him, and most of Macky Steinhoff's former night pilots were reassigned and tasked with converting to the 110 heavy fighter. The Bf 110 was chosen for no other reason than it had a much greater range than the Bf 109 and could therefore stay airborne for longer periods, and as it had a second crewman on board it was thought that he could navigate as well as operate the radio and therefore leave the pilot free to concentrate on the tricky job of flying at night. The 110 was far from perfect though, as Heinz Philip realised: "We didn't have any planes specifically for night fighting, so at first the Me 110 was equipped and put into operation as a night fighter, but it couldn't fly for long enough and didn't carry enough guns." Philip himself was a crewman on the Junkers Ju 88 medium bomber:

> In order to carry more weapons the Ju 88 was used. Trials with other planes were made but they were ineffective. We didn't carry bombs, in our bomb bay they put an additional fuel tank so we could keep flying for hours. I sat at the guns on the Ju 88. There were four 2cm guns at the front and the magazines were in a position so I could remove them when they were empty and replace them with fresh ones.[7]

The Junkers was a popular choice with its Luftwaffe crew. "You felt as comfortable [in it] as though you were at home by the fireplace." In all, three staffeln of Ju 88s were allocated to NJG 1, along with a number of Dornier Do 17 medium bombers, nicknamed 'the Flying Pencil' by the British due to its slender airframe. The Do 17 was already obsolete at that early stage of the war, but was thought better than nothing, and NJG 1 needed all the help it could get.

As it was, NJG 1 didn't have long to wait before its first success. The Germans had been trialling a new innovation against the British night raids that involved placing a number of flak and *Scheinwerferregimenter*, searchlight regiments, in a line, the *Helle*

*Nachtjagdsriegel* – illuminated night fighting barrier – around anticipated targets. Fighters would then patrol the area and when an enemy bomber was illuminated by the searchlights they could attack visually. They christened it *Helle Nachtjagd*, *Henaja* for short – bright light night fighting, and in the early hours of 20 July NJG 1 got its chance to try out the new tactic. Earlier that night *Oberleutnant* Werner Streib and his radio operator, *Gefreiter* Lingen, had taken off from Gütersloh in western Germany in their Bf 110. Reaching their patrol height, they took up station over the city of Gelsenkirchen in the centre of the Ruhr. Searchlights were probing the sky and there was just enough light for Streib to spot something about three hundred yards to starboard and a little below him. Turning towards it, the young German sought to get closer when Lingen cried out, "It's one of ours, a 110!" A similar mistake had been made by another crew on an earlier mission, and they had ended up shooting down and killing their fellow fliers. But Streib wasn't sure, so in he went, creeping ever closer until he was almost within touching distance of the aircraft's wingtip. At that moment he saw a gun turret and an RAF roundel – it was a British bomber.

"I never saw an enemy plane so close and clear. Not wanting to be shot point-blank by its rear gunner, I darted away in a 90 degree turn to starboard." It was a Whitley with twin tail fins just like the Bf 110, hence Lingen's confusion. Slowing down to let the bomber move away, he positioned himself behind it and went in for an attack from astern. But he had been spotted, and when he was about 250 yards away the rear gunner opened fire. Streib ignored it, letting fly with two short bursts of cannon and machine-gun fire. "His starboard engine was burning … Two dots detached themselves and two parachutes opened and disappeared into the night." Abandoned by some of her surviving crew, the stricken aircraft was doomed, even as the pilot fought to save her. "The bomber turned and tried to get away … I attacked again, aiming at the port engine and wing … Two more bursts and engine and wing immediately blazed up." The Whitley managed to hold its course for another few minutes, then suddenly turned over and dived, hitting the ground and exploding in a flash of fuel and bombs. Werner Streib was officially credited with the first ever *Henaja* victory.

Two nights later he scored again, closely followed by successes for his fellow night fighter pilots *Oberleutnant* Walter Ehle and *Oberfeldwebel* Paul Gildner, but bomber sightings were few and far between as the short summer nights kept most of Bomber Command on the ground. It was only with the arrival of autumn that the number of raids began to increase and once more it was Streib who made the running, shooting down no fewer than three Wellingtons inside a frenetic 40 minutes on the night of 1 October, in what was NJG 1's most successful sortie to date.

The onset of autumn coincided with a fresh initiative on the ground in Germany, with the roll out of the new *Führer-Sofortprogramm* (Führer Emergency Programme) to build 6,000 air raid bunkers across 92 German cities for civilians and essential personnel. Intended to be the largest public works programme the Nazis had ever undertaken, it required the lion's share of the output from the German concrete industry, and even a re-design of railway timetables across the country. The programme was a good start in providing safe havens for the population, but it would need to be repeated several times over to cover the whole country, and there wasn't the appetite for such a commitment. After all, only Britain was still resisting in the West, and the Nazis were now firmly focused on the east and the Soviet Union. The result was a lack of manpower and materials dedicated to the shelter programme, which continued in a rather desultory fashion into the new year.

The end of 1940 saw the Luftwaffe on top in the battle over Germany. RAF Bomber Command had lost 810 aircraft, and casualties among its trained crews were severe. Most of its aircraft types had been found wanting and it had been forced to abandon daylight bombing. The difficulties in switching to a nocturnal campaign were mammoth, and Bomber Command realised it was not equipped or prepared to fight at night, but nevertheless it had continued to attack, the bravery of the air crews pushing the Germans into a response. That response had been pretty haphazard, but in Wolfgang Falck and Josef Kammhuber, Luftwaffe high command had accidentally stumbled on two men who would go on to define and dominate Germany's night fighting operations for the next three years.

# 2

# 1941

# STALEMATE

"When *Barbarossa* commences the world will hold its breath..."
This was Adolf Hitler's declaration on his longed-for invasion of
the Soviet Union in June 1941. For the Nazi dictator *Barbarossa*
was what his national socialist revolution was all about; the
destruction of communism and its masters in international Jewry,
and the establishment of a German Empire in the east that would
provide the *lebensraum* – living space – and resources to sustain
the Aryan race for a thousand years. The enemy the Germans faced
in the East possessed the largest long-range strategic bomber force
in the world at that time, but in the course of a single summer,
in what the senior Luftwaffe general Albert Kesselring dubbed
the *Kindermord* ('Slaughter of the Innocents'), it was so utterly
eviscerated that it never again posed a threat during the war.

In light of that, the ongoing battle in the air with RAF
Bomber Command seemed of limited interest. In preparation for
Barbarossa, Goering shifted his gaze and his forces eastwards,
massing over two-thirds of the Luftwaffe in east Prussia and
occupied Poland, effectively stripping the majority of Germany's
fighter force from the homeland. One exception, however, was the
130-strong night fighter force which stayed where it was – mainly
in the Netherlands. In many ways this eastwards switch was

understandable. The Soviet Union was a colossus, and defeating it meant concentrating every drop of combat power the Reich could muster. Plus, the greatly feared bombing of Germany that was the stuff of every senior Nazi's nightmares had not materialised. Much of Bomber Command's effort had been directed into dropping propaganda leaflets – *Nickelling* as it was called by the air crews – hoping to persuade the German people to rise up against the Nazis and end the war. A plan that the acid-tongued commander of No. 4 Group – a certain Arthur Harris – thought achieved nothing more than fulfilling "the Continent's requirements for toilet paper".

Apart from leaflet drops, the British had focused on Germany's navy and its harbour installations, and as the Heligoland Bight battle had shown the Luftwaffe had proved more than capable of seeing them off. True, the latter half of 1940 had seen the RAF shift to bombing industrial targets inside Germany itself, but casualties had been light and the populace didn't seem unduly concerned, quite the opposite in fact, as the previous year's exodus of city children – the *Kinderlandverschikung* programme (Children's Evacuation to the Countryside) to over 2,000 camps run by the Hitler Youth and the National Socialist People's Welfare (*Nationalsozialistische Volkswohlfahrt* or NSV) had gone into reverse, with most of the youngsters returning home. Germany's anti-aircraft batteries were also getting bigger, firing hundreds of shells into the air at the merest hint of a bomber overhead, and providing the people with visible and audible proof of their government's determination to keep them safe. That, and the establishment of the Nachtjagd, would seem to have put Germany into an unassailable position. But all was not what it seemed.

No lesser figure than Adolf Galland, when interviewed by the Allies after the war, said of Germany's aerial defences at the time:

The necessary signals facilities [along the Dutch, Belgian and French coasts] for defensive aerial fighting operations were neglected in 1939 and 1940 because of the offensive role of the fighter force in these years ... the period of need could have been bridged with sufficient fighter forces, but these were just what was lacking.[1]

The *General der Jagdflieger* could have been more critical. Falck's NJG 1 was still in its infancy and was only reinforced in November 1940 when NJG 2 was created from a cadre of existing aircraft and crews. In the meantime, Falck did the best he could, modifying NJG 1's aircraft for night operations, a rudimentary process that consisted mainly of fitting flame dampers to the exhausts, altering cabin illumination to eliminate tell-tale lighting, and painting each aircraft black. He also organised training for his crews, which included emphasis on the importance of the crews' night vision. "We knew the English night pilots were called 'rabbits' because they ate so many carrots, and that in the prep rooms they wore dark glasses so they could quickly become accustomed to the darkness, so we, too, wore dark glasses to prepare ourselves." One of Falck's future night fighter pilots, Peter Spoden, testified to the practice:

> We sat in dark rooms as it was very important to be able to adapt to the night. Some pilots prepared before they flew by wearing dark glasses. Then there were some of us who ate carrots because of the vitamin A content and because the doctor recommended it. Nobody ever tested our night vision, but it was a fact that those with better night vision were better able to shoot successfully.

While Falck concentrated on his fighters, his boss Josef Kammhuber – now promoted to the rank of *Generalmajor* – busied himself with overhauling the Luftwaffe's entire night fighting infrastructure. As Walter Knickmeier recalled, "Priority was given to setting up a ground organisation." The system he would put in place would become the mainstay of Germany's western defence for almost three years and became known to the allies as the Kammhuber Line. The man himself was a fully qualified pilot, and, like Falck, had been sent to train secretly at Lipetsk. Later on, he was appointed to command a bomber geschwader during the Battle of France. Shot down, he ended up in a French PoW camp until the end of hostilities. A protégé of Walter Wever – the Luftwaffe's first Chief of Staff – he excelled at staff work and was recognised as a brilliant organiser with a strong personality. That personality occasionally tipped over into stubbornness and an inability to work in collaboration with others, but on first taking up his post those were exactly the traits required.

The organisation he inherited was a mess. Germany's flak, searchlight and aircraft detection units were all under separate command with no single reporting chain – as Hermann Diehl had discovered at Heligoland – and much of what did exist seemed to him to be in the wrong place. The searchlight units were the worst. The Nazi Party chiefs in charge of Germany's administration – called *Gauleiters* – insisted that the searchlight regiments be grouped around their cities to provide the light needed by the flak batteries to try and shoot down the bombers and prove to their citizens they had their best interests at heart. But that meant Falck's night fighters couldn't operate over those same cities as they would risk being hit by their own guns. Kammhuber wanted a different approach, and he trialled it with the authorities responsible for the city of Münster. Chosen because it sat astride the main flight path into Germany by the British bombers, Kammhuber positioned the searchlights out to the west in a protective screen, allowing the fighters to engage the bombers without fear of being shot at by their own flak. He then concentrated his aircraft detection units to give early warning of any incoming bombers and provide an accompanying fighter control facility, and he centrally controlled it all from his new divisional operations room at Döberitz near Berlin. Effectively, this was Helle Nachtjagd on a large scale.

This new approach worked – to a degree – unwittingly helped by the British tactics of the time. Firstly, there weren't that many bombers, and they were usually tasked to attack several different targets on the same night. This meant they were dispersed across the night sky, so a 'defensive wall', as it were, would give the Luftwaffe night fighters the ability to hunt multiple bombers all at once. But the bombers soon learned to avoid the area and simply fly around it to their targets. Kammhuber's counter to that move was to expand the system out to either side and create a defensive line that would eventually become some 30 kilometres wide and stretched for almost 900 kilometres from northeast to southwest, but it was far from perfect.

The Light Night Fighting technique itself also had significant problems, as *Leutnant* Hans Autenrieth discovered on the night of 12/13 August 1941. Having flown two previous sorties without any luck, he took off with his two crew, Rudi Adam and 'Schorsch' Helbig, in their Bf 110 and after half an hour got the call from ground control: "Otto, Otto". This was the signal that a bomber was illuminated in his sector. "I flew towards the searchlight cone but was unable to recognise the target within it … it took a long time before I was close enough to make out the coned aircraft in the haze." The bomber desperately tried to escape the searchlights as Autenrieth tried to get into a firing position. "I was worried that the Tommy would soon have escaped from them [the searchlights] and also from me … I fired short bursts at the wildly twisting Tommy who then succeeded in getting out of the searchlight's cone."

Frustrated at his failure, 20-year-old Autenrieth was almost immediately given another opportunity. "I received the report of a second sighting which I was able to spot at once." Racing to lock on to his intended victim, the over-eager pilot suddenly realised, "I had been in an ever-steepening dive. My engines screamed, I never got the chance to fire, and I levelled out gently." Even worse for the pilot, "Whilst I dived past [the bomber] through the searchlights, I was blinded by one of them, which shone directly in my face." Swiftly recovering his vision, Autenrieth tried again, this time being engaged by the bomber's tail gunner. "But the bullets passed to port of my cockpit. I pressed all the buttons at once and aimed the first burst at the rear turret. When this had been silenced I went for the starboard engine and wing." Again, his inexperience cost him, as his superior speed forced him to pull up to avoid ramming his target. Losing his victim in the darkness he desperately searched the sky but "the Tommy had escaped the searchlights and I climbed back to 6,000 metres and called it a day."

Finally, his luck changed and towards 3am he was "directed to another Tommy". Getting in close, he "opened fire on his starboard engines and wing with my machine-guns and cannon, and turned away to port for a second attack". The bomber disappeared from view but was confirmed as having crashed by ground control. "It was our first *Abschuss*" – literally a 'shooting' or 'firing' but better translated as a 'victory'. Autenrieth later learned that "the seven crew members all baled out, but five drowned in a bog."[2]

Kammhuber realised the shortcomings of Henaja, knowing how dependent it was on weather conditions, with thick cloud and smog from the industries of the Ruhr blinding it. He cast about for an answer. The answer Kammhuber was searching for was technology, and more specifically *detection* technology. Despite having a raft of leading scientists, Nazi Germany had fallen behind Great Britain in the field of radar, with the Germans relying more on sound locators to provide early warning of air attack. Those locators were mostly based on the coast of occupied Europe, but from 1939 onwards were increasingly supplemented by an infant radar network. Indeed, it was one such radar facility – Hermann Diehl's in fact – that had alerted the Germans in time to fight the Heligoland battle. Now running to catch up, the main two radar systems German industry was working on were the *Freya* and the *Würzburg*. The former was a general area machine, able to detect aircraft out to a range of about 100 kilometres, but with little ability to determine their altitude. This made it of limited value at night, with fighters groping around in the dark as bombers either passed over or under them.

By contrast, the newer Würzburg was far more accurate, but with a limited range of about 30 kilometres. Kammhuber had managed to get his hands on six of the new sets back in the autumn of 1940, and early results had been promising, but far from conclusive. Pondering the problem, Kammhuber decided the best way to optimise both radar was to combine the two into one single system.

Leaning on his earlier experience in combining searchlights and night fighters in a defensive line, Kammhuber now matched his fighters directly with radar in an initial series of six aerial 'boxes', each with its own animal-related codename, such as *Tiger* or *Lobster*. Each box usually covered a zone 30 kilometres long north to south, and 20 kilometres wide east to west. A radio beacon was situated in the centre of each box, around which a single night fighter would loiter, with a secondary night fighter available as a back-up and a long-range Freya providing early warning of a bomber's approach. A ground control officer – Walter Knickmeier was one – sitting in one of the now three operations rooms and known as 'Kammhuber's Cinemas' by their staff – would then use two shorter range Würzburg sets; one locked on the bomber and the other on the allocated night fighter, to vector the fighter to its target, supplying instructions on direction, height and speed via the radio. This then was *Dunkel* (Dark) *Nachtjagd*, as opposed to *Helle Nachtjagd*.

Just as with Kammhuber's earlier effort, the system evolved, at first focusing on the main bomber pathways and then expanding outwards to cover the entire Ruhr valley and further afield. Eventually, the Line became shaped like a sickle with the handle running through Denmark, north to south, and the blade curving through northern Germany, the Netherlands, Belgium and eastern France to the Swiss frontier. This then was *Himmelbett* – literally *heaven bed* but usually translated as *four-poster bed* – the first integrated night fighter air defence system.

The Germans' opponents were changing, too. In terms of Bomber Command's aircraft, the Hampdens and Whitleys were being phased out, and while the much-adored twin-engine Wimpys were still in favour, a new generation of four-engine bombers, the Avro Manchester – forerunner of the Lancaster – and the Handley Page Halifax and Short Stirling, were coming on stream. Major investments were being made in technology, especially in the fields of navigation and bomb aiming. The reasoning was clear; with a rigidly enforced black-out in place and European weather being what it is, finding the target and then hitting it accurately was a daunting task. One RAF crewman remembered what it was like at the time in the pre-operation briefings.

The main target would usually be an armaments factory, or harbour installations ... there'd probably be a secondary target, something like a railway station ... clear and easy to find – though it never was – and in recognition of that fact the instructions always ended with the same thing; after that, *'anything that opens and shuts in Germany'*, and everyone always cheered.[3]

The first big breakthrough was *Gee*, which used two radio signals to produce a locational fix and was accurate out to 350 miles. Gee had its maiden operational outing on the night of 11/12 August and was all its developers hoped, but its success came against a bloody backdrop for Bomber Command. The two bombers that tested Gee on 11 August got home safely, but a Gee-equipped Wellington that went out the following night to hit Hanover failed to return. Being shot down, the Wimpy was just one of 106 bombers lost in August. September would prove fractionally worse, with 2,501 sorties flown at a cost of 108 aircraft destroyed, of which 68 were lost to the increasingly effective German night fighter force.

Ominously for Bomber Command, one of the aircraft lost that August was a Wellington shot down on 9 August by *Oberleutnant* Ludwig Becker and his *Bordfunker* (radio operator) *Unteroffizier* Josef Staub, who were guided onto their target by a new airborne radar array built into the nose of their Dornier night fighter – the *FuG 202 Lichtenstein*. Still being tested, the radar array stuck out of the nose of the aircraft like a bunch of very large television aerials. It was disparagingly nicknamed the *Drahtverhau* (barbed wire fence) by suspicious crews, who were annoyed by its drag, which reduced their air speed by as much as 20mph. Nevertheless, the Lichtenstein had the potential to tip the balance in the air war further in Germany's favour.

Becker's victory on 9 August 1941 was only his second, his first being during the night of 16 October 1940 in what was then the first ground radar-directed victory for the Luftwaffe. On that occasion, he had been vectored onto his target by none other than Hermann Diehl and his experimental Freya radar station at Nunspeet in the Netherlands.

I was guided very well at the correct height of 3300 metres with constant corrections towards the enemy at his starboard rear, and suddenly saw, about 100 metres above me to my left, an aircraft in the moonlight … I closed in slowly behind him and gave him a burst of about five or six seconds, aiming at the fuselage and wing roots. The starboard engine caught fire at once … then the fire went out and I watched him spinning downwards and finally crash. I observed no-one baling out.

In fact, two crewmen did manage to get out, but the pilot and the remaining three crew were all killed.

Becker would go on to refine his hunting technique, with the Westphalian becoming a leading night fighting tactician, eager to pass on his knowledge and expertise to other pilots. He became so good at it that he was nicknamed 'the Night Fighting Professor' by his comrades. His preferred method of attack would begin by climbing above the expected height of the incoming bombers and using his on-board radar to home in on a target. Once locked on, he would drop below the bomber so it would then be silhouetted against the night sky by any ambient light. He would then slowly creep ever closer until only a matter of yards away. Still underneath his victim, he would be out of sight to any of its gunners, and his black painted fuselage and wings would act as camouflage against the darkness of the ground. He would then pitch his nose up ever so slightly and fire a burst at a point in front of the bomber so that it passed through the hail of shells and bullets, inevitably being torn apart by the gunfire.

The tactic was adopted by many other night fighter pilots and was christened the *von hinten unten* – meaning 'from behind and below'. The only significant drawback of the von hinten unten was that it could lead to a huge explosion in the bomb bay of an inbound aircraft, which could inadvertently destroy the fighter, although this obviously wasn't an issue on the homeward bound leg. To avoid such a scenario, some pilots first disabled or killed the bomber's rear gunner and then finished the aircraft off at their leisure from dead astern.

Becker would go on to become one of the leading proponents of what was an increasingly specialised field of combat. The list would include Helmut Lent, Werner Streib, Paul Gildner – the only

NCO on it – and Egmont Prinz zur Lippe-Weissenfeld. Each would score dozens of *Abschüsse* and together with their ever-loyal crewmen would be lauded in the Nazi press as poster boys for the Nachtjagd.

Helmut 'Bubi' ('Little laddie') Lent was the near perfect Nazi pin-up for the Nachtjagd. Born in the village of Pyrehne in Brandenburg – now Pyrzany in western Poland – the youngest of five, he joined the *Deutsches Jungvolk* ('German Youngsters' – a branch of the Hitler Youth for younger boys) in 1933, and within a year was promoted to Troop Leader, organising and leading 60 to 70 other boys. Most activities were based around sports and outdoor pursuits such as camping and hiking, but also included a weekly indoctrination session held every Wednesday evening – the *Heimabende* (Home Evenings) –– where the boys would be lectured on Nazi politics and ideology as well as the Party's racial theories. Boys were also encouraged to inform their adult leaders if their parents' expressed beliefs or views contrary to Nazi policies. For the blond-haired and blue-eyed Lent this posed something of a problem as his father was the local pastor and he himself held strong Christian beliefs. The Nazis were not in favour of Christianity, mistrusting its central message of peace, love and the brotherhood of man, and intensely suspicious of its Jewish origins.

The young Lent kept his counsel, and two years later reported for training at the *Luftkriegsschule* (Air Warfare School) at Gatow in southwest Berlin. Strongly attracted to a career in military service and passionately committed to flying, Lent had opted to become a pilot and spent the next year and ten months qualifying for his *Flugzeugführerabzeichen* – his pilot's wings. Starting out on the Heinkel He 72 *Kadett* (Cadet) – similar to a Tiger Moth – he soon moved up to the Focke-Wulf Fw 44 *Stieglitz* (Goldfinch) two-seater biplane and got his single-engine A licence. Along with all other cadets he was also taught to drive a car and a motorbike, both skills in short supply in pre-war Germany. He graduated in time to fly in the annexation of the Sudetenland in the autumn of 1938, and in the subsequent takeover of the remainder of Czechoslovakia the following year. He learnt to fly the Bf 108 but converted to the heavy fighters in the run up to war.

Lent scored his first Abschuss in Poland and two more at the Heligoland fight, before being sent to join the Nachtjagd, a decision he was not happy with, as he made clear in a letter home: "We are currently converting to night fighting. We are not very enthusiastic. We would sooner head directly for England [and the Battle of Britain]." Lent's aversion to his new role was understandable given that a posting to the night fighters was seen within the Luftwaffe at the time as something of a punishment. The pill was, however, somewhat sugared by promotion to command of a staffel, and he and his radio op Walter Kubisch – with whom he would fly for most of the war – soon settled into their new base at Leeuwarden in the Netherlands. Thereafter, the pair steadily built their score against the crews of Bomber Command, and on 30 August 1941 Lent was awarded the Knight's Cross for reaching 21 victories, two-thirds of them at night.

With good news eluding the Luftwaffe over the skies of England on account of the heroics of RAF Fighter Command, efforts were made by Nazi Germany's propaganda machine to showcase the successes of the Nachtjagd to the German people. Lent was chosen as just such a good news story and the war correspondent Josef Kreutz was sent to shadow him. Kreutz witnessed Lent utilise the von hinten unten approach at first hand.

A British bomber has crossed the flight path of the searching night fighter. The range is getting shorter and shorter. Will the enemy crew see the fighter? But there is not a single shot. The Tommy is now within attacking range ... he [Lent] wants the first attack to blow the enemy to pieces ... then it is time. The cannon hammer out in short bursts, then there comes the lighter rattle of the machine-guns. His aim is good! A flurry of bright fragments from the aircraft swirl through the air ... all around night turns to day. *Hauptmann* Lent pulls his aircraft away...[4]

In many ways Lent would come to typify the German night fighter arm. A relentless and focused flier, he would be showered with the kind of awards that the Nazis loved to bestow, including the

Iron Cross, the German Cross in Gold and the Knight's Cross with Oak Leaves, Swords and Diamonds. His personal life was less to the Nazis liking. He married a Russian, Lena Senokosnikova, and both his elder brothers, Joachim and Werner, got into hot water with the Party because of their strong Protestant faith. It was a faith that Lent also stuck with, although not to the same extent as his siblings. Wolfgang Falck knew him well. "We had a very fine personal relationship as he came from the same part of Germany where my family lived ... [and] we were both sons of Protestant ministers. I liked him, understood him and liked to fly with him."

A predator in the air, on the ground Lent was respectful of and generous to his enemies. He once wrote that "War is a horror, but if it has to be, then it should be fought in fairness, with honour and chivalry to preserve something human." On one occasion he visited the hospital ward where a surviving RAF crewman from one of his victories was being treated. The German asked if there was anything he could do for the wounded airman, to which he replied yes there was, could he arrange for the window next to his bed to be unsealed so he could get some fresh air. Lent had the window opened forthwith. After entertaining the crew of a shot-down Halifax in his mess at Leeuwarden one evening – a practice not uncommon on both sides during the war – he wrote to his parents, "It really is a cause for regret that we have to fight against such men."[5] But fight they did, and with ever greater fury.

Then the unexpected happened. In August 1941 a report commissioned by Winston Churchill's Chief Scientific Advisor and close friend, Lord Frederick Cherwell, was circulated to a chosen few at the top of Government and the military. The document in question – called the Butt Report after David Bensusan-Butt, a civil servant in the British War Cabinet's Secretariat and formerly Cherwell's Private Secretary – was highly confidential and made for very uncomfortable reading for the men in charge of Britain's war effort. Butt and his team had undertaken to analyse the effectiveness of Bomber Command's raids and had studied a mass of over 650 photoreconnaissance images from a hundred night attacks on 28 different targets over June and July. What they concluded was shocking: half of all bombs dropped came down in open country and did no damage, only one in three crews who had claimed to reach their target actually did so, and overall only 5 per cent of the bombers had dropped their payloads within five miles of their assigned target.

Butt highlighted a raid launched on 21 July against the city of Frankfurt in western Germany as typifying the problem. A total of 71 bombers set out on the raid; half Wimpys and half Hampdens, and the after-action reports from the crews were positive, painting a picture of a successful attack. The Germans, however, disagreed, with the authorities in Frankfurt hardly mentioning the bombing and reporting little damage, while the city of Darmstadt – some 15 miles away – stated that in fact *it* had been the target, with severe damage to a number of buildings and 16 citizens killed.

Unsurprisingly, the RAF disputed the report and its findings and sought to dampen down any criticism of its performance by commissioning its own study. Completed in less than a month, the new document did not address what bombing had or had not achieved so far – that was conveniently left out of the picture – but focused instead on what bombing *could* achieve in the future, which was – apparently – to win the war for Britain in six months as long as the bomber fleet was more than quadrupled in size to a gargantuan 4,000 aircraft, most of which would need to be the new four-engine heavies. The RAF's demand for an increase in strength of that order of magnitude was met with ashen faces. In cash terms alone it would mean Bomber Command receiving massively more funding than the entire British Army, and that wasn't on the cards.

Historians have long argued over the real influence of the Butt report on British bombing policy and practice, being as it was just one report among many at the time, but on reflection it is difficult not to view it as the instigator of a crisis of confidence within the RAF and Bomber Command in particular. Churchill himself wrote that "It is an awful thought that perhaps three-quarters of our bombs go astray." Not that all was rosy on the German side of the fence either. Since his appointment Josef Kammhuber had pushed the idea of using long-range night fighters to go on the offensive by hitting the RAF's bombers as they took off from their own airfields, then as they approached Germany over the North Sea, and finally as they landed back at their home bases in England following a mission. The practicalities of the first two of those three separate operations proved difficult to achieve, but the third was far more promising. The bomber pilots and crews would be at their most vulnerable; tired after a sortie lasting eight hours or more, low on fuel and unable to manoeuvre, many of them damaged and carrying wounded.

To trial the concept a new headquarters had been established – NJG 2 – and a gruppe of Ju 88s and Do 17s assigned. Called the *Fernnachtjagd Gruppe* (Far night hunting Group), a Condor Legion veteran, *Major* Karl-Heinrich Heyse, was put in command and charged with leading night-time intruder operations against the bomber bases. The first success was achieved on the night of 24 October 1940, when *Feldwebel* Hans Hahn shot down a Whitley bomber over its own airfield at Linton-on-Ouse. The British got their revenge one day short of a month later when Heyse himself failed to return from a mission, almost certainly having been shot down by a Hampden tail gunner. Hahn would go on to achieve twelve victories in his Ju 88 and be awarded the Knight's Cross in July 1941. One of Hahn's fellow fliers – *Oberfeldwebel* Hermann Sommer – described a Fernnachtjagd sortie he flew in the early hours of 30 April 1941: "I saw an English aircraft fire recognition signals and flew towards it where I found an airfield – illuminated and very active. I joined the airfield's circuit ... and after several circuits an aircraft came within range. I closed to between 100 and 150 metres and fired. After a short burst the aircraft exploded in the air and fell to earth." Not content with his success, he flew off but loitered within sight of the base. He was rewarded when only a few minutes later another bomber came into land. "I attacked from behind and above at roughly 80 metres. The aircraft crashed after my burst, hitting the ground and catching fire." His night further improved when by the "light of the flames from the two wrecks I saw 15 to 20 aircraft parked on the airfield. I dropped my bombs on them." Luck continued to go Sommer's way when he went on to shoot down a Blenheim as it landed at RAF Hucknall, and finally a Bristol Beaufort twin-engine bomber over Norfolk on his way home.

Despite the success of Hahn, Sommer and other NJG 2 pilots such as Willi Beier and Heinz Völker, the intruder concept never won much favour in Luftwaffe high command. With only one gruppe actually in NJG 2, there were rarely more than 20 serviceable aircraft available to it, and when Kammhuber lobbied Hans Jeschonnek as Luftwaffe Chief of Staff for an increase in intruder strength – and in the night fighter force overall – he was pointedly rebuffed: "At this rate the night fighters will absorb the whole of the Luftwaffe." Kammhuber was flabbergasted. By the end of August, NJG 2's single gruppe had claimed a total of 135 victories, more than any other night fighter unit, and two of its members had been awarded the Knight's Cross – what more did Jeschonnek want?

As it turned out, September was a quiet month for the intruders, and then October brought disaster. On the eleventh of the month Hans Hahn proved over eager when shooting down an Airspeed Oxford trainer flying over Grantham in Lincolnshire, colliding with it even as he riddled it with gunfire. Both aircraft crashed to the ground. No-one survived. Worse was to come for the intruder offensive when Hitler called Kammhuber to a conference two days later and declared that "If the long-range night fighting plan really produced results the British would have copied it a long time ago as they imitate anything good that I do." In a baffling decision, given his offensive mindset, Hitler ordered Kammhuber to cease all intruder operations, giving as his reason that "the German citizen, whose house has been destroyed by a British bomber, would prefer it if the British aircraft were shot down by a German night fighter and crash next to his burning house." The NJG 2 fliers were incredulous, understandably believing themselves to have not only mastered their role but become the élite of the night fighter arm. Their resentment then turned to anger when they were told that the gruppe was being transferred to Sicily, where it would act as convoy escort for troops and supplies en route from Italy to Erwin Rommel in north Africa.

November 1941 was a strange month for the Luftwaffe's defence of Germany. The threat was still from RAF Bomber Command, and in that fight the German night fighter arm was winning. An

RAF raid on the night of 7 November was savaged, with 37 aircraft lost out of the 400 dispatched. Losses on that scale were simply unsustainable and operations were noticeably wound down from that point onwards as the RAF licked its wounds. Then, as dawn was breaking on the morning of 17 November, Ernst Udet picked up the phone and called his girlfriend, the young and beautiful Inge Bleyle. He had spent the night alone, drinking himself sober with two bottles of cognac. "*Ingelein* [his nickname for her], I can't stand it anymore, I'm going to shoot myself. I wanted to say goodbye to you. They're after me." *Ingelein* pleaded with him and begged him to wait. "I told him I would be right there. I heard the shot over the telephone. When I got there he was dead." Accounts differ, but scrawled in red on his bed's headboard was either "Iron One, you are responsible for my death" or "*Reichsmarschall*, why have you deserted me?" Both meant the same thing, the 'Iron One' being the Nazi Party's propaganda name for Udet's boss, *Reichsmarschall* Hermann Goering. Ernst Udet was forty-five years old when he committed suicide and a darling of both the Luftwaffe and the German public. The second highest scoring German First World War fighter ace after the legendary Red Baron, he had been an early convert to Nazism and subsequently a totem for the rise of the Luftwaffe. Goering, his final First World War commander, had hugely overpromoted him, eventually handing him the job of Chief of Procurement and Supply for the entire Luftwaffe in 1939. Technically in charge of 26 different departments and several thousand staff, it would have been difficult to find a role he was more unsuited for. At one of the infant service's most critical junctures the man responsible for all aircraft production, armament and supply was an affable playboy with no real interest in anything apart from flying. The mistakes he made during his tenure were colossal and would haunt the Luftwaffe until its demise. However, at the time, Udet's death was a real blow to morale among the ranks of an air force that idolised him, and a public that adored him. His State funeral brought more grief for the Luftwaffe, when Werner Mölders – the 28-year-old head of the Luftwaffe's fighter force and originator of much of its operational doctrine – died after a plane crash on his way to attend the ceremony.

Robbed of its brightest star, the new head of the Luftwaffe's fighter arm was the 29-year-old Adolf Galland. 'Dolfo' Galland was the second eldest of four brothers born into a family of French Huguenot descent in western Germany's Westphalia region. He would go on to become a hugely important figure in the Luftwaffe's daylight battle with the bombers, his influence also spilling over into the night campaign. A leading fighter ace during the invasion of France and the Battle of Britain, his fellow flier, Otto Stammberger, remembered him as "a fighter pilot with great successes, who hourly put his life on the line and was a wonderful example." A keen hunter and excellent marksman, "he was the same in the air, he was at one with his machine and always shot at exactly the right moment." Technically gifted as a pilot, he projected a relaxed and rather rakish image with propaganda photos often catching him playing with his beloved dog *Schweinebauch* (Pork Belly) or smoking his ever-present cigars. That image was sometimes at odds with his behaviour, as his successor to the command of *Jagdgeschwader* (Fighter Wing) 26 recalled, in his dealings with other pilots: "A certain feeling of superiority to other people arose from his skills [and he] kept his distance and didn't open up."

Essentially a day fighter man, nevertheless, Galland could feel relatively happy with Germany's night fighter arm and the situation in the skies over Germany as he took up his new role. Two more Nachtgeschwader had been established; NJG 3 covering the north German ports and naval installations, and NJG 4 to help protect the country's interior, and overall the Luftwaffe's night fighters had been responsible for shooting down more than 400 of Bomber Command's total loss for the year of 1,631 aircraft. Not that there wasn't room for improvement. Just as the Butt report had made for sobering reading for the British about the efficiency of their bombing, so an internal report into the effectiveness of the Nachtgeschwader gave pause for thought for Luftwaffe high command as well.

After studying after action reports it concluded that of some 3,500 sorties flown, less than 7 per cent reported even seeing a bomber, and only 2 per cent ended in an actual attack. The figure for a successful Abschuss was even lower. This partly explained why it was that despite the losses inflicted on the bombers, they had still kept on coming, dropping almost 32,000 tons of bombs on the Reich, an almost three-fold increase on the previous year's total. There was another cloud on the horizon as well. If November had been a month of swings and roundabouts for the defence of German skies by the Luftwaffe, December was a month heavy with ill omens. On 7 December the forces of Imperial Japan attacked the home base of the US Pacific Fleet at Pearl Harbor in Hawaii. Four days later, in a rambling speech to the *Reichstag* – the Nazi parliament – Hitler declared war on the United States of America. At a stroke the dictator had totally transformed the future of the war over Germany.

# 3

# 1942

# THE TIDE TURNS

"If we haven't won the war by December we have no prospect of doing so." So said Hans Jeschonnek, the Luftwaffe's Chief of Staff at the beginning of 1942. It might appear shocking that a senior Nazi could make a statement that could be interpreted as defeatism at worst and lacking faith in victory at best, but in doing so the Prussian staff officer, once lauded as the air force's *wunderkind*, was only following in his master's footsteps. Hitler himself repeatedly made doom-laden prophecies. In June that same year he confided in Friedrich Paulus, commander of the German Sixth Army, that "If I don't get the oil of Maykop and Grozny [in the Soviet Caucasus] then I must end this war." Two months later coking coal, and not oil, was the dictator's direst need. "If, due to the shortage of coking coal, the output of the steel industry cannot be raised as planned, then the war is lost."[1]

As it transpired, Hitler didn't get the Soviet oil, or the planned rise in steel output, but the war didn't end. Hitler and Jeschonnek were correct, however, in seeing 1942 as a defining year in the war. It most definitely was in the air war over Germany. What made it so important a year was how the Germans let slip the crown they had fought so hard to retain since the war's beginning. Having chased the British bombers out of the sky during daylight, and then built an efficient and deadly night defence umbrella, the Reich's leaders allowed their focus to wander at precisely the time when the British were finally getting into gear, and the Americans began to arrive on the scene.

The first nail driven into Germany's coffin that year was the arrival at RAF Bomber Command's High Wycombe headquarters of Air Marshal Sir Arthur Harris on 14 February 1942 – Valentine's Day. Rather short and somewhat thick round the waist, Harris had the demeanour of a bulldog, and would come to personify Britain's bombing campaign to such an extent that he will be forever known as 'Bomber' Harris. Recalled from his post as head of the RAF delegation in the United States to replace Richard Peirse, Harris had watched with increasing concern from Washington as Germany's night defences had slowly gotten the upper hand in the campaign. He was determined to redress the balance and use the bomber fleet as the "potentially decisive weapon" he was totally convinced it was. One bomber pilot described him as "a rough, tough, vulgar egomaniac. He was just what Bomber Command needed."[2]

Back in 1918 when the RAF had first been established, the President of the Air Council – William Weir – had told the RAF's first commander, Hugh Trenchard, that it wasn't necessary to worry about accuracy during bombing raids, to which Trenchard replied, nodding, that "all the pilots drop their eggs [bombs] into the centre of town [anyway]." Trenchard applied this truism to the RAF's founding doctrine, which stated that the principal use of air power was to gain control of the air – crucially, Trenchard further insisted that this aim included the use of a strategic bombing force 'to *destroy the enemy's means of production and his communications in his own country*'. Harris believed in this approach utterly. He thought precision attacks a mirage, and that the key to victory lay in massive area bombing that would shatter an enemy's morale and destroy his ability to wage war.

Hitherto, Bomber Command had operated under a strict set of rules that had limited its attacks firstly to German shipping and coastal naval installations, and then allowed night-time precision raids on war industry targets in western Germany. The Butt report had shown the latter was an illusion. The technology to deliver such a campaign simply didn't exist at the time. The point was finally conceded on 22 February 1942, when the Air Ministry issued its Directive No. 22. What became known as the 'area bombing directive' was issued to Harris and was very clear: "You are now ... authorised to employ your forces without restriction." From now on, attacking "the morale of the enemy civilian population and, in particular, of the industrial workers" should be the "primary object" of bombing.

The Directive was reinforced by another report from Lord Cherwell. It was called the *Dehousing Paper* and took the line that what the Butt report proved wasn't that the bomber offensive was a failure, but rather had been directed at the wrong targets. What was required was additional resources – although not up to the Air Ministry's 4,000 aircraft mark – and a focus on bombing working class neighbourhoods in German cities where housing was densely packed. In conclusion, the report estimated that if Bomber Command could destroy 30 per cent of homes in the Reich's 58 largest cities and towns, the German people would break. This astonishing claim was based on an analysis of German raids on cities such as Hull and Birmingham, but since those same raids had failed to destroy British morale it was difficult to see why the Germans would react any differently.

Regardless of the veracity of Cherwell's claim, Directive 22 provided Harris with official permission to do what he believed was necessary and right anyway, and he immediately set about ensuring he had the men and equipment to deliver the campaign he envisaged. On taking up his appointment he had discovered that Bomber Command had lost some 2,331 aircraft and 7,448 aircrew either killed in action or accidents or taken as POWs since the war began, and morale was low. As it stood, he had the sum total of 378 serviceable aircraft, of which only 69 were the newer heavy type. If he was going to hit Germany as hard as he wanted, Harris knew he needed bigger aircraft able to carry more bombs, and a lot more of them; plus, he needed men prepared to risk their lives night after night in some of the toughest conditions imaginable. He was considerably aided in this endeavour by production decisions taken before his tenure, as the new four-engine Halifax and Stirling bombers began to arrive in significant numbers, allowing the smaller Whitleys, Hampdens and Wellingtons to be phased out from frontline duty and moved to training duties.

Not that everyone was happy with the move to the new fleet, as one pilot made clear: "It was terrible in the Stirlings, I mean they were always crashing." But it was the arrival of one aircraft in particular, that would transform Bomber Commands night-time campaign – the Avro Lancaster. Able to carry a payload of 14,000lb while flying 8,000 feet higher than the Stirling, the Lancaster's first outing was a relatively tame sea mine laying sortie on the night of 3 March, but the following week it was sent in to hit the city of Essen in Germany's Ruhr valley. It soon became a crew favourite – "once you got in a Lancaster you'd feel safe"[3] – and with its advent Harris began to revitalise his men's battered spirits. His way of doing so was extraordinary and unique to himself, as one of his group captains described.

> Harris didn't come and see us and hand out cigarettes or anything else, he sent the most amazing signals for you to read out to your crews at briefing. One I'll always remember said 'tonight you go to the Big City [Berlin] and you have the opportunity to light a fire in the belly of the enemy and burn his black heart out.' Well, after the crews stopped cheering they didn't want aircraft, just fill their pockets with bombs and point them towards Berlin.

Against every tenet of accepted military leadership Harris eschewed personal contact with his men, rarely leaving his High Wycombe headquarters and visiting their stations. But his concern for their welfare was genuine and heartfelt, and they knew it. His real connection with them, however, was his obsessive commitment to victory over Nazi Germany by any and all means available at whatever cost, and the men and women of Bomber Command knew that, too. Harris's faith in regarding the civilian population of the Reich as a legitimate target was no empty act of bombast. On the wall of his office in High Wycombe he pinned a list of over

100 German cities and large towns compiled by the Ministry of Economic Warfare, each individually rated according to size of population and the existence of factories and industrial sites scored from 1 to 3 depending on certain criteria. The cities were then ranked from No. 1 in importance as a target; Berlin with a score of 545, down to lowly Wittenberg in Saxony at No. 104 with just nine. Harris's habit was to put a mark through each city as it was attacked, and he would invariably refer to the list when selecting destinations for raids.

The men and women he led instinctively understood his stubborn, combative nature, and also respected the detachment he exercised, which enabled him to send so many of them to their deaths, and so they affectionately nicknamed him 'Butch' – short for 'Butcher'. An oft-repeated anecdote concerning Harris relates how he was stopped by a policeman as he raced at manic speed in his sports car between his headquarters and the Air Ministry one night, with the young constable berating him by saying that at that speed he could have killed someone, with Harris replying sardonically; 'Young man, I kill thousands of people every night.' What Harris needed now was an opportunity to demonstrate to his own side – and especially the naysayers in the War Cabinet – what his new Bomber Command could achieve.

The ancient Baltic port city of Lübeck is named for the Slavic word *Liubice*, meaning 'lovely'. The de facto capital of the medieval Hanseatic League, famous for its trade, wealth and culture, Lübeck sits astride the mouth of the River Trave where it empties into the sea. In 1942, its ancient streets were narrow, the buildings mostly built of wood and densely packed together. Far from the forges and blast furnaces of the Ruhr, it wasn't considered an important wartime production centre and was only lightly defended by a handful of flak batteries. All of those factors made it the perfect target for Harris to put his stamp on Bomber Command's rejuvenated offensive. As he said himself in his post-war memoir, "It seemed to me better to destroy an industrial target of moderate importance than to fail to destroy a large industrial city." On the night of 28 March 1942, Harris sent 234 aircraft to do exactly that.

When the air raid sirens sounded out there was a great deal of surprise among the citizenry – 'What could the English possibly want to bomb here?' The answer, in Max Hastings apt turn of phrase, was that it wasn't "bombed because it was important, but important because it could be bombed". Easily identified due to its position at the river mouth, a 10-strong force of Wellingtons dropped flares over the city to mark the target and were followed up by 40 bombers dropping incendiaries to start thousands of mini-fires among the houses. Then came the main force, dropping yet more fire-starting incendiaries as well as building-flattening 4,000lb high explosive 'cookie' bombs. On the ground, smaller fires merged into bigger ones and raced through the city's wooden houses, burning almost fifteen hundred to the ground and damaging almost 4,000 more. Some 320 people were killed and another 785 injured. The region's gauleiter, Karl Kaufmann, told Berlin that it took 32 hours to put out the fires and that in his opinion the raid was the heaviest suffered by anywhere in Germany ever. The Luftwaffe's night fighters were caught off-guard, their main force positioned for the RAF's usual attacks on the Ruhr, not the Baltic coast. Nevertheless, they and the flak gunners accounted for a dozen bombers, but the night undoubtedly belonged to Harris and Bomber Command.

Just under a month later, it was Rostock's turn. Another Hanseatic port city lying on a river mouth, this time the Warnow, it was pretty much a carbon copy of the Lübeck raid with hundreds of civilians killed. Again, the defenders were caught unprepared and only a dozen bombers were shot down, as one of the bomber pilots recalled: "Night fighters claimed some victims, but we didn't see one, and the flak over the target didn't worry us much." There were, however, differences in the two raids. Rostock was home to both an Arado and Heinkel factory producing aircraft for the Luftwaffe and so was far more of a military target, plus a lot more bombers were sent – some 521 in all. There was another alteration to the Lübeck template as well, and that was the use of return raids, with the first on the night of 24 April being followed by more over the next three consecutive nights, overwhelming the city's emergency services and leaving it a smouldering ruin.

German public opinion went into shock. Having been told by Nazi propaganda that the authorities had the bomber threat well in hand, they were now hearing that two of the country's most historic cities had been nigh on incinerated. Wild rumours swept around that hitherto neutral Sweden had declared war on Nazi Germany and been responsible for the bombing, and when a further alarm mistakenly sounded in the city on the fourth day, terrified residents panicked and could only be controlled by cordons of armed SS men. Frightened, the public cast around for answers. Joseph Goebbels – Reich Minister for Propaganda, and the Nazis' media mastermind – understood why they were angry after seeing the devastation for himself. "'Community life there [in Rostock] is practically at an end ... the situation in some sections is catastrophic ... seven-tenths of the city has been destroyed ... more than 100,000 people had to be evacuated ... there was, in fact, panic." Sensing the change in public mood, he gave the people what they wanted — someone to blame.

The raids were now *Terrorangriffe* (terror attacks), and the RAF bomber crews, hitherto always portrayed as dandified aristocrats, were now *Terrorflieger* and *Luftgangsters* – terror fliers and air gangsters. In Rostock itself the authorities also acted with remarkable shrewdness; loudspeaker vans toured the city calling for calm, while mobile kitchens were set up in badly hit areas to hand out bowls of hot soup, while chocolate and butter – having long since disappeared from German larders – were distributed from Government emergency stores.

For Kammhuber and his night fighters the twin raids hastened the end of Henaja Light Night Fighting. Across the Reich, the local Nazi gauleiters demanded the return of their searchlight batteries, and Hitler – a Party man through and through – felt beholden to his old comrades and ordered the searchlights returned to the cities. Those same batteries were now equipped with over 3,000 searchlights, mostly of the standard 150cm type, projecting a beam equivalent to one million candlepower. Each battery now had a so-called 'master searchlight' which was of the 200cm bigger and newer variety and was radar-controlled. Standard procedure was for the master searchlight to locate and fix an aircraft, and then for the rest of the battery's 150cm types to join in, coning the bomber so that the gunners could concentrate their fire on it.

Those anti-aircraft batteries were expanding all the time as part and parcel of what was named the Führer Flak Programme. Given high priority by the Nazis, the idea was to build a ring of steel around the Reich's cities, through which the bombers could not break. That meant an increase in the allocation of guns and ammunition that saw the flak arm absorbing fully 28 per cent of the entire Wehrmacht weapons budget and 17 per cent of the munitions budget at the time. In March alone, Germany's now 4,500 heavy and 7,500 medium and light flak guns would fire 800,000 rounds at the bombers. All those guns and searchlights needed people to man them, and consequently the number of personnel in the service grew from 255,000 in 1940 to 439,000 in 1942.

The demands of the gauleiters stripped the Henaja system of one of its key components, and the whole system was more or less dismantled by the summer. In the meantime, the Dunaja Dark Night Fighting concept became the norm, although the relatively slow production of the necessary radars was proving an issue. Regardless, German night fighter strength was growing steadily and would reach 342 aircraft by the end of the year, almost all Ju 88s and Bf 110s. This was a modest proportion of the 15,700 aircraft German industry produced in the year, but with the majority going to the ever-hungry Russian Front, Kammhuber's men could count themselves lucky to get even that. The Nachtjagd was, however, getting the bulk of Germany's radar production, and the Himmelbett system now covered northern and western Germany, as well as the occupied Low Countries and northern France. Many of its older and less suitable aircraft had been retired and replaced by newer models with more weaponry and better on-board equipment, and its pilots, crews and ground staff had grown ever more experienced and proficient in their role. In particular, the core of highly successful fliers around which every branch of the Luftwaffe was built, was growing.

Two such pilots were Werner Streib and Egmont Prinz zur Lippe-Weissenfeld. Streib, a native of Pforzheim – the 'gateway to the Black Forest' – had renounced a promising career in business to join the Army, before transferring to the Luftwaffe on its creation. His introduction to night flying had been under his friend Wolfgang Falck's command at Aalborg in 1940, when Falck had trialled efforts to attack passing British bombers at night. He had gone on to score the Nachtjagd's first Henaja success in July the same year, and on 7 October was awarded the Knight's Cross for achieving seven night victories. Viewed as one of the Nachtjagd's most promising pilots, he was allocated to a prime approach route into Germany for the RAF's bombers, so ensuring a steady stream of potential targets. Streib lived up to the billing and by the end of 1941 his score stood at twenty-two, putting him at the top of the Nachtjagd tree. Technically gifted as a pilot, Streib was an enormously popular character among his peers and superiors, renowned for his sense of humour and fun despite the terrific strain night fighting put on him.

Streib's brother-in-arms, Prinz Egmont, was quite different from his ebullient compatriot, being a minor Austrian aristocrat and one-time heir to a tiny principality in the German Empire. When Germany became a republic after defeat in the First World War, his family – along with all other German royal houses – was forced to abdicate, but the bonds and behaviours of class run deep. He loved hunting at the family castle at Alt Wartenburg, and when not flying he was rarely happier than when sailing on the Ijsselmeer near his base in the Netherlands. A Bf 110 pilot like Streib, he claimed his first Abschuss – a Wellington – on the night of 16/17 November 1940, but it was another two months before he would score again. "On 15 January 1941 I was briefed to fly a Dunaja in the area of Den Helder [Netherlands]." After several unsuccessful intercepts, "I saw a dark shadow at a distance of about 150 metres. I altered course towards it and approached with a high speed advantage ... I pulled up and recognised the target with certainty as a Whitley-Armstrong [Armstrong Whitley]." Edging closer while trying not to overrun his victim, at 300 metres out, "I could no longer see my target because my bulletproof windscreen was almost completely obscured by frost. At this moment the enemy saw me." The British bomber flung itself into a series of evasive manoeuvres "and the rear gunner fired several long bursts without actually hitting me." Pressing home his attack, he was able to see "the two exhaust flames from the twin engines at a distance of about ten metres. I fired a short burst and as I pulled away I could see the bomber was on fire. After about two minutes the wing came off and the aircraft went down."

Quickly marked out as a potential future star, he enjoyed a good relationship with Josef Kammhuber, in particular. When he crash landed at sea after a training sortie went wrong, after being picked up by a Kriegsmarine launch he received a signal from Kammhuber asking him "Who gave you permission to go swimming?" From then on he scored regularly and was awarded the Knight's Cross on 16 April 1942 after his twenty-first victory. By that date the Luftwaffe's award system had continually been adjusted upwards, so Werner Streib's seven victories was enough to earn the coveted medal in 1940, but nowhere near the mark in 1942.

Lauded in the Nazi press, Streib and zur Lippe-Weissenfeld joined the likes of Falck, Lent and Ludwig Becker as pin-ups of the night fighter arm. Heaped with praise and awards, they also mostly managed to maintain their humanity in what was a gruelling war of attrition. Helmut Lent wasn't the only one to visit his victims in their hospital beds after he shot them down. Zur Lippe-Weissenfeld did exactly the same, in mid-July 1941 expressing regret to the survivors of a downed Wellington that his actions on the night had resulted in the death of their pilot, and explaining he was shooting down the bomber, not the men inside it. Warm words though these were, they couldn't hide the fact that zur Lippe-Weissenfeld, Streib, and all the rest, were predators, and they were getting better and better at their job. The figures spoke for themselves. In 1940, flak had accounted for over 80 per cent of bomber losses, the Nachtjagd for just 15 per cent. The following year the figures were fifty-fifty.

Now the German night fighting arm would face off against an RAF Bomber Command reinvigorated under Harris's leadership, increasingly equipped with new and bigger bombers, and with far better navigation and guidance technology. The scene was set for a bloody summer. The question was who would land the next blow, and the answer was Bomber Command.

Even before his arrival to take over the helm at High Wycombe, Harris believed that the key to a successful bombing campaign was mass and concentration – the so-called 'one night, one main target' principle. He was also keenly aware that the Lübeck and Rostock raids had bought him time in the eyes of his detractors, but the deal was still far from being sealed. What was needed was an even more powerful demonstration of Bomber Command's capability and potential. This was the genesis of the Thousand Plan. In May 1942, increases in production and crew training meant Bomber Command was now able to get over four hundred serviceable bombers into the air every night from a total force of between six and seven hundred, but Harris wanted more. The only avenues he could turn to were Coastal Command and his own Operational Training Units (OTUs).

With the U-boat threat at its zenith the Admiralty understandably refused to let Coastal Command participate, so it was down to Harris's semi-trained crews to take up the slack. Pretty much every aircraft and crew that could fly would take part to bump the numbers up to the magic Thousand Bomber total. Codenamed *Millennium*, the date selected for the raid was the night of 30 May – a full moon, and the target for the world's first ever thousand-bomber attack would be Hamburg – Germany's second city. Gathering as usual for the morning briefing in his sparsely furnished office, the grandfather clock loudly ticking and the wall map of Europe dominating the room, Harris was given the bad news; cloud cover over Hamburg made the city unsuitable for the raid that night. Harris shrugged, the secondary target it would be then – Cologne.

For their mission briefing, Harris sent his crews a special message telling them just how big the attack would be and demanding of them the utmost determination. He ended by exhorting them to "Let him have it – right on the chin." An incredible 1,047 aircraft took off for the attack, and just under 900 bombed the city in three successive waves. Over fifteen hundred tons of bombs rained down in one and a half hours, levelling 600 acres of the city and rendering 60,000 of the city's 770,000 inhabitants homeless. As one German Red Cross nurse recalled, "I came out of the shelter and Cologne was a wall of flames." Twelve thousand homes were either destroyed or damaged, industry was badly affected and 474 people were killed – an astonishingly low number given the size of the raid and the scale of the devastation. It didn't seem that way to those who had to live through it.

> The digging parties hauled the dead out and laid them at the side of the road. Those who'd been killed by high-explosive bombs were propped up, their skin was a grey, pallid colour and their hair stood off their heads like wire nails, while those who'd died from incendiaries you could only find bits of bone, which were gathered up in washtubs, big zinc baths.[4]

One Cologne *hausfrau*, Käthe Breuer, described how one of her neighbours in the apartment block she lived in had "a bad case of asthma" and refused to go down to the cellar to shelter. After the raid Frau Breuer's husband went to check on the man: "He'd been shot through the temple and the pistol was lying on the ground. He couldn't bear it any longer and had shot himself." In an act of kindness Herr Breuer got rid of the weapon. Later, the dead man's wife said to him "Thank you Herr Breuer … the doctor said it was a bomb fragment [that killed her husband], otherwise I would have had no claim to supplementary insurance." Soldiers on leave from the Front asked after their relatives and "you had to tell them they're dead – your wife is dead, your children are dead, your grandparents are dead."

Albert Speer, the architect-cum-Nazi armaments supremo, was shocked. "We really didn't expect in 1942 such a heavy raid … we were used to smaller attacks and so when I got the news that about a thousand bombers were attacking Cologne it was incredible." Speer and his Luftwaffe production head Erhard Milch went to see Goering the morning after the raid to discuss what to do, only to find the boss of the Luftwaffe on the phone screaming in rage at Cologne's gauleiter: "[The report from] your Police Commissioner is a stinking lie. I tell you as the *Reichsmarschall* that the figures cited are simply too high. How dare you report such fantasies to the Führer!"⁵ To both Speer and Milch's dismay, Goering simply "didn't want to believe it", understandably petrified that he and his Luftwaffe would bear the blame for the disaster. He was right to worry.

At Hitler's situation conference that same day, Jeschonnek – standing in for his boss – told the subdued attendees that "According to preliminary reports we estimate that 200 enemy aircraft have penetrated our defences. The damage is heavy ... we are still awaiting final estimates." Witnesses to the conference said the Luftwaffe Chief of Staff's hands were shaking as he read out the lines from his papers. As well they might. Hitler exploded. He had received a different report. "I thank the Almighty that I can rely on my Gauleiter, even if the Luftwaffe deceives me." Then he drove the dagger home. "There were a thousand or more English aircraft ... do you hear? A thousand."⁶ Towards the end of the war this type of rant had become commonplace, but in the summer of 1942 it was still a rarity, and Jeschonnek visibly quailed. In London, Churchill sent a signal to Harris congratulating all of Bomber Command on the raid and declared it as "proof of the growing power of the British bomber force". However, despite the undoubted success of the attack – and the propaganda value was at least as great as the material impact - the authorities and people of Cologne proved far more resilient than Berlin feared and London hoped.

Within hours of the bombers passing, trucks were pouring in from across the Ruhr bringing in aid. The NSV – the National Socialist People's Welfare – got into gear alongside the city authorities; those rendered homeless were found shelter, streets were cleared of rubble, and within days thousands of glaziers and builders were at work repairing the damage. In a month all damage claims had been paid and life was beginning to return to some sort of normality. Local authorities were able to report to Berlin that the city was functioning and the public mood was one of 'we can take it.' Speer himself conceded that "the morale of the people [in Cologne] wasn't shattered too much, it was a shock, a shock that passed away."

But what of the Luftwaffe's much-lauded night fighters, where had they been as the bombs whistled down? *Leutnant* Helmut Niklas was one of them, and he had been in the air in his Bf 110 with his *Bordfunker*, *Unteroffizier* Heinz Wenning. With no victories to their name, the two men were not the primary fighter for their allocated box, so had been forced to sit on the ground and watch as the raid unfolded. "The waiting was agony, but at last we got the order to scramble." By the time they reached their patrol altitude, Cologne was burning, producing enough light – the flames were actually visible from the air some 125 miles away – to enable Henaja fighting. "We saw the first one [bomber] at 1,000 metres ... we recognised it as a Wellington. The enemy saw us almost simultaneously." Overshooting the Wellington as it tried to shake off its pursuers, Niklas managed to put a burst into the port engine. "It caught fire and we could see a faint glow." Coming around for another go, Wenning saw his pilot "fire another burst into the fuselage and wing, which now began to burn brightly". The Wimpy pilot tried to hold her steady, but in vain: "It tipped over and went down like a comet, trailing a banner of fire behind it. There was an explosion just above the ground." The two men were elated, with Wenning slapping his pilot on the shoulders – "our first Abschuss!"

They went off in search of another target and found one almost immediately: "another Wellington ... we went straight into the attack." Closing fast on the bomber, Niklas waited and then "from point-blank range our guns fired into him, sawing into the fuselage and wing. I immediately saw flames coming from the stern." Wenning thought they had scored another victory unscathed, only for his pilot to shout, "I'm wounded." The fire the radio op had seen was the bomber's tail gunner bravely defending his aircraft and crew. Niklas and Wenning were now in desperate trouble, even as the Wellington plunged to its doom. Niklas was badly wounded, "his left arm was hanging down, lifeless ... he could feel the blood pouring down and asked me to bind his arm." Niklas tried to steer them home, despite most of his instruments being shot to pieces.

Nearing the airfield, he asked for the landing lights to be put on to guide him in, but ground control refused, citing the danger from the bombers. Faint with blood loss, Niklas kept on slumping forward, only to repeatedly pull himself together. With Wenning directing his pilot in between black outs, they somehow didn't crash, then *Leutnant* Niklas fell forward again. "There was a cracking noise, but quite soft. Soil was flung up against the cabin ... the cracking and banging got louder, then there was a jerk. I was flung to one side, all then was quiet." Incredibly, both men survived, although Niklas would be out of action for several months. He wasn't the only night fighter pilot to claim two victories that night, Werner Streib did the same – his twenty-fifth and twenty-sixth.

Overall, Bomber Command lost 41 aircraft in Operation *Millennium*, far and away its biggest single loss of the war so far, with 16 shot down by flak, two colliding, and the rest falling to the Nachtjagd. Another 116 were damaged, almost all hit by anti-aircraft fire. However, while these were not losses that could simply be shrugged off, Harris felt vindicated and ordered a further two bomber raids on the same scale as soon as was practicable. The first was just two nights after Cologne, on the city of Essen, on the night of 1 June. Home to the enormous Krupp armament works, Essen had been a prime target for Bomber Command since the start of the war.

After the losses over Cologne, particularly the level of damage to so many aircraft, the British fell just short of putting a thousand bombers into the air, for what was still a remarkable achievement. The results though, were unremarkable. Low cloud and haze obscured the target and the marker flares, and in the end only a paltry 11 houses were destroyed, with more buildings lost in the surrounding cities as bombs went astray. Another 31 bombers were shot down. The last of Harris's thousand-bomber raids had to wait until the end of that same month, when the city and port of Bremen was attacked. On the night of 25 June, Bomber Command sent a stunning 1,067 aircraft – 20 more than against Cologne – to saturate the target. Once more, low cloud – Bomber Command's most frustrating enemy at the time – sheltered the target, but this time the bombing was far more deadly than at Essen, and large parts of the city were razed.

The cost was again high. Forty-eight aircraft were shot down, exceeding the losses over Cologne. At least one of the bombers was shot down by 20-year-old Hans-Heinrich 'Skittle' König, piloting a Bf 110. Along with his radio op, König had a war reporter on board that night, keen to describe the glory and bravery of the night fighters to the German public. The reporter must have had mixed feelings that night, given Bremen was his hometown, and as he took off and climbed he could clearly see the "core of raging red fires". Alerted for an intercept, they homed in and "There he is ahead! ... It is a Lockheed Hudson." Coming in from slightly below to hide from the tail gunner, König got into position and "The fighter is snatched upwards and fires from all barrels ... for a moment we gaze into a fountain of deadly fireworks." Damaged but still flying, the Hudson dived away, but König followed him and made two further attacks. "He's burning König, he's burning! ... a burst goes into his starboard wing ... the machine disappears reeling into the white veil, there is a flash." Immediately called on for another target, König sped away as his piggy-backing journalist mused on "how ghost-like is the confrontation with the enemy in the sky at night."

Then all hell was let loose as König called out, "I'm attacking!" It was a Wellington, and as the young blond-haired German opened fire he was matched by a return burst from the sharp-eyed tail gunner. In disbelief, the reporter heard König say over the intercom: "I'm wounded! I'm finished! Get ready to jump!". Both the pilot and radio op were bleeding from head wounds, with "a gaping hole in the glass cockpit roof" where the Wellington's gunner had hit home. Somehow composing himself, and to the reporter's relief, König then changed his mind. "My right eye is gone, but I can still hold the machine. I will try to get you home." Nursing his aircraft back to base, König made a safe landing: "A small bounce on the grass, then the machine completes its run and stops."[7] One hundred and twenty bombers were lost in the three raids and, although the British press trumpeted their success, Harris dropped the idea of launching any more giant raids – for now.

Without knowing it, the Germans had bought themselves some breathing space, but they failed to use it to its fullest advantage.

Kammhuber was astute enough to recognise that the three raids were more than just a change in scale, they were also a major change of tactics. At the Heligoland Bight the British had come on "like Cromwell's Ironsides" shoulder to shoulder, when switching to night attack they had acted almost independently, choosing their own routes and bombing as and when they arrived over the target. Now came the 'bomber stream'. Aircraft would fly independently as before, but at the same speed and along a common route and be given a height band and a time slot in which to bomb. This would significantly reduce the length of the raid, which previously could have lasted several hours, and concentrate the effect of the bombing into 40 minutes or less. The sheer mass of the stream would overwhelm the German defences and provide safety in numbers for the bombers. Given staggered take-off times and the speed of the aircraft involved, one such bomber stream for a 'maximum effort' raid, involving most of Bomber Command, could typically be 150 miles long and over a mile deep, with stragglers making it even longer. But the true secret to the bomber stream as a challenge to Germany's defences was its relative lack of width. This meant the bombers could breach the Kammhuber Line through as few as four air defence boxes and – even with a matrix of boxes – the result would be that the vast majority of German night fighters would be neutralized, their pilots and crew sitting on the ground waiting to be scrambled, or even worse aimlessly loitering around their control beacons, burning up fuel before landing after another fruitless sortie.

The target-rich bomber stream would provide excellent pickings for the few night fighter pilots it would charge through and back, but with each box designed to vector a single fighter onto a single bomber, more than 40 other bombers could fly in, through and out of a box during a single intercept time. If the Germans were lucky – or especially skilled – they could perhaps carry out two or even three interceptions before the stream disappeared, but it wouldn't be enough.

This was the conclusion that Kammhuber didn't appreciate. The stubbornness he had needed in the campaign's early days, to win out against internal opposition to night fighters and create his country's night-time air umbrella, was now an obstacle to the necessary evolution of that same umbrella. To keep the upper hand, it was essential to bring the Luftwaffe's growing night fighter strength to bear and shoot down so many bombers at a time that the British would be forced to call a halt to the offensive. Kammhuber didn't see it – or rather he refused to believe it.

Cologne and its aftermath gave the opposing supremos, Josef Kammhuber and Arthur Harris, a lot to mull over. In the meantime, the bombers kept on coming, albeit in far smaller numbers, and the Nachtjagd kept on meeting them in the skies. With the nights shortening, Bomber Command prioritised Germany's northwest coast and the Ruhr – both within reach during the shrinking hours of darkness. Having been subjected to the last of the three one-thousand-bomber raids, Bremen was hit again several times, and then it was the turn of industrial Duisburg. The Ruhr city was attacked four times in under a fortnight. Far fewer bombers – typically around 2-300 – made for far easier pickings for the Nachtjagd, and they recorded 102 victories in July.

However, amidst the almost nightly battles, a chain of events was occurring that would profoundly alter the course of the campaign over Nazi Germany – the Americans were coming.

In their first meeting after the Pearl Harbor attack and Hitler's declaration of war on the United States, Churchill had persuaded Roosevelt to adopt a 'Germany First' strategy. This committed the American President to a massive build-up of the US Army Air Force and Army in Britain, while the Navy and Marines held the ring against the Japanese in the Pacific. Britain would now, once again, fulfil its role as a concentration area and unsinkable aircraft carrier for the Americans.

America's initial aerial contribution to the campaign over Germany would be the VIII Bomber Command, although it would soon become forever known as the Mighty Eighth – the Eighth US Army Air Force. Established in January 1942, the first personnel and equipment began to be shipped to Britain by convoy in April. At the same time, one of Britain's largest ever construction programmes was begun. While it was envisaged that the first US units would use existing RAF airfields and facilities, the sheer size of the American command meant new air bases were needed on a massive scale. Each new base was designed to accommodate between 20 to 50 bombers and needed a total of 640,000 square yards of concrete for runways, taxiways, hard standing and so on. That was enough concrete to build a road 18 feet wide and 60 miles long. Each base would take several months to build – the largest up to ten – and would typically use 1.5 million man-hours of labour.

In early June, US ground personnel took up residence at RAF Polebrook in Northamptonshire, to be followed a month later on 6 July by the very first B-17 bombers. The B-17s would be joined by B-24 Liberators, but it was the Flying Fortresses that would epitomise the US bombing campaign over Germany. The Boeing B-17 Flying Fortress was a four-engine heavy bomber and a veritable flying armoury. While the Heligoland Bight experience had convinced RAF Bomber Command that unescorted bombers operating during daylight were easy meat for fast and agile fighters, the Americans still wholeheartedly believed in precision bombing by day. Their faith rested on their bombers' ability to defend themselves, and that came from firepower and flight discipline. Unlike the British four-engine fleet, which relied on darkness as its main form of protection, the Flying Fortress bristled with heavy .50-inch machine-guns, the legendary M2 Brownings. The Americans were also trained to fly in huge 'boxes' with aircraft rigidly positioned in a tight formation in the air, enabling them to act as a unit and bring as many guns as possible to bear on attacking fighters.

The first US bomber mission was flown on 17 August 1942 against the industrial zone of the French city of Lille. More French targets were attacked over the next few weeks to allow the crews and staff to acclimatize themselves to a war that had already been going on for almost three years. For the very first time Luftwaffe day fighters were coming up against US bombers, and they succeeded in shooting down a Flying Fortress over northern France at 6.55pm on 6 September, swiftly followed by a second ten minutes later. One US pilot described being shot at by a Bf 109 as "rather like sitting in the boiler of a hot water heater and being rolled down a steep hill", while another saw a German cannon shell "tear a hole in the skin [of a wing] you could shove a sheep through. The entire wing was just a goddamn bunch of holes."[8] Truth be told, the Nazis didn't have a high opinion of the fighting ability of Americans in general, believing them lacking in the necessary resolve. The appearance of the US Air Force over France however, gave them pause for thought. The German day fighters hadn't seen a British bomber in over two years and were used to a diet of aerial jousts with the aircraft and men of RAF Fighter Command. Clashing primarily with Spitfires, the Germans had held their own, even as more and more of their number were ordered east to the titanic struggle in Russia. Now they were faced with a dramatic change – the huge, four-engine Flying Fortresses. They initially called them 'bluebottles', a reference to the metallic shine of their unpainted air frames, and they would nickname them *dicke Autos* – 'fat cars'. Otto 'Stotto' Stammberger, an *oberleutnant* in JG 26 covering the Channel coast, was involved in one of the first clashes with the Americans on 9 October, as B-17s and B-24s headed once again for the steel and locomotive works in Lille.

> We spotted a large formation of formidable fat bluebottles and they weren't flying in tight formation ... We came in from behind, charged into the single vees [the B-17s flew in a V-formation] in pairs and attacked like wild men; approach from behind, full throttle and dive away. The things got bigger and bigger and all our attacks were begun and broken off much too early as we feared colliding with these 'barn doors'.

After several unsuccessful attacks, Stammberger realised what was wrong: "40 metre wingspan! I then approached much closer and saw hits on the left wing. By my third attack both left engines were burning, and I fired freely at the right outboard engine as the crate spiralled down in broad left turns."[9] Five bombers were lost at the cost of two Luftwaffe pilots killed.

This was just a foretaste of things to come, but the Americans were learning. They realised that most German attacks came from the rear, where the B-17's high tail fin obstructed the top gunner's ability to provide effective fire, so they lowered it in later variants. In response, *Hauptmann* Egon Mayer trialled frontal attacks, aiming to destroy the cockpit and kill the pilot and co-pilot. His first opportunity came on 23 November when he led his gruppe against a 44-strong US bomber force attacking the drydocks and naval installations at St Nazaire on France's Atlantic coast. Identifying a clutch of five bombers, Mayer went head on with a wingman on either side. One German fighter pilot later described what it was like to make a head-on attack.

> Everything went very quickly with this tactic, every second bringing us 200 metres closer together, and of course we didn't want to collide but pull up over the bomber. To pull up we needed the whole last two seconds, so our guns were adjusted to 400 metres ... we didn't have more than a second to fire our guns ... a very dangerous business.

The Fortresses had no nose guns and although the German pilots only had a split second to fire before taking evasive manoeuvres to avoid a collision, they managed to shoot down four bombers for the loss of just one of their own. Again, the Americans adapted and a nose gun turret was added, raising the number of machine-guns on board to thirteen.

While the likes of Stammberger and Mayer were beginning to test out their new enemies, decisions were being made back in the Reich that would have a calamitous impact on their future ability to combat America's growing bomber strength. The first had actually been made back in March, before the first convoys of American Air Force personnel had reached Britain. Knowing that America's vast industrial potential would soon be brought to bear against Germany, Erhard Milch – Ernst Udet's successor as head of production and supply to the Luftwaffe – had presented a plan at a high-level conference in Berlin to his boss, Goering, and Hans Jeschonnek as Luftwaffe Chief of Staff. Milch's presentation was extraordinary. He proposed the wholesale junking of the Luftwaffe's current supply ethos, and the takeover in all but name of the entire German aircraft industry. Jeschonnek was left open-mouthed, and even Goering, no stranger to political power grabs, was astounded. What especially took both men aback was that the current set-up was Milch's brainchild anyway and bore his name – the Milch System. At a stroke, the man infamously known as having one of the largest egos in Nazi Germany's military hierarchy was admitting fault on a colossal scale. This was very 'unNazi' behaviour, and they knew it. What had driven Milch's conversion?

The answer was an urbane architect from Mannheim in southern Germany; Albert Speer. Speer and Milch had long recognised each other as kindred spirits; ambitious, unscrupulous and ruthless, but also possessed of talent. A favourite of Hitler, for whom he had designed several prestige projects including the *Zeppelinfeld* stadium in Nuremburg as home for Nazi Party rallies, Speer had succeeded Fritz Todt as Minister for Armaments and Munitions on the latter's death in a plane crash on 8 February. In this role, Speer's remit only covered the Army, with the Luftwaffe and Kriegsmarine in the hands of others. This was not a situation to his liking and he did everything in his power to change it. With Hitler's support, less than a month after taking office, he inveigled Goering to name him 'General Plenipotentiary for Armament Tasks' in the Nazis economic Four Year Plan. This move increased his influence but he needed allies, and Milch proved a willing accomplice.

In discussion, both men realised that the widely held image of German industrial efficiency was a myth. Speer related how not long after assuming his new role he left his office in Berlin late one afternoon and went on a surprise visit to an armaments factory in the city only to find it locked up and only the nightwatchman on duty – everyone had gone home for the day and a night shift was unheard of. Worse still, not long after his Berlin jaunt, he met Junkers' General Manager, Dr Heinrich Koppenberg, at his large manufacturing plant in Dessau in Saxony. Speer said Koppenberg "took me into a locked room and showed me a graph comparing American bomber production for the next few years with our own. I asked him what our leaders had to say about these depressing figures, and he replied, 'That's just it, they won't believe it,' whereupon he broke into uncontrollable tears." There is more than a whiff of personal aggrandizement in this recollection, and Speer was a man who created a powerful post-war myth about himself, but what can't be denied is that in confronting the future American aerial threat, the major problem was one of scale.

This was the nub of the issue. The Milch System embraced a throwaway culture, with the emphasis on replace rather than repair, and no thought given to the kind of exponential increases in production that Britain was committed to, let alone the United States. The Nazis instead envisaged a series of quick campaigns where industry would provide new aircraft to keep frontline strength at an acceptable level, so damaged and worn-out machines could simply be discarded in aircraft graveyards. Overall production was indeed increasing, from 10,826 aircraft in 1940 to 11,776 the following year, but this could hardly be described as a manufacturing revolution. Not that the sector could produce such a revolution, even if it wanted to. Composed of a mass of competing companies, the industry was riddled with inefficiency on a grand scale, and the diktats of the *Reichsluftfahrtministerium* (Reich Air Ministry – RLM) only made matters worse, with bureaucrats constantly demanding minor changes that continually halted production. More than a few aircraft works were still 'craft' orientated rather than organised for mass, assembly line production, with an emphasis on highly skilled, high specification, manpower intensive manufacture. With no centrally directed targets, companies found it in their interests to overestimate their requirements for raw materials and hoard whatever they were given, rather than be encouraged to innovate their way out of scarcity.

BMW's radial 801 engine was a classic example of the malaise. The jack-of-all-trades engine for the German aero industry, some five tons of high-grade metal were allocated to each manufacturer to build one, and yet half a ton of that precious metal was then lost in the machining process. Valuable hours were spent machining down aircraft bulkheads and non-vital fittings, and minor non-load bearing parts were finished to exact tolerances that spoke far more of engineering obsession than practical manufacturing. Even the crew seats were obsessed over, with Luftwaffe backsides sitting on the finest upholstery of any aircraft in the world. All of this at a time when British aircraft manufacturing was increasing at pace and Washington was placing orders with its own producers that had Boeing building factories to accommodate a staggering 100,000 workers each to meet the Government's targets.

In place of the existing system, Milch proposed centralised control of the industry, with resources directed towards those manufacturers that hit set targets. Modern, high-volume manufacturing would become the norm, plants would concentrate on single model production and the hoarding of raw materials would be punished. The size of the workforce would be increased – up to 2,300,000 by 1944 – but skill levels would be reduced to speed up production, and the standard 48-hour working week would be replaced by round-the-clock shifts. Milch's presentation then reached its climax. He knew his audience, and with a flourish announced the new plan would be called the *Goering Programme*.

Before a flabbergasted Goering could respond, Milch then played his ace: "Herr *Reichsmarschall*, your total demand is for 360 new fighter aircraft per month. I fail to understand. If you were to say 3,600 fighters, then I would be bound to state that against America and Britain combined even 3,600 are too few! We must produce more." Jeschonnek dived in: "I do not know what I should do with more than 360 fighters!" Clearly, the Luftwaffe's Chief of Staff was out of his depth in the burgeoning air war, and Milch knew it. He and Speer were co-conspirators in their mutual drive for ever greater personal power. For Speer, the prize was to supplant Goering as the Reich's economic supremo, and for Milch it was premiership of the Luftwaffe.

Goering accepted much of Milch's plan, paving the way for the increases in production that were such a feature of Germany's war effort from then on. Milch, admired and disliked in equal measure by his contemporaries, was in his element; touring factories, meeting with officials, cajoling and persuading managers. His peer, *Generalmajor* Klaus Uebe, said of him, "Taken in the right way and assigned to the right position he was a motor without equal." Crucially, however, Milch's '3,600 fighter' boast was shrugged off by Goering, who continued to believe that the aerial threat posed by America was a chimera.

One man who didn't agree with Goering on the looming danger was the celebrated bomber pilot Hans-Joachim Herrmann. Awarded the Knight's Cross in the autumn of 1940, 'Hajo' Herrmann had gone on to take part in the near destruction of the Russian-bound PQ17 Arctic convoy, and then hit the headlines again in April 1941 when he blew up the British ammunition ship, the *Clan Fraser*, in Piraeus harbour near Athens. The resulting explosion sank a number of other ships in the port and made the whole facility unusable for months. A committed Nazi, he believed utterly in the offensive principle and the crucial role of the bomber in delivering German victory. His appointment to the Luftwaffe staff in Berlin in July 1942 was – as far as he was concerned – a heaven-sent opportunity to press the case for increased bomber production, and on his arrival in the Ministry he participated in a number of meetings concerning RAF Bomber Command. To his utter dismay he was told that "the British had an annual production potential totalling 15,500 twin and four engine bombers, while our night fighter capacity totalled just 1,700 per year." On further investigation with colleagues, he was even more shocked to find out that "In a year the Western Allies were producing 29,000 twin-engine and four-engine aircraft against which our own fighter production of 10,000 a year appeared rather pathetic." He also discovered that the same enemy "would be able to call on cover from their forecast fighter production of 19,000 per year ... a ratio of five to one against us."

All thoughts of fighting the bomber's corner went out of the window, as the tall and imposing flier "saw no unified view of production based on the threat and an overall plan to combat it". Herrmann came up with his own plan to "ruthlessly cut bomber production, and from the released capacity fighter production should be greatly increased." He went further and tried to persuade colleagues that "70 fighter gruppen could be formed from 35 bomber gruppen and a further nine fighter gruppen could be formed from nine Stuka gruppen." Officials at the Ministry were dumbfounded, and Herrmann's erstwhile bomber comrades more or less ostracised him. His proposal was swiftly dismissed as "a naïve fallacy".

Adding to all this turbulence within the senior echelons of the Luftwaffe was the upheaval caused by the introduction of a new aircraft into the inventory of the day fighter arm – the Focke-Wulf Fw 190. Going into the war, the Bf 109 was, of course, the mainstay of the fighter staffeln, and, apart from the British Spitfire, the finest fighter in the world at the time. However, a 42-year-old former Prussian cavalryman had other ideas. Kurt Tank was head of the design department of the famous Focke-Wulf aircraft company and had built a prototype of a new single seat fighter that he believed could supplant the Messerschmitt – the Fw 190. Intrigued by Tank's claims as to its capabilities, Goering himself went to Bremen in 1940 to see a test flight, and he was hooked. He famously told Tank to "turn these new fighters out like so many hot rolls".

Tank took the head of the Luftwaffe at his word and starting in 1941 the new fighter was rolled out to frontline units. It was a hit with the vast majority of its pilots, being more forgiving to fly than the Bf 109 and more rugged, a key attribute in the new campaign in the Soviet Union where the airfields were usually bumpy grass strips on the sun-baked steppe. It excelled at low and medium altitude where the overwhelming amount of dogfights with the Soviet Air Force occurred, and it had a far greater ability to absorb punishment and keep flying – vital when ground fire from Red Army troops was a constant factor in Russia and brought down many a German pilot.

Indeed, the failure of the Nazis Barbarossa offensive to defeat the Soviet Union in 1941 was now beginning to be felt in the aerial campaign over Germany, as well as in every other facet of Germany's war. It had been anticipated that shifting the greater part of the Luftwaffe to the east was only going to be a temporary measure, and that following a German victory the bulk of her forces could once more be focused in the west. This was the reasoning behind Goering's demand of his slimmed-down western command to hold down the fort for now. "All such tomfoolery will be unnecessary once I get my *geschwader* back to the west ...

but first the Russians must be brought to their knees." This was as close as Goering would come to an admission that the Luftwaffe was stretched too thin to cover both the Russian theatre and the home front.

By the summer of 1942, the Fw 190 was firmly established among the Jagdwaffe, while the Bf 109 had gone through two major evolutions, from its Battle of Britain 'E' for 'Emil' variant, to the 'F' for 'Friedrich' model, and then on to the 'G' for 'Gustav' model, coming on stream. The G-model was a world away from the original 109 with its ultra-sleek lines and rapier outline, instead the Gustav was heavier upfront, with more armour and far more armament, and designed less for speed and nimbleness and more for resilience and firepower. Pilots' views on it were mixed. Some sang its praises but not all, and one memorably described it as a *Scheissbock* – a bucket of shit. In truth, the Gustav was a compromise. At the time the head of the Luftwaffe's Technical Office held a meeting with Willy Messerschmitt to express his view that while the 109's speed was fine, it needed greater range and a better rate of climb, to which the aircraft designer testily shot back, "What do you want? A fast fighter or a barn door?" The official deferred to the engineer. But that didn't resolve the issue. By 1942 more than a few of Germany's aero engineers thought the 109 airframe at the end of its useful lifespan, and trying to develop it further would lead to significantly reduced returns, but the timing of such thinking couldn't have been much worse. Milch's Goering Programme was clear: to increase production, there would be a ruthless focus on existing aircraft, and investment in wholly new models would be kept to a minimum.

With battle raging in the corridors of the Air Ministry as to where the balance of the Luftwaffe should be, and what was the right mix of aircraft types in the fighter arm, another crisis of even greater import was making its impact felt – fuel. Germany's lack of oil deposits and the Royal Navy's ability to block its access to world markets had long been known to be a significant weakness in the Reich's military capability. The Nazi plan had been to stockpile as much as possible before the war, and then win in as short a time as possible – or at least before the taps ran dry. Barbarossa's failure in Russia had thrown a rusty spanner in the works. With the Wehrmacht now committed to a longer than anticipated war in the East, Hitler had based his summer campaign of 1942 against the Red Army on the premise of seizing Russia's oilfields in the far-away Caucasus and thus solve his dilemma. With German forces consuming huge amounts of fuel as they advanced towards the Caucasus and Stalingrad, pressure on the Reich's dwindling supplies grew alarmingly.

The lifeblood of every fighter in the Luftwaffe – high octane aviation spirit – was especially hard hit. Always a rare commodity, the established reserve of three month's supply had been drained down to just two weeks' worth by September. In a state of near panic, the Air Ministry desperately tried to cut back on consumption, reclassifying the Luftwaffe's units in western Europe as 'non-essential' users and restricting the fuel available to them. Aircraft manufacturers were also caught in the net, with supplies drastically reduced. The result was that instead of every aircraft coming off the assembly line receiving a full flight check, only one in five did, with the others making do with a perfunctory 20 minutes in the air before being shipped off to their frontline units.

The most damaging cut in the long term, however, was the impact on pilot training. Flight schools were also deemed non-essential, with the number of volunteers accepted onto training programmes cut right back. One such would-be flier was Richard Onderka. "I wanted to join the Luftwaffe because my civilian job involved helping design and build gliders, but at the recruiting office they told me everybody who came in wanted to be a flier so there were no vacancies." Like so many others, Onderka went elsewhere. "I was very disappointed and on the way out I spotted a poster for the paratroops and the recruiter said go for it, so I signed up." As for those that did get in, they found themselves and their instructors stranded on the ground and missing out on invaluable flying hours. It was a decision the Luftwaffe would come to rue in the skies over Germany.

In those same skies the war went on. Autumn brought longer nights and Bomber Command took the opportunity to launch raids against Karlsruhe in southwestern Germany on 2 September,

Bremen again two nights later, and then Düsseldorf in the Ruhr on 10 September. The northern port city of Kiel was attacked in October, and then the target was Cologne once more, only this time the city suffered little damage, and it wasn't down to the Nachtjagd, but because of a decoy site which lured the main bomber force away. The Cologne decoy was actually part of an increasingly sophisticated ground defence system built around western Germany's cities. At first, the idea had been to fool incoming bombers by lighting huge fires in large enclosures in the countryside outside each possible target, so that when the bombers approached the crews would see the flames and – thinking the objective already on fire – would proceed to drop their bombs on it, thereby saving the city, which would be several miles away. When this proved not only successful but also cheap, the programme evolved, with smoke generators brought in to blur the real target and help convince the bombers to hit the dummy sites.

As Bomber Command got wise, the Germans went one step further, building replica factory complexes on the sites, complete with fake railway stations and tramlines fitted with electrical circuits to simulate the sparks for the overhead lines. The sites would even be dimly lit, as if from poor blackout discipline. The largest single decoy site was, unsurprisingly, a doppelganger of the Krupp works, built outside Essen. The Germans estimated that over half of all bombs intended for the huge armaments site fell instead on the dummy. Stuttgart was also well protected, having no fewer than nine decoys, its main one was codenamed *Brasilien* and located 20 miles north of the city outside the town of Lauffen. So successful was Brasilien that at the end of the war the Allies discovered it had been bombed no fewer than 37 times in place of Stuttgart. Berlin even topped that, with 16 separate decoy sites encircling it, with elaborate measures taken to simulate the real thing, including the covering of an entire lake west of the city with green netting overlaid with a wide band of grey canvas across it to resemble a major road. Major landmarks such as the famous Brandenburg Gate were incorporated, in its case it was replicated in wood and canvas and erected on one dummy site along with all the other buildings surrounding the original.

The icing on the decoy cake as it were, was the deployment of anti-aircraft batteries to 'defend' them. If nothing else at a site like Brasilien convinced a doubting pilot, then heavy flak most certainly did. These guns were a relatively small part of the huge increase in flak batteries across Germany in 1942, as Albert Speer described: "We were forced to build up a strong defence with all these anti-aircraft guns stationed in every town, and because we never knew who'd be next we had to stock all the ammunition there for a heavy attack." Speer's real gripe, however, was that all this damage and disruption was "diminishing my production by 20 to 30 per cent".[10]

He could have added that it wasn't just any old guns the Germans were having to use, but perhaps the finest cannon they produced during the war – the 88mm. Originally developed as an anti-aircraft gun, the '88' was soon found to be a tank killer par excellence, and not only as a stand-alone weapon but fitted into an armoured chassis and called the Tiger tank. The Army just couldn't get enough 88s, but 75 per cent of all of them were kept in the Reich in the anti-aircraft arm. The fire they produced was greatly feared by the bomber crews, despite the fact that relatively few bombers were actually shot down by it. One RAF crewman recalled a flak barrage as resembling "a big box in the air that might be a couple of miles long [and] about a couple of thousand feet deep". Pilot John Whiteley said there were two types of barrage, "one was predicted flak and the other was barrage flak. If you were flying towards a target area where they were predicting flak, you dived away … With barrage flak there's nothing much you can do about it, you just had to keep going straight and level and hope for the best."[11]

Poor weather severely curtailed Bomber Command operations in November and December, with just two major raids on Hamburg and Stuttgart – or rather Brasilien – in November, and two more on Mannheim and Duisburg in December. For the Germans, the lull gave them the opportunity to reflect on the previous year.

At the start of 1942 the Luftwaffe felt it had the upper hand against the British, with the homeland covered by Kammhuber's radar boxes and the Nachtjagd becoming increasingly proficient at shooting down the bombers. Indeed, the RAF tail gunner, Alec Ollar, told his girlfriend, "The crews of these night fighters are the cream of the Luftwaffe. They are the thing we fear the most." Revealingly, he also expressed his sadness that "we have to fight good people [the night fighter crews] so like ourselves." Perhaps Ollar would have been comforted to know that those same crews weren't as marvellous as he feared they were. *Major* Wilhelm Herget, a Bf 110 pilot who had converted to the Nachtjagd in '42, explained how he almost shot down one of his own one night. "Once I followed a Ju 88 for 20 minutes thinking it was a Lancaster and I got very close before seeing it was a Ju 88, I saw underneath four exhaust flames and thought, ah, four motors, nearly a terrible mistake." Narrowly avoiding shooting down the Junkers, he correctly identified a Handley Page and went in to attack from below. "I must shoot as quickly as possible [he wrongly believed the bomber had a belly gun], which I did, and then the plane exploded because it was full of bombs and ... I nearly had to bale out as I was spinning around all the time ... after that I told all my pilots never, ever attack into the bomb bay – shoot in the motor."[12]

Regardless of Herget's wobbles, the Germans felt they had the measure of the British, until the two devastating attacks on Lübeck and Rostock shocked them out of their complacency. It was clear now that they were in a fight and, belatedly, the Nazi leadership stepped up their defensive measures. Decoy sites sprang up and became increasingly complex, the flak arm was significantly expanded, and so was the Nachtjagd, reaching a strength of well over 300 aircraft by year's end and with more on the way – a lot more. That wasn't the end of the saga. Nazi ideology demanded revenge – it screamed for it – and the result was a renewed bombing campaign of their own against Britain. On Hitler's express orders, the Luftwaffe was instructed to launch a series of air attacks against British cities to 'punish' them for Lübeck and Rostock. These *Vergeltungsangriffe* – revenge attacks as Hitler called them – were christened the 'Baedeker raids' after Gustav Braun von Stumm, a press official in the German Foreign Office, announced to the world's media that "we will go out and bomb every building in Britain which is marked with three stars in the Baedeker Guide." (Baedeckers were popular travel guides published at the time by the German company of that name, and they still are.) With the Luftwaffe stretched thin, and the fighting in Russia soaking up men and planes, it was a costly diversion Germany's air force could do without. Several months of attacks cost the Luftwaffe precious aircraft and crews, while achieving nothing of significance. By the time the raids were called off, the Luftwaffe had dropped 2,320 tons of bombs on English cities – Bomber Command dropped more than 45,000 tons on Germany in 1942.

German confidence took another hammering in May when Harris's first Thousand Bomber raid ravaged Cologne. Bomber Command couldn't maintain a force of that size, and most raids for the remainder of the year would usually involve between one and three hundred aircraft, but Berlin's Air Ministry was forced to react, for the first time recalling units back from the frontline to help defend the Reich. In defiance of logic, the failure of Kammhuber's system over Cologne didn't lead to a radical revision of Germany's night defences. Instead, the Luftwaffe general doubled down, insisting his system was correct and expanding his radar boxes until there were 1,500 covering everywhere from Scandinavia down through western Europe and on to Italy, and adding a further two underground central control stations to his original three. He now had his own at Döberitz near Berlin, one at Arnhem-Deelen in the Netherlands, another at Stade on the lower River Elbe, one at Metz in Alsace-Lorraine and the last at Schleissheim near Munich in Bavaria. Galland described the atmosphere inside these 'battle opera houses': "Bad air, cigarette smoke, the hum of ventilators, the ticking of the teletype and the subdued murmur of countless telephone operators gave you a headache." They would be needed, especially as it became obvious to Luftwaffe high command that the British were investing heavily in their bomber force.

Target identification and bombing precision were still huge issues – as Brasilien's success demonstrated – but the British were getting better, and bigger, as the old two-engine fleet was phased out in favour of the four engine behemoths, particularly the magnificent Lancaster. This new bomber in particular gave Wolfgang Falck sleepless nights. "It didn't only make the fighting more difficult; it was the beginning of the end of the air war as far as I was concerned ... that's when we began to feel the superiority of the RAF."

By the end of 1942 some 11,000 German civilians had been killed in British bombing raids. A tragedy, but to put it into context, the Wehrmacht was losing on average 37,000 men killed every month in that same year. What really made 1942 stand out was the arrival on the battlefield of the Americans. Nazi Germany's air defence was overwhelmingly geared towards combating a night-time threat. From now on they would have to fight the bombers during the day, too. It wasn't something they were prepared for, as Adolf Galland admitted of his day fighter force: "At the beginning of the first attacks by four engine bombers ... only three fighter geschwader were on the Channel coast and in Holland ... in Germany itself at this time there were no fighter units."[13]

# 4

# 1943

# EIGHTH USAAF AND BOMBER COMMAND'S BATTLE OF THE RUHR

"The first massed daylight attack by the Americans on Germany marks the opening of a new phase of the war in the air."
Heinz Knoke, Fw 190 fighter pilot, Jagdgeschwader 1.

On 26 January 1943 *Generalleutnant* Max Pfeffer led the few starving survivors of his 297. *Infanterie-Division* into Soviet captivity. The battle for Stalingrad had a few days to run. For the first time in the war, Nazi Germany was about to lose an entire field army – Friedrich Paulus's Sixth. They would be joined in oblivion by the Romanian 3rd and 4th, the Hungarian 2nd and the Italian 8th Armies. The Nazis do or die struggle with Russia would be forever changed as a result.

The following day dawned bright and clear over northern Germany as 64 Flying Fortresses and 27 Liberators climbed into the sky over East Anglia and headed out over the North Sea. This was to be the Americans first ever raid into Germany. Previously limited to attacking military targets in occupied France, Ira Eaker's Eighth Army Air Force had come under increasing pressure to expand its reach into the Reich itself, and the Casablanca Conference of the Big Three had proved a turning point. With Stalin demanding more direct action in the West, including the opening of a second front, Roosevelt and Churchill confirmed a new phase in the air campaign over Germany. The British delegation had tried to convince the Americans to join them in night raids against the Nazis, only for the Americans to refuse and insist instead on their own philosophy of precision bombing by day. The resultant Casablanca Directive was issued to both countries' senior air force commanders and listed U-boat construction yards and the German aircraft industry as priorities for bombing. For Eaker, it meant the focus of his campaign would be on "the progressive destruction and dislocation of the German military, industrial and economic system, and the undermining of the morale of the German people". Harris was a little more prosaic. "It allowed me to attack pretty well any German industrial city of 100,000 inhabitants and above."

The 27 January raid was to be Eaker's first step in achieving the Casablanca Directive, and the selected target was the German naval base and shipping yards at Wilhelmshaven on the west German coast. On board the B-17s, the crews switched on their oxygen as they reached 8,000 feet and the waist gunners pulled their hatches open and felt the icy blast of air as they swept towards the coast. Standing in the freezing cold they tested their guns and scanned the sky for any sign of German fighters. They wouldn't have long to wait. The Russian invasion had hollowed out the Luftwaffe's day fighter strength in the West, leaving only Jagdgeschwader 1 and 26 covering from Denmark all the way to northern France, with JG 2 defending the U-boat bases on France's Atlantic coastline. With the bombers flying more or less directly over their airfield at Jever, it would be *Oberstleutnant* Dr Erich Mix's JG 1 who would be the first to strike with its Bf 109s. Gustav Rödel was a 109 pilot and remembered that "seeing these huge aircraft was enough to really scare you, their firepower was incredible." The fighters attacked but found *die Boeings* – as the Germans called them – seemingly impervious to their relatively light weaponry. One Fortress was eventually destroyed, but at a cost of four Messerschmitts, with three of the pilots going down into the cold waters of the North Sea. None were recovered.

The Liberators weren't as lucky as their Flying Fortress cousins. Getting lost almost from the start, the B-24s flew across the northern Netherlands trying to get a fix on where they were, only to then give up and jettison their bombs in the sea, where they were met by a staffel of Fw 190s from JG 1. Manoeuvring ahead of the bombers, they managed to make one head-on pass, *von Schnauze auf Schnauze* – snout to snout – successfully shooting down a single Liberator. Defensive fire claimed one Fw 190 which, as it plummeted downwards, sliced the tail off another bomber, taking it with it to its doom. There were no survivors.

Eight days later, the Americans were back, this time aiming for the Ruhr city of Hamm. Sixty-five B-17s groped their way through heavy cloud and failed to find it, settling instead for Emden on the northwest coast. A dogfight between the Boeings and the Fw 190s of JG 1 left six 190s and four Fortresses as burning wrecks, before the intervention of an unexpected player, *Hauptmann* Hans-Joachim Jabs and his eight Bf 110 night fighters flying out of Leeuwarden. These were Helmut Lent's men, although he personally was banned from taking part lest he be shot down and killed – the Nazis didn't want to risk their Nachtjagd poster boy. Erich Handke was a radio operator in one of the Bf 110s:

> The Eisbär [Himmelbett control station in northern Holland] controller directed us over the Zuider See ... we were the last to make contact with the enemy at 23,000 feet, 12 miles west of Texel ... Suddenly we saw the Boeing Fortresses ahead in a great swarm. I confess the sight put me into a bit of a flap, and the others felt the same. We seemed so puny against these four engine giants ... we'd been ordered to attack only from head-on, but no-one did that ... we attacked from the beam following the pair leader.

That pair leader – *Unteroffizier* Scherer – exclaimed, "Contact with 50 bandits, *Pauke, Pauke!* [literally Kettledrums, Kettledrums but meaning attacking, attacking], only to be swept by heavy machine-gun fire from the massed B-17s. Scherer and his radio op were both wounded and only survived because Jabs led his wingman right into the bombers to draw their fire away from Scherer's damaged fighter. Handke's Bf 110 hadn't been able to fire and "we passed behind the formation with everyone firing at us." Then another pair, *Leutnant* Karlheinz Völlkopf and his wingman Karl Naumann, attacked *von Schnauze auf Schnauze*, causing one bomber to drop out of formation, bleeding smoke from one engine. Naumann attacked again, this time from the rear, to finish off the bomber, only for the B-17s determined tail gunner to rake him with fire. Both aircraft went down in flames. Neumann managed to crash land in shallow water just off Ameland island; the Fortress had no such luck.

Finally, it was Erich Handke's turn. His pilot, Josef 'Schorsch' Kraft, led his pair in, aiming for a bomber that had fallen behind the rest. "We attacked ... alternately from behind and above until we were both riddled." Repeatedly hit, the B-17 went into a spin, but both attacking Bf 110s were hit in return. "We had to feather our port engine as it began to smoke. Both port tanks and the starboard rear one were shot through, the coolant and petrol pipes to the port engine and Schorsch's bulletproof windscreen were also gone." In the end, one crewman was wounded and all eight specialist night fighters were damaged and put out of action for quite some time. It was a high price to pay to shoot down three B-17s. Erich Handke ruefully remarked that he and his comrades had been learning on the job, "attacking from the side, from the rear, above and below" and had "mostly fired from too great a range".

Just over three weeks later, after a couple of raids on French targets, the Americans were back once more, heading for the Focke-Wulf factory in Bremen, but on failing to find it, going for their secondary target of Wilhelmshaven instead. They had already had a run in with Eberhard Burath over the North Sea, in his "first contact with the heavies". He had been "flying on the far right of my formation" and then "lost it during a left turn". Flying on alone, he sighted his comrades and headed their way at full throttle. As he got closer, "Their silhouettes grew larger and larger – far too big for fighters." It was the Americans, *Viermots* [four engines – German pilot slang for the heavy bombers] 60 or

70 in tight formation." Without hesitating, Burath prepared to engage: "Fear comes from experience, which I lacked, so without thinking I turned into the formation and attacked." Going in from head on, he found himself "flying through a cloud of bullets and tracer". Firing back, he suddenly saw "a burst coming towards me from the left, as red as a tomato". He veered off and then attacked again. Taking hits on his engine, he finally realised the danger and running low on fuel, headed home. "What did the Amis [German nickname for the Americans] think of this attack by a lone German fighter?" He returned to base "on 13 out of 14 cylinders".

On the ground was Heinz Knoke. Knoke, a pilot in JG 1 just like Burath, was a veteran of the Russian Front, and was now "enjoying the warmth of the first spring sunshine ... the weather is ideal, the sky a clear and cloudless blue." Then, "Attention all! Attention all!" Shaken out of his reverie by the base's loudspeaker, Knoke and his fellow fliers ran for their aircraft. "Canopies close. Mechanics swing the starters. My engine at once thunders into life." Swiftly climbing to 25,000 feet, the German fighters were ordered to loiter and wait for the bombers. Then they could see them. "It is an impressive sight. Some 300 heavy bombers are grouped together [there were actually 93], like a great bunch of grapes shimmering in the sky."

Picking out a Liberator, Knoke decided to make a frontal attack. "The Yank is focused in my sights. He rapidly grows larger. I reach for the firing buttons on my stick." Before he could fire, the Liberator's engineer and top turret gunner, Robert K. Vogt, opened up on Knoke, and was joined by navigator Wayne Gotke and assistant radio operator James W. Mifflin firing from the nose. "Tracer came whizzing past my head, they've opened up on me!" Knoke's first pass wasn't a success: "My aim is poor, I can see only a few hits register on the right wing." He dived below the bomber and then climbed up steeply and broke away to the left. Going in for a second attack, "this time from a little below. I keep on firing until I have to swerve to avoid a collision." Getting in close had done the trick. "Flames are spreading along the bottom of the fuselage of my Liberator. It sheers away from the formation in a wide sweep to the right." Knoke went in to finish off the crippled bomber. Gotke later claimed that the Liberator's gunners shot down three German fighters. "Vogt ... shot down the first fighter, and I shot down the next one ... Sergeant Mifflin shot down the third from his waist position." In reality they didn't hit any. Knoke pressed home his attack and watched as the right wing was covered in flames: "Suddenly the wing breaks off altogether. The body of the stricken monster plunges vertically, spinning into the depths ... One of the crew attempts to bale out, but his parachute is in flames. Poor devil! The body somersaults and falls to the ground like a stone."

On board, Gotke felt as if "someone pushed me from behind and everything went black. I woke up falling through space and I pulled my rip cord, but with no results! I reached back and tore the back off my chute and quickly pulled as much of the material out as possible until it opened." Incredibly, Gotke survived and was found "dangling between two trees about 20 feet in the air". James Mifflin also lived. As for Knoke, he landed back at Jever where his ground crew carried him shoulder high to the dispersal point. "That was my fourth combat victory on my 164th operational mission and 1,004th flight." Knoke, a fervent Nazi, had earlier landed at the bomber's crash site to help the recovery and had seen the bodies of the dead US crewmen. Now the inevitable question came to haunt him. "When will our turn come?"

Using the Nachtjagd, and their precious aircraft and crew, to supplement the day fighters back on 4 February had been a mistake, but Luftwaffe high command were sometimes slow learners and once again, after Knoke and his comrades had broken off their attacks, Jabs and his men were scrambled to intercept the bomber force as it headed home after its bomb run. A dozen Bf 110s soon caught up with the bombers and went into the attack. With them on his very first daylight sortie was the renowned night fighter ace and leading tactician, Ludwig Becker, and his radio op Josef Staub. The 'Night Fighting Professor' already had 44 victories to his credit, and that very day had been informed he had been awarded the *Eichenlauben* – the Oak Leaves – to his Knight's Cross. The night fighters attacked and succeeded in shooting down a single Liberator before turning for home. There was no sign of Ludwig Becker. He had last been seen at the beginning of the fight. Together with Josef Staub, he was never seen again.

There is no record of Hermann Goering's reaction to the news of Ludwig Becker's death. The appearance of the Americans over the skies of Germany was the most significant event in the air war since the British had switched from day to night bombing, and the Luftwaffe needed to respond decisively, but Goering was suddenly *hors de combat*. The reason wasn't hard to find. *Der Dicke* – the Fat One – as he was generally known, had been Hitler's closest confidant for years. The dictator had been drawn to the muscular, bemedaled fighter ace, finding in him a ruthlessness and ambition that matched his own. Alone among senior Nazis, Hitler held Goering in something akin to awe, and had bestowed enormous powers on him that gave him responsibility for the German economy, the state of Prussia, and much of the country's police service. But the jewel in the crown was the Luftwaffe. Whereas the Army and Kriegsmarine were headed up by their own officers, men with decades of command experience, Goering was given a free hand to create a service arm entirely in his own image. He knew his man though. When asked whether he supported the development of a long-range strategic bomber force within the Luftwaffe, he replied, "The Führer does not ask how big the bombers are, but how many do we have."

Belying his later reputation for sloth and self-indulgent excess, it had been Goering's drive and energy that had largely established the Luftwaffe in record time. But if Goering had indeed created the most fearsome air force in Europe in a few short years, it was also an edifice riven with fault lines. Paranoid about potential rivals within his own service, he set up a sort of kitchen cabinet, derisively called the 'Little General Staff' by just about everybody. Packed with cronies such as his old First World War comrade Bruno Loerzer, and even his own doctor, they became Goering's sounding board and first port of call, bypassing the chain of command and obsequiously reassuring the Luftwaffe supremo as to his own rectitude and wisdom.

Goering was increasingly distracted by luxury and opulence – the panzer general Heinz Guderian described how at a dinner party he once cried out "I adore splendour!" – and adore it he did. Surrounding himself with grand residences on the Leipziger Platz in Berlin, an alpine house on the Obersalzberg near Hitler's own, a villa on the island of Sylt, and two castles at Veldenstein and Mauterndorf. Unlike Hitler, he also loved field sports, securing himself the positions of Master of the Hunt and Reichsminister for Forestry. To indulge his passion he had a hunting lodge at Rominten in East Prussia, now Krasnolesye in Russia, which he named *Emmyhall* after his second wife, Emmy Sonnemann. But it was his first wife – Carin von Kantzow – whom he still idolised. After her death from a heart attack in 1931, he commissioned a famous architect to build *Carinhall* northeast of Berlin in the Schorfheide forest in her honour. The country-mansion-cum-hunting-estate-cum-private-zoo eventually boasted a sauna, a bowling alley, galleries crammed with looted art works, and even a huge 321-foot-long model railway set complete with tunnels and bridges that the *Reichsmarschall* could play with for hours. Goering threw lavish parties at Carinhall, regularly appearing to his guests wearing his favourite purple toga complete with gold laurel wreath and wrist guards. His bonhomie was legendary, although it wasn't to everyone's liking, including Macky Steinhoff. "I found him annoying, exhausting and intrusive ... he loved to grab you, almost hug a man and slap your back."

He could be astute, and even enjoyed being the butt of public humour, choosing to see it as a sign of popularity among the people. He always wanted to hear any jokes about him doing the rounds, "no matter how rude", and he loved it when told they said he would wear an admiral's uniform to take a bath, or that he was so fat "he sits down on his stomach." A personal favourite piece of mockery has him carrying out an official visit to meet the Pope in the Vatican, after which he wires Hitler to say, "Mission accomplished. Pope unfrocked. Tiara and pontifical vestments are a perfect fit."

But Stalingrad marked a turning point. Unwilling to face up to the disaster, Hitler had ordered Goering to lead the official public mourning for the loss of the Sixth Army. Regular programming on Nazi State radio was replaced by the brooding tones of the

Adagio movement from Anton Bruckner's Seventh Symphony, and Goering himself delivered a eulogy. In so doing he became the public face of defeat, and the jokes about him were now tinged with bitterness and anger. His morphine addiction – begun when he was wounded in the failed Beer Hall Putsch of 1923 – grew worse, and he retreated more and more to Carinhall. Guderian remembered that:

> His style of dress grew more eccentric, he adopted the costume of ancient Teutons [pagan Germanic tribesmen] when hunting and his uniforms were unorthodox; he either wore red boots of Russian leather with golden spurs or else he'd appear at Hitler's conferences in long trousers and black patent leather pumps, he was strongly scented and painted his face [and] his fingers were covered with heavy rings.

Mussolini's son-in-law and foreign minister Galeazzo Ciano also noticed Goering's increasingly erratic behaviour. He recalled meeting him in Rome: "At the station he wore a great sable coat, something between what motorists wore in 1906 and what a high-grade prostitute wears to the opera."

Just when the Luftwaffe needed him most, its creator more or less absented himself, and when he did act it was usually to the air force's detriment. For instance, his previous lack of interest in technology now became a serious handicap. On radar he remarked that "I have frequently taken a look inside such [radar] sets. It does not look all that imposing, just some wires and a few other bits and pieces. The whole apparatus is remarkably primitive." Concerning the effort to increase production he suggested to an exasperated Milch that perhaps women could do factory work at home so they could still watch their children at the same time. Little wonder that Guderian believed "his influence was uncommonly disastrous."

Marianne Hoppe was somewhat kinder, recalling visiting Goering at one of his homes at the time when his young nephew, a pilot, was there on leave. Goering started talking about flying to Britain and attacking it when his nephew "suddenly turned white as a ghost and said 'the planes we have to fly are all nothing but a bunch of old crates, we're going to get shot down,' but Goering dismissed him saying 'Where would we be today if we'd talked like that during the First World War?' ... Somehow he was never able to detach himself from World War One."

In his absence, the response to the entry of the Americans into the war over Germany fell to Dolfo Galland as head of the Luftwaffe day fighter force, but his gaze was firmly fixed a thousand miles to the south. He wrote of the Allied Torch landings in French North Africa in late 1942: "Thanks to this operation the war for Germany had taken another fundamental turn for the worse ... from the south the enemy knocked on the doors of Europe for the first time." Even as the Eighth Army Air Force began to launch regular raids into western Germany, Galland flew to Tunis where "The situation of the two fighter geschwader fighting there was desperate." The fighter general's fixation on the Mediterranean front was a significant error. Precious pilots and aircraft were pitched into what was in reality a subsidiary theatre of war, despite its tremendous cost to both sides. The transfer achieved little and put further strain on an already overburdened Luftwaffe.

Back on the home front it was left to the likes of Heinz Knoke to try and improvise a defence against the new foe. "Why not try using our own aircraft to drop bombs on the close-flying American formations?" Unbelievably, he and his friend Dieter Gerhard's rather absurd suggestion was taken seriously, and on 22 March Knoke released a 500-lb bomb over a formation of B-17s on their way home from attacking Wilhelmshaven. "My bomb goes hurtling down ... then it explodes, exactly in the centre of a row of Fortresses. A wing breaks off one of them, and two others plunge away in alarm." On landing Knoke was feted by both his comrades and senior commanders, who demanded he "do it again with the whole Staffel!" But Knoke himself thought it probably a fluke and was amazed to be telephoned that same night by Goering himself, who said he was delighted for the "initiative you have displayed" and wished to express to him his "particular appreciation".

Not that all Knoke's superiors felt the same. Josef Kammhuber called the young airman the day after, and in Knoke's words was "incoherent with rage". Knoke "held the telephone at arm's length from my ear until the din subsided". The night fighter supremo evidently considered the young pilot's actions as something akin to insubordination, but Knoke told him that *Reichsmarschall* Goering didn't seem to have a problem with it, and in any case Knoke was no fan of Kammhuber, calling him a "poisonous little twerp, commonly known as *Wurzelsepp*", a play on Sepp being short for Josef, roughly translated as 'Sepp the hayseed'. Knoke's unit continued with the bomb tactic for a time, but it didn't prove worthwhile. What was needed was a huge reinforcement of the day fighter force defending Germany, and a serious plan on how that defence was to be conducted – in the absence of strong direction from the top, both were missing.

In the meantime, the Luftwaffe continued to see the main threat coming from Bomber Command during the hours of darkness. Their concern was understandable. April and May saw a return of daylight raids by the Americans on the Kriegsmarine's U-boat bases on the Atlantic coast, with Lorient and St Nazaire both getting hit, and relatively few attacks into Germany, but the same could not be said for the British. As the Americans took their first tentative steps onto the battlefield over Germany, Arthur Harris was preparing to hit the enemy where it hurt.

Coal had been mined in the Ruhr valley in western Germany since the thirteenth century, and, along with large scale iron ore deposits nearby, had fuelled the industrial revolution in Germany. Massive orders for barbed wire of all things, had then meant boom time during the First World War, along with a huge demand for weapons and ammunition that had made the Krupps' family factory complex in Essen the largest manufacturer of armaments the world had ever seen.

Turned away from the Krupp's behemoth as a sightseer in 1928, Hitler returned six years later as Chancellor and dictator and was welcomed by Gustav Krupp himself. Touring the workshops and assembly lines of the two-square-mile site, Hitler knew he was in one of the most important enterprises in the Reich if he was going to realise his vision of a global Germanic empire. Critical as it was, Krupp's was still only one piece of the Ruhr jigsaw. Even Essen wasn't the whole. It was the valley in its entirety that was crucial.

The 3 million Germans living and working in Essen, Cologne, Duisburg, Dortmund, Düsseldorf, and the other ten or so towns and cities that clustered in the valley were all interconnected; the coal mines feeding the coking plants, those plants supplying the blast furnaces of the pig iron and steel mills, and that iron and steel then transformed into panzer turrets, field howitzers and U-boat crankshafts. Arthur Harris recognised that network, and in it, saw opportunity. In his office in High Wycombe he had a large table covered with a photographic mosaic of the entire Ruhr.

Hitherto, Bomber Command had made a significant number of raids on the Krupp works in particular, but most aircraft had bombed off-target, lured away by a decoy factory, built in the open countryside more than two miles south near the Baldeneysee reservoir. The reservoir itself had been drained in 1941 to accommodate several miles of lights strung up to resemble a badly blacked-out factory site, with goods stations, unloading docks and assembly halls. A pillbox in the valley centre acted as the control room, doing such a good job that up to the beginning of 1943 over 70 per cent of the payload intended for Krupp's had actually landed on the Baldeneysee decoy. The plan now was to mount a sustained campaign against Krupp's and the entire Ruhr valley. Harris intended to strike at the very heart of the weapon smithy of the Reich.

"At long last we were ready and equipped ... on the night of March 5th ... I was at last able to undertake with real hope of success the task which had been given to me ... a little over a year before, the task of destroying the main cities of the Ruhr." Harris had already said, "If I could send 20,000 bombers over Germany tonight, Germany would not be in the war tomorrow; if I could send 1,000 bombers over Germany every night, it would end the war by autumn." Cologne had proven Bomber Command couldn't sustain that level of force, but it did have access to around half that number on any given night, and now they would be focused on the Ruhr valley, starting with Essen and the Krupp works that very night. This was the opening act of the Battle of the Ruhr.

When the crews were briefed earlier that day on their home airfields, there were groans and grumbles. Of greatest concern to the assembled airmen was that "to attack any town or city in the Happy Valley [the Ruhr], as we called it, you had to fly through 20 miles of concentrated flak."[1] Sergeant Robb's concern was not misplaced. In January that year the Nazis had 1,089 heavy and 738 light flak batteries protecting the homeland, usually with four guns per battery. To increase each battery's firepower, trials had been undertaken using six guns per battery, but it had been found that a more effective method was to link three normal batteries together under the control of a centrally located fire director. These *Grossbatterien* (super batteries) became standard across the Reich in the autumn of 1942. Some 1,680 barrage balloons were also deployed around major cities, while the number of searchlight units expanded from 174 in 1942 to 350 a year later.

The effectiveness of flak versus night fighters has been hotly debated ever since the war and was also a major point of discussion at the time. Flak's detractors point to the enormous resources poured into the arm that otherwise could have gone to the front and the number of aircraft shot down compared to that of the Nachtjagd. They also, quite rightly, highlight Hitler's emphasis on the importance of flak from the point of view of civilian morale rather than military logic. There is more than a grain of truth in these arguments. However, not all can be taken at face value. Hitler did indeed believe flak was good for morale, but also believed in its effectiveness, and the RAF's own figures go some way to support his view. Bomber Command lost 696 aircraft from July to December 1942, with 169 going down to fighters and 193 to flak. A shocking 334 were lost in accidents or scrapped due to damage – much of that from flak. In the first three months of 1943 the fighters did better, shooting down 96 bombers against 90 for the flak, but when damaged aircraft are counted, the airmen sent a mere 81 limping home versus an incomparable 724 for the gunners. In terms of manpower, the flak arm was huge, with over 1 million personnel in uniformed service at the beginning of 1943 – unsurprising given a heavy gun battery required between 130 and 150 people to man it. But then, the days of those personnel being young, fit men who could have been better employed at the front were gone.

On 13 January 1943, Hitler issued a directive entitled *Comprehensive Employment of Men and Women for Duties in the Defence of the Reich*. It called on all German citizens "whose labour capabilities are not at all or not fully utilised ... to bring their abilities to bear". In practical terms, all males aged between 16 and 65 and all females between 17 and 50 were now liable for call-up. Overwhelmingly, they would become *Flakhelfer* – flak auxiliaries. The Luftwaffe's *Luftnachrichtendienst* (Air Signals Service) was a major beneficiary of the influx of manpower – or rather girl power – with its commander, *General* Wolfgang Martini, informing Goering that the service was "mostly delivered by young women". These women – nicknamed *Blitzmädel* or *Blitzmädchen* (Lightning Girls) – acted as telephone, telegraph and radio operators, as well as performing key tasks in the co-ordination of day and night defensive operations. For most, it was their first taste of life outside the family home, and with it came real responsibility and, somewhat bizarrely given the circumstances, a sense of personal freedom.

The Air Signals Service was not the only branch of Germany's aerial defence that benefited from the influx. More and more women in their late teens and early twenties were deployed to searchlight batteries, and even to the guns – mostly on the communications side. This did lead, however, to complications of a sexual nature, with large numbers of romantic liaisons, but also instances of sexual harassment and bullying. Goering himself was obliged to issue a warning to his ground commanders that anyone found guilty of abusing their position in relation to the girls would be punished with the "fullest severity of the law".

As for the remaining men of military age manning the guns, many were redeployed to the front and their places taken by the teenaged boys of years 6 and 7 in German high schools. On Monday 15 February 1943, all across Germany, these 15- and 16-year-olds reported to their local town or city hall with their parents and were duly sworn in to service. In the Ruhr city of Krefeld, 150 boys gathered in the city hall, where they were told by a local dignitary that "you are wood of our wood, flesh of our flesh." In nearby Cologne another youngster said being called up filled him with "a feeling of pride ... that I too can take part in the defence of the *Heimat* [Homeland]." In Berlin, Karl Damm was drafted five days before his sixteenth birthday: "I reported, like almost all my classmates, to the 2nd Battery of the 267th Heavy Anti-Aircraft Battalion for service in the flak auxiliary." At first, he found it "fascinating ... we were impressed by the fact that we were now soldiers." As "almost all of us had been wearing uniform since we were 10 ... with the *Jungvolk*, and then when we were 14 in the regular Hitler Youth," he didn't find it such a wrench. Some were not so pleased. The devout Catholic teenager Joseph Ratzinger was sent to join a battery defending a BMW factory outside Munich. The future Pope Benedict XVI had been conscripted against his will and would end up digging anti-tank ditches in his native Bavaria as the war finally came to an end.

Many parents were not only concerned for their offspring's safety but also their academic future if they missed out on so much schoolwork, so the authorities compromised, with teachers ordered to carry out lessons on the gun positions themselves. Herbert Mittelstädt remembered how his regular teachers "held 22 hours of classroom instruction a week, literally between the guns – you can imagine how excited we were about that."[2] Teenagers weren't the only draftees, older men were also called up, as were – controversially – forced labourers and PoWs. These last categories were almost exclusively from the occupied east – *Ostarbeiter* (East workers) – and had been press ganged into working in the Reich, where they endured brutal conditions. But at least life was better on the gun batteries than it was in the Ruhr's coal mines, and over time their numbers on the guns grew and they took over more and more of the work. A battery commander – one of the handful of posts still reserved for professional gunners – took to starting his daily briefings to his troops with, "Ladies and gentlemen, fellow workers, schoolboys and *tovarischi* [comrades]".

This then was the ground-based defence waiting for Bomber Command as it began its latest offensive. Some 442 bombers took off on the Essen raid, with 412 making it to the city. The sirens sounded at 8.45pm and 15 minutes later the Mosquitoes of the

Pathfinder force began to drop red target markers. In the Krupp complex – equipped with its own air raid warning system and fire-fighting service, complete with 21 fire engines of various sizes – a total black-out went into operation as soon as the sirens sounded. The majority of workers on site went to their designated shelters below ground, leaving only a few key personnel in place until just before the bombing began, when they, too, headed for shelter. For the bombers, identification was good, it was the first time the British used *Oboe* – a new radar tracking guidance system – and in just under 40 minutes three tightly bunched waves of bombers dropped over 1,000 tons of high explosives and incendiaries. In between, more Pathfinders dropped green markers to ensure the follow-up bombers could see the aiming points among the fires.

Harris rather grandly declared that the attack had "inflicted such vast damage that it will in due course take historical precedence as the greatest victory achieved on any front." Hyperbole for sure, but Essen was indeed hit hard. One hundred and sixty acres of the city had been reduced to rubble, along with 3,000 homes. Hundreds more acres suffered damage and 50,000 Esseners – over 13 per cent of the population – were left homeless. A thousand citizens were wounded and 457 killed. However, the main target of the raid – the Krupp works – wasn't smashed. Post-attack reconnaissance two days later identified damage to several large buildings and more than 50 workshops, but little else. Fourteen bombers were lost, just over 3 per cent of the force, with Bomber Command attributing five to flak and the same number to night fighters. As for the others, they weren't sure.

Joseph Goebbels immediately sprang into action in his role as chair of the Inter-Ministerial Bomb Damage Committee, co-ordinating as much of the response on the ground as he was able, although in typical Nazi fashion responsibilities were divided, with Goering controlling civil defence bodies, Heinrich Himmler the police and fire services, and the city's gauleiter all Party organisations on the scene.

The Essen raid was the first act in the battle of the Ruhr, but the second, third and fourth were attacks over three subsequent nights on the cities of Nuremburg, Munich and Stuttgart, far to the south. Launched to throw the Germans off the scent and stop them concentrating their defences in the Ruhr, they collectively cost Bomber Command 27 bombers, one of which was shot down by *Leutnant* Johannes Engels and his Lichtenstein-equipped Bf 110. His 21-year-old *Bordfunker*, *Unteroffizier* Karl-Ludwig Johanssen, described how they closed in on their prey as he sat hunched over the Lichtenstein's radar screen. "The ground controller continued with his orders, but now the pilot only responded to my instructions. 'Rolf [code for height and/or course] – more Rolf – Stop – Marie 2 – a little Lisa - same height ... with a jerk of the controls the pilot called, 'There he is! Pauke, Pauke!'" Attacking from "about 200 metres aft and to starboard we fired our first burst but apparently without effect. But we'd been spotted and the Viermot fired and took evasive action." They attacked again and a third time, the bomber beginning to burn even as it twisted and turned to escape its pursuer. The bomber's tail gunner stuck to his task and there was "a crackling in our aircraft, the starboard engine trailed white smoke – coolant! But it was still running." Engels bore in one last time, his four machine-guns were "on target", but then the Bf 110's starboard engine "packed up and stopped". The hunt had taken the two Germans down to 3,000 feet, and then the "cockpit was suddenly lit up. The enemy aircraft had crashed and its fire lit up the wooded and hilly countryside." Johanssen was about to give his pilot a course for home when the intercom blurted "Jump Johanssen! I can't hold the machine." The emergency lever released the cockpit roof and the young crewman "climbed, no, rolled out of the cabin".

Coming down – God knows where – he walked rather gingerly into a nearby town's main street where a passing soldier helped him find a phone so he could tell his base what had happened. He found out Engels was OK and in Weiblingen at the Gasthof zum Ochsen hostelry. He was then arrested by a local bobby on suspicion of being a downed RAF crewman, his guilt appearing ever more obvious when he couldn't produce his identity card or remember if Heidelberg had an airfield! After an uncomfortable night more or less under guard, he was reunited with Engels at the bomber's crash site and then flown home in his commander's Storch. The downed Halifax's pilot and five of the crew had baled out safely and were taken prisoner. The only one killed was the tail gunner who had so stoutly defended his aircraft, Sergeant Robert Moore.

The following night it was Essen's turn again. Oboe was employed once more and the 457 bombers hit the city hard. Another 40,000 Esseners were made homeless this time, with 648 killed. A petrified teenager cowering in a shelter as the raid commenced recalled that "with every bomb that fell the 'Our Fathers' sounded louder."[3] This time the Krupp complex was badly damaged, with the locomotive shops and rolling stock works burnt out. Of greater immediate import for the Nazi war effort, the panzer construction sheds had also been smashed, which may have contributed to the delay of the planned *Zitadelle* offensive at Kursk in central Russia.

For the next three months Bomber Command was relentless. Time and again, the cities of the Ruhr were attacked by 'maximum effort' raids of 400 aircraft and more. Duisburg, with its iron and steel foundries, was a favourite target, and the end of April saw the largest armada launched against it yet – 561 bombers – which deluged the city with nearly 1,500 tons of high explosives and incendiaries. Also hit were Gelsenkirchen, Bochum, Dortmund, Oberhausen, Mülheim, Düsseldorf and Mönchengladbach. In between the Ruhr raids, Bomber Command attacked Berlin twice. Hans von Luck, a decorated panzer commander stationed in the capital at the time, described his personal air raid routine:

Each evening the apartment had to be blacked out. The little suitcase always stood ready. It contained my most important papers as well as my stock of coffee and cigarettes ... as soon as the sirens wailed – and that happened almost every day – I hurried with the suitcase to the air raid shelter. In Berlin's sea of houses I couldn't stay outside during air raids, the danger of being hit by debris or bomb fragments was too great, besides, everyone had to comply with the instructions of the air raid wardens.

One non-Ruhr raid that went awry was flown against the giant Skoda works in Pilsen in far-off Czechoslovakia on the night of 17 April. The unfamiliar target proved deadly, with 36 bombers lost and another 57 damaged from the 327 that went on the sortie.

Bochum was hit again on 13 May, after which there was a lull of a few days before Wing Commander Guy Gibson led 617 Squadron on the famous Dambusters raid. Two dams were breached by Barnes Wallis's 'bouncing bombs' for the loss of eight Lancasters and 53 crew; and something like 1,400 civilians, at least half of them not Germans but enslaved labourers from Poland, the Soviet Union and Ukraine, alongside French and Belgian PoWs.

Just over a fortnight later the citizens of Cologne feared they would again be the target on the first anniversary of the Thousand Bomber raid that had devastated the city. But for once they could breathe a sigh of relief; it was neighbouring Wuppertal's turn. Hitherto relatively untouched, Wuppertal was not a centre for war production as Essen was, but it still had its tube and sheet metal plants, its wire-rolling mills, and workshops churning out parts for panzers, artillery, and the Luftwaffe's aircraft. Bomber Command dispatched 719 aircraft, with 611 reaching the target. Lothar Carsten – a local member of the Hitler Youth – remembered that "In the middle of the night, at 12 o'clock, the sirens sounded."

The Pathfinders succeeded in effectively marking the Barmen section of the city (Wuppertal was created by the merger of Barmen and Elberfeld), and 2,000 tons of bombs rained down. The leading wave dropped incendiaries which started the fires, followed by high explosives which blew open the buildings. This helped the fires spread, which then sucked in the surrounding oxygen and created a firestorm. The temperature shot up and people began to pass out from lack of oxygen in the shelters. On the streets, those trying to flee found themselves stuck in the melting tarmac and were burned to death. Everywhere was chaos, flames and smoke. Carsten left his shelter after the bombers departed and saw that "the whole horizon [was] blood red." Barmen was effectively destroyed. Over a thousand acres of the city centre were torched, with 80 per cent of the buildings razed. One hundred and eighteen thousand people were made homeless and 3,400 were killed, the most by far from a single raid up until that point.

The next morning the clear-up began, with rescuers making the gruesome discovery that the intense heat of the firestorm not only burnt off people's clothes and hair, but also caused human body fat to melt, meaning three 'fatless' bodies could usually fit in a washtub, and up to eight in a bathtub. A local Nazi Party member noted that on the morning after the attack he greeted 51 people in the city with his customary 'Heil Hitler', but only two returned it in the same manner.

Worryingly for the authorities, the Wuppertal incident wasn't a one-off. Despite Goebbels's propaganda trumpeting the success of the Nachtjagd and the Ruhr's citizens seeing the searchlights and hearing the guns, the people were beginning to blame the Nazis for their suffering. When Krefeld, the largest producer of high-grade steel in Germany, was bombed on the night of 21 June the destruction was so great that over 80 per cent of the city's centre was burnt out, and 40 per cent of its entire housing stock was lost. A fireman said, "The heat was so great that we couldn't touch the metal on our helmets."[4] The next day, under the mailbox of a surviving Post Office, a crudely printed poster declared 'People Awake! [a play on the Nazis own 'Germany Awake' slogan] down with Hitler, Goebbels … These swine have plunged us into misery; every night these raids. Do we need to stand for that?' Days later more posters appeared, this time calling for 'No more of these raids, unite, arise, down with the Hitlerian murderers!'[5] Goebbels himself acknowledged the strain on his fellow citizens, writing in his diary that "reports to me … indicate that the population of one or another city is gradually getting somewhat weak in the knees. That is understandable. For months the working population there has had to go into air raid shelters night after night, and when they come out they see a part of their city in flames." Albert Speer was even more outspoken:

People can't take anymore, they're just getting numb … I was seeing them going through the streets in the morning to work and they were like ghosts, they looked terribly bad but they carried on … in the Ruhr valley where almost every night there were bombing alarms for weeks and weeks and only when it was pouring with rain they maybe had one night's sleep.

He also recognised the people weren't at breaking point, however. "But work still went on in spite of it all, morale was still there."[6]

The last act in the Battle of the Ruhr would be an attack on the city of Remscheid on the night of 30 July. An eyewitness remembered that "it was a summer night, the telegraph spread the word that enemy bombers were on their way to the Raum area of Koblenz. There was also talk of Kassel." It wasn't to be. "At about 11.20pm the air raid warning was sounded." In fact, a raid was indeed hitting Kassel that night, but only as a diversion to draw the night fighters away from Remscheid. The city's flak was now its only defence. "The men who manned the guns often glanced towards the centre of town, which was getting redder and redder with fire. The local youngsters on the guns kept looking towards their burning town with anxious eyes, and a feeling of unknown regarding their relatives. They did their best, but with little success."[7]

Over a thousand of Remscheid's inhabitants were killed in the raid, and when the survivors left their shelters after the 'all clear' was sounded at 2.45am, they were dumbstruck at the devastation. Remscheid was gone. More than 11,000 of its 14,000 houses were rubble and burning timbers. The engineering works, the goods depot and the main railway station were all destroyed.

Remscheid brought an end to the battle of the Ruhr, although it must be stressed that didn't mean an end to the bombing, it simply meant Bomber Command moved on to other missions – indeed it was landing its heaviest blow elsewhere in Germany even before Remscheid was obliterated. As for the citizens of the Ruhr, during the battle they had endured 43 major raids and a number of smaller ones and felt the weight of 34,000 tons of bombs. No town of any size escaped unscathed. Cologne was attacked on four separate occasions by a total of 1,600 bombers; its west bank centre was flattened in the second raid, its industrial areas on the eastern bank on the third, and its marshalling yards in the north on the fourth. Essen suffered even more, as Goebbels acknowledged in his diary. It was scant consolation to the men, women and children of the Ruhr that their night fighters and flak crews had shot down 640 bombers and damaged another 2,000.

Ordinary Germans reacted to the offensive in different ways. A joke doing the rounds at the time indicated that people knew the authorities were lying to them about the effects of the bombing. 'A man took his radio to confession in Cologne cathedral – because it had been lying so much lately.' The raids even coined a ditty popular among the residents of the Ruhr at the time:

*Lieber Tommy fliege weiter,*
*Wir sind alle Ruhrarbeiter,*
*Fliege weiter nach Berlin,*
*Die haben alle 'ja' geschrien.*

"Dear Tommy fly on, we are all Ruhr workers, fly on to Berlin, they all screamed 'yes.'"

Most couldn't even summon up that kind of black humour. With so many civilians newly homeless there was a massive shortage of accommodation, and tens of thousands had no choice but to move out to towns and villages away from the cities. They then had to commute to work on already crowded trains. With so much sleep lost to the air raids it was a common sight to see people fast asleep on rail platforms and in ticket halls, and trains and trams would often arrive at their destinations with every passenger snoring away in the carriages. For many Germans in the Ruhr and further afield, the bombers' obvious success created gloom and despair. One soldier wrote home to his mother from the Russian front, "I have talked with comrades who returned from leave in Cologne. They told me that one third of the city is a pile of rubble and there is much anguish and misery ... it is no use for us to defeat the Russians while the English destroy our homes."

The Germans – or more specifically their night fighters – were, however, fighting back. Their numbers were steadily growing, and would reach six full geschwader by September, offering the potential for more fighters to engage more bombers at any one time. But the very system so painstakingly put in place over the preceding eighteen months was now a major part of the problem. Himmelbett was simply too rigid. For a chosen few in the Nachtjagd, it worked to their advantage, ensuring they were allocated the boxes most likely to be flown through by the bombers – such as Walter Knickmeier's highly sought after *Raum 5B* (Room 5B) over Venray in the Netherlands – thus helping them build big scores, while the majority of crews were condemned to endless patrols resulting in nothing.

On completion of his night fighter training *Feldwebel* Herbert Koch and his crew were posted to Grove air base in November 1942 as one of that unlucky majority. "Grove was the most northerly operational airfield of any Nachtjagd Gruppe ... we immediately asked for a transfer to another area of operations but were turned down ... Only on my nineteenth operational sortie, on the night of 20 April 1943, did I finally get into combat with an enemy aircraft for the first time." Sticking with the system as it was, effectively meant the increase in overall night fighter numbers was almost pointless as the new boys didn't get a sniff of a bomber.

Technology was the answer. If the fighters could be freed from dependence on the ground stations then they could potentially bring their expanding numbers to bear – that was *freie nachtjagd*, or 'free night hunting' as it was called, and it came courtesy of the on-board Lichtenstein radar system. With Lichtenstein fitted the fighters could be inserted into the bomber stream en masse by the ground stations, and then actively hunt. They would then be helped by a wonder weapon developed at Parchim in northern Germany.

The mastermind behind the new weapon was a blond-haired former merchant seaman. Rudolf Schönert spent five years in the Merchant Navy before he decided his future lay in the air instead. Trained at the Air Transport School in Braunschweig, he flew for Lufthansa before the war, and then transferred over to the Luftwaffe and became a night fighter pilot in June 1941. He proved a success in his new role, scoring his first victory on 9 July 1941. As an experienced flyer he had heard stories of First World War fighter pilots fitting upward firing guns to their aircraft, only for the war to end before the idea really took off. He now thought it was time to try it again. The usual attack approach for the Nachtjagd was from behind, using the fighter's greater speed to close in on the enemy and then fire – normally at the engines. An Fw 190 pilot captured by the British and secretly taped talking to a comrade in his room described one such attack on a two-engine bomber:

> I put the rear gunner out of action first ... you could see him firing quite plainly from the tracer. I pressed the button for a very short burst, he crumpled up – that's all, not another shot, the barrels were sticking right up. Then I put a short burst into the starboard engine, which caught fire. I then turned on the port engine. The pilot very probably got hit at that point – I kept my thumb on the button the whole time – it went down in flames.

Bomber Command's own analysis estimated that up to 90 per cent of night fighter attacks up to February 1943 had been made from the rear. But attacking from behind exposed the night fighter to fire from the bomber's rear gunner. What Rudi Schönert realised was that the British bombers didn't have belly guns, so – theoretically – it would be possible for a night fighter equipped with upward firing guns to come up underneath a bomber and get into a firing position without being detected. The pilot could then fly straight and steady, engage the bomber and then peel away safely – all without the unfortunate bomber crew knowing what hit them. In August 1941, Schönert, an *oberleutnant* at the time, put his thoughts down on paper and sent them to Josef Kammhuber. Kammhuber wasn't a fan of the concept but talked it through with Helmut Lent and Werner Streib to get their take. The two aces rejected it out of hand, telling their boss it was impractical. Kammhuber told Schönert to drop it. But he wasn't put off so easily, continuing to secretly experiment with upward firing guns in his own Dornier Do 17. In late July the following year, he reached 22 victories – although none were from his upward firing guns – and was told he'd cured his *Halsschmerzen* (throat ache) as it was called and was awarded the Knight's Cross – nicknamed the necktie or *Blechkrawatte*. None other than Kammhuber himself made the formal medal presentation, at which point the irrepressible former seaman once again brought up his upward firing guns idea. Reluctantly, Kammhuber agreed to have them installed in three Dornier's for trials at the weapon testing site at Tarnewitz on the Baltic coast.

It didn't go well. Using towed drogues as targets the test pilots found that trying to get into position to fire meant having to lean backwards and look up while still trying to fly straight and level – not only uncomfortable but disorientating. Approach after approach had to be broken off until it was discovered that the guns were just as effective when the angle was reduced so the pilot could still look forward to a degree as he lined the target up.

Partway through all this, Schönert was promoted to command of a gruppe and posted to Parchim. His new unit flew Bf 110s but he took one of the Tarnewitz Dorniers anyway. Wilhelm Johnen – 'Wim' – was one of his new charges and liked him instantly. "The 'old man' … was on free and easy terms with the whole mess." Schönert's command was positioned to help defend Berlin, and his first weeks at Parchim were quiet. He didn't dawdle and used the time well, working with one of his armourers, *Oberfeldwebel* Paul Mahle, who suggested replacing the twin machine-guns in the Dornier with heavier Oerlikon 20mm cannons. Mahle had been Helmut Lent's armourer back at the Heligoland battle, and now he brought his experience to bear in helping to create what became known as *Schräge Musik* (best translation would be 'Jazz Music'). Schönert was completely taken by the prototype and had a number fitted to his men's machines. It wasn't long before he would use them in action.

On the night of 30 March he and his faithful radio op, Johannes Richter, were credited with shooting down a Lancaster using *Schräge Musik* during a raid on Berlin.[8] Soon, conversion kits for the new weapon were ready and more and more night fighter pilots opted to have them fitted. Further trials had resulted in the mounting of an optical reflector sight in front of the pilot so he could position himself between 50 to 100 metres beneath a bomber and then open fire using the sight while maintaining level flight. Peter Spoden – one of Schönert's pilots – remembered how his boss told him the British weren't "bad fellows" and had "ended up in this bloody mess just like we have", and then told him to fire into a bomber's fuel tanks between the engines, as "It only takes a few rounds to set the tanks alight, and what's more, the crew still have time to bale out when a wing is on fire." Doing so also avoided the danger of firing into a bomb bay full of high explosive and potentially blowing yourself, your crew and your aircraft to bits. The new weapon soon became markedly popular with night fighter crews – particularly the newer ones who found it easier than the technically more difficult *von hinten unten* method favoured by the older, more experienced pilots.

The first daylight raids by the newly arrived Eighth Army Air Force were of course a wake-up call for the Luftwaffe, but the Americans were still in the process of building up their strength and so the attacks were containable with the number of fighters the Germans were able to put in the air – for now. What the Germans couldn't see – and didn't want to think about – were the endless acres of aircraft assembly lines springing up all over the States, and the tens of thousands of pilots and air crew in training in the cloudless blue skies of the US southwest. The Luftwaffe's focus was still firmly fixed on Britain and the threat from Bomber Command. That threat was very real.

The battle of the Ruhr proved traumatic for a significant segment of the German population. The Thousand Bomber attack on Cologne the previous year could be almost written off as an aberration, a one-time event that could never happen again, but the constant stream of raids over more than four months in the spring and summer were proof positive that the British hadn't just got lucky over Cologne, they could now attack – and keep on attacking – almost at will. For the Nachtjagd, somewhat counter-intuitively, these were still the good times. Karl-Georg Pfeiffer was a night fighter pilot based at Leeuwarden in the Netherlands and considered himself lucky to be in "the best night fighter unit in the Luftwaffe". He recalled how he and his comrades fought it out in the dark skies, and then, "We could nip into town and have an ice cream on the roof of *Vroom und Dreesmann* [a department store] or go dancing in the *Valhalla* and have some fun."

The advent of *Schräge Musik* and the increasing supply of on-board Lichtenstein radar sets made a big difference, helping sustain a night fighter force that could not beat the bombers, but could inflict heavy losses and maintain something of a balance in the air. But even as Pfeiffer enjoyed his ice cream he looked up at the growing American bomber armadas with a sense of foreboding.

Future gazing was one thing, the cataclysm of the present was altogether different, and all Germany saw just how different in late July over Hamburg.

# 5

# 1943

# GOMORRAH

*Die Katastrophe* – the Catastrophe – that's how the offensive on Hamburg of late July and early August 1943 has burnt into German folk memory. Even the Thousand Bomber raid on Cologne isn't recalled with anything like the same horror and anguish. Nazi Germany's second city – *Red Hamburg* – home to nearly 2 million people, the country's biggest port and its gateway to the world – eviscerated.

Before the war, like most German cities, Hamburg was something of a conundrum for the Nazi regime. The Great Depression had almost destroyed Germany as a functioning state. Millions were unemployed and grinding poverty was commonplace. Erwin Bartmann remembered how growing up in Berlin, "I didn't have shoes, I had one pair of wooden clogs and wore them to school every day, including in winter when I walked through the snow." While many Germans – the northern Protestant middle classes especially – saw Hitler and the Nazis as their salvation, millions of others hadn't. Despite the 'Socialist' in their party's title, the Nazis were viewed with mistrust by large sections of the German working classes, who viewed them as being capitalist stooges in the pockets of rich industrialists and bankers. A great number of them turned instead to communism for solutions to their economic and political woes. There had been a number of communist revolts in German cities in the turbulent '20s, and Hamburg's 14,000 card-carrying Communist Party members had staged a short-lived uprising in 1923 that had been brutally suppressed. Almost a decade later, in mid-July 1932, a vicious street battle between local communists and their bitter rivals in Hitler's brownshirts had left 17 people dead and dozens wounded in what became known as *Blutsonntag* – bloody Sunday. Ernst Thälmann, the head of the German Communist Party, was himself a native of the city and represented it in Germany's Reichstag parliament until he was arrested and imprisoned by the Gestapo in 1933. After that, the city's radical tradition was pushed underground, but when the French journalist Daniel Guérin visited Hamburg, he wrote about the workers' "worm-eaten wooden houses" being daubed with slogans declaring 'Death to Hitler!'

Regardless of the discontent of some, the build-up to war had treated Hamburg well. Straddling the mouth of the mighty River Elbe as it flows towards the sea, the ancient Hanseatic city had always been a bustling centre of commerce and industry. When Hitler seized power and pressed ahead with German rearmament, Government contracts, and the money that went with them, flowed into the city, its oil refineries and shipyards. Foremost among the beneficiaries was the mammoth Blohm & Voss yard, which not only built the cruiser the *Admiral Hipper* but also the mighty *Bismarck* battleship, and one in five of the growing U-boat fleet. The downside to the economic boom was, of course, it made the city a prime target for the bombers.

The first to fly to the city were the British, when a small raid on the night of 17 May 1940 seemed to achieve little except "robbing them [Hamburg's citizens] of their sleep", according to the American journalist and war correspondent William Shirer. The RAF returned repeatedly, but never in great numbers, and the number of Hamburgers killed or injured from 1940 to the beginning of 1943 was few. However, the city's authorities didn't sit on their hands during those early years. The Gauleiter, Karl Kaufmann, worked closely with the local SS leader; *SS-Gruppenführer* Georg-Henning Graf von Bassewitz, and the city's fire, police and emergency services, to prepare Hamburg for anything they feared the RAF could throw at them, as well as dealing with the impacts of the first raids. For example, the attack during the night of 15/16 September 1941 was far heavier than the city was used to and left 600 people homeless, so Kaufmann petitioned Hitler to allow him to deport local Jews so he could confiscate their property and rehouse the bombed-out 'Aryans'. Hitler agreed immediately, and the deportations began on 26 October, with 1,034 Jewish residents loaded onto cattle trucks at the formerly disused Hannoversche railway station and transported to the Lodz ghetto in Poland. Most were dead by the year's end from cruelty, starvation and disease. Kaufmann had also overseen the Führer Emergency Programme in Hamburg, but the building of enough air raid shelters for everyone to fit into had been problematic to say the least. Fifteen-year-old flak auxiliary Klaus Kühn described the one in which he was stationed:

> The bunkers were built three to six feet below the surface of the ground and consisted of two to four large tubes about 150 feet in length. The tubes, which were pretty far apart from each other, were connected by fireproof doors. You got into the bunker by a stairway ... once you got downstairs you had to walk down a long hallway ... benches sat on either side and each tube was separated from the others by thick concrete walls so that if it got a direct hit it would be the only one destroyed.

With nowhere near enough bunkers for everyone, improvisation was the order of the day, with large numbers of Hamburgers living in areas above the prevailing water table told to use the *Keller* in their apartment block or house. Keller translates literally as *cellar* but is better taken here as *basement*. The 40 per cent who couldn't avail themselves of a Keller were allocated a place in a public shelter, such as the 15 *Winkeltürme* – or Winkel Towers – named after their architect designer Leo Winkel and nicknamed 'Concrete Cigars' by the bemused residents. The storage basements of city centre department stores and office blocks were also used. The city's Block Wardens were tasked with ensuring every resident under their watch knew what to do in the event of an air raid, to keep a roster of those responsible for firefighting, and maintain buckets of sand and water on every floor of all apartment buildings. To supplement the fire service, there were no fewer than 402 mobile water pumps manned by trained volunteers, and all businesses had to have firewatchers on duty during the hours of darkness, with factories and shipyards required to have their own fire teams.

The Nachtjagd's Himmelbett system covered Hamburg of course, as did the flak arm, with 22 searchlight units, 54 heavy and 26 light batteries containing 166 88mm and just under one hundred 105mm guns. As in Berlin, the Nazis had constructed flak towers – *Flaktürme* – in the city, which rose above the skylines and were topped with huge dual-barrelled 128mm guns – the biggest the flak arm possessed. These flak towers were gargantuan, built from reinforced concrete, their lower storeys available for use as air raid shelters and their upper floors designed to house the gunners and their ammunition. The mass of the defences was positioned to intercept incoming bombers from the west and extended some 20 miles out from the city centre.

Direct fire wasn't the only trick up the defenders' sleeves of course, and, as elsewhere across the Reich, subterfuge was important. Dummy sites were built outside the city – 11 in all – with stone enclosures filled with combustible material ready to light to mimic a burning city, fake railway lines and replica factory buildings, and three smoke generator units to fill the sky with acrid smoke and confuse bomber crews flying through a dozen or more minutes of heavy flak.

Precautions against attack and the frequent blaring of *Meier's bugles*, as the air raid sirens were now sarcastically described, were far from the only changes to normal life in the busy city brought on by the war. The teenaged Hitler Youth member and part-time RLB messenger Uwe Köster explained how he and his schoolfriends would "have six hours of school a day, then we were sent out to collect junk that could be recycled. In our district we collected scrap metal, old newspapers and bones. Oil was made from the bones, which was made into grease for weapons." More noticeable even than the gangs of teenagers roaming the streets dragging barrows like rag and bone men, was the general lack of food in the shops and on Hamburg's dinner tables. A port that used to offload goods and food from across the world now handled mainly iron ore from Sweden and fish from German trawlers that had managed to dodge RAF Coastal Command's mines and patrols. Germany was gripped by rationing, with everything from clothes to coal, horseshoes to bicycle tyres, all requiring the proper authorisation and documentation to purchase, provided the buyer had the money of course. But it was food, and the lack of it, that dominated the lives of ordinary Hamburgers.

By the spring of 1943 an adult in the city was limited to nine kilos of bread per month, along with just under two kilos of meat and 600 grams of cereals. Fats and cooking oil were in ever shorter supply, and whole swathes of foodstuffs were now made from replacement or *ersatz* ingredients, coffee being the most obvious, with Germany's hot drink of choice now almost entirely made from ground acorns or roasted chicory. A running joke at the time pointed out that Germans could no longer commit suicide by hanging themselves as they didn't weigh enough. As in Britain the feeling of shared privation helped bind much of the population together in common cause, although it also rankled among ordinary Hamburgers that while most went hungry, the well-heeled and Nazi Party bigwigs could still dine out in the exclusive Four Seasons grillroom or Schumann's Oyster Cellar.

Alongside food and goods, young men were also disappearing from Hamburg, as the fighting, particularly in Russia, ground on. The list of occupations eligible to be called up for conscription grew ever longer and protected professions fewer, as more young men were hauled in from offices, farms and factories. Their places were taken by older men, or those deemed unfit to serve in the frontline. Even then the gaps in the labour force were huge, and so – as in every other city, town and village in Germany – *Fremdarbeiter* (foreign workers) came in to fill the holes. Some were volunteers from countries the Nazis deemed of at least limited racial value, *Gastarbeitnehmer* (guest workers) as they were called, one of whom was the young Fleming Jef Beutels, who went to Kassel as a volunteer worker in the Henschel engine factory. Beutels and his fellow workers even got involved in the city's air defence: "The local police used us as helpers for the bombing raids and we were always on standby." The Nazis were keen to show their gratitude for the help. "We were all awarded the War Service Cross 1st Class in recognition of what we did."

Volunteers like Beutels were, however, a minority, with most workers transported against their will to the Reich. These forced labourers were mostly from the conquered countries in the east and the Soviet Union, where Nazi policy was increasingly draconian and whole villages were being rounded up, packed into cattle trucks and shipped west to the Reich like so many human chattels. A few ended up working in the flak batteries, but most worked in factories and farms in often miserable conditions. One such *Ostarbeiter* was 15-year-old Irena Chmiel from Lublin in Poland. Irena worked in a lemonade factory of all places, where "Frau Niemayer, our foreman at work, was very nice, she gave me clothes and brought me bits of food." Others weren't so kind: "An old man [in the factory] called us *Polen Schweine* [Polish pigs] and spat at us." Irena and the other girls saw for themselves how the war had taken most men by that time: "There were only three men in the factory, one had three fingers missing … and one was mentally deficient who carried dirty pictures to show us." Even in their spare time, the Ostarbeiter were singled out. "Off-duty we were allowed out as long as we wore our 'P' badge [the letter P on a cloth badge sewn onto their clothing like the Star of David Jews were forced to wear to identify themselves], but some of the children spat at us and threw stones when they saw the badge." Rations for Ostarbeiter were poor. "The food was very bad, fit for pigs. I got sick of strong sauerkraut but we had to eat it. We got one slice of bread a day, it was so thin we used to say we could see Warsaw through it."

By the spring of 1943 there were 66,000 foreign workers in the city, over three-quarters being men, so that whenever Lusie Schmolz ventured out she always heard "a confused babble of languages wherever you hear people speaking". Life for the Ostarbeiter was harsh, with very long hours and often back-breaking labour, but it was almost a holiday in comparison to the conditions suffered by the poor souls brought in to work from the nearby Neuengamme and Fuhlsbüttel concentration camps. The two camps were not death factories like Auschwitz-Birkenau or Treblinka, but they were still places of untold savagery and brutality. The inmates, formed into *Aussenkommandos* (External units), were given the dirtiest and most dangerous jobs, including removing unexploded bombs left over after air raids, and clearing out bodies from under the rubble.

The *Aussenkommandos* were kept busy as Bomber Command persisted with its attacks in the first couple of months of 1943, thereafter launching only a few nuisance raids, mainly with fast-flying Mosquitoes that caused some sleepless nights but little damage. In fact, the city's skies stayed quiet for the best part of five months as spring turned into a baking hot summer. People had not become complacent though, as Louise Schäfer described: "Summer nights always meant a threat of raids, there was constant fear … But it was a fear we had learned to live with, a case of what can't be cured must be endured." June was a warm month, and July saw the thermometer continue to climb, with weeks of sunshine and only the odd splash of rain. With a scant few days to go before August arrived, the temperature in the city's streets topped an unusually high 27°C.

As spring had blossomed in Berlin, all the talk in military circles had been about the forthcoming offensive in Russia. The Wehrmacht always favoured fighting in the summer, and after the Stalingrad disaster it was no secret to anyone that Hitler planned to attack in the East and regain the initiative. Bad weather delayed the start of the attack, codenamed *Zitadelle* (Citadel), and then the loss of numbers of newly manufactured panzers – including Panthers – during the Ruhr battle, had imposed further time penalties. There was also vacillation on the part of Hitler. The pressure was on among army command and its planning staff to launch the offensive as soon as possible to destroy the Kursk salient and the million or more Soviet soldiers inside it, but disagreements about the viability of Zitadelle at the top table were intense, with frontline commanders such as Walter Model and Erich von Manstein expressing serious doubts, and Heinz Guderian -- the Inspector of German Armoured Troops – calling on Hitler to abandon the attack: "Do you think anyone even knows where Kursk is? The entire world doesn't care if we capture Kursk or not."

In this febrile atmosphere, Josef Kammhuber flew to Hitler's headquarters in Rastenburg in East Prussia to present his plan to radically improve the Reich's air defences and defeat the growing threat of Bomber Command. His plan called for the unification of all Germany's night defences under a single command – his own – and the rapid expansion of the Nachtjagd to well over 2,000 aircraft. The diminutive Bavarian had already gained approval for the proposal from Goering and Milch, and he thought the weight of his arguments would surely be enough to persuade the dictator. He was wrong. Hitler – with Speer's warnings about the problems German industry was having in producing the weapons needed for Zitadelle still ringing in his ears – didn't even let him finish his argument. He rejected the plan out of hand, accusing Kammhuber of overestimating Bomber Command's strength and Britain's ability to replace its losses.

Those losses were indeed substantial. In 1940 the RAF had lost 42 bombers to night fighters, that grew tenfold to 421 in 1941 and then increased again to 687 in 1942. The introduction of airborne radar and *Schräge Musik* in particular, had further boosted the effectiveness of the Nachtjagd, with 316 bombers shot down across April and May 1943, and another 235 in June – the highest monthly score they had ever achieved. Taken aback by Hitler's reaction, Kammhuber desperately looked around the room for allies, and found none. Wilhelm Keitel – chief of the Armed Forces high command – was present and knew from his own staff that Kammhuber's forecasts of growing British strength were accurate, but Hitler's habitual yes-man was unwilling to contradict his master and stayed silent. In the gangsterish feuding and politicking that always characterised Nazi Germany's upper echelons, Josef Kammhuber had overplayed his hand and his star would wane from then on. Germany's night-time air defences would remain fragmented. The Nachtjagd had pretty much reached its zenith in terms of overall numbers.

Two days after Kammhuber's plan was flatly rejected, Harris ordered the circulation of Operational Order No. 173 to his six

Group Commanders. The order was headed *Intention – To destroy HAMBURG*. The idea was to put into practice Harris's long-held belief that to achieve maximum impact it wasn't enough to bomb on a single night, the key was to return to the same target several nights in a row – for up to a week or more – and totally overwhelm the city's authorities and emergency services, causing damage that just couldn't be repaired. Headquarters staff at High Wycombe and across Bomber Command began to carry out detailed planning for the operation, even as the battle of the Ruhr continued over the skies of western Germany.

At around 09.15am on the morning of Thursday 22 July, Harris convened his usual morning conference at Bomber Command headquarters and announced the time had to come to implement Op Order 173 – Hamburg would be attacked with a whole series of 'maximum effort' raids. Every aircraft that could fly would be involved, loaded up with every bomb they could carry. The operation was codenamed *Gomorrah*, Sodom's twin city destroyed by God in the Old Testament for its sins. It was due to begin on the night of Saturday 24 July. As the 5,000 or so Bomber Command pilots and air crew went through their usual pre-mission routines on the Saturday, a huge logistical effort swung into action. More than 10,000 ground staff busied themselves on the aircraft, loading over 2,000 tons of bombs and 1.3 million gallons of high-octane aviation fuel into the 791 aircraft being readied for the relatively short flight to Hamburg – a short flight meaning less fuel and more bombs.

That same day, hundreds of miles away in Rome, the Italian Fascist Grand Council held its first formal meeting since 1939. In a marathon 10-hour session, leading members of the Fascist Party lambasted Benito Mussolini for his disastrous conduct of the war and voted by a majority of 19 to 7 to remove him from office. When Hitler heard the news, his gaze turned from the massive battle still raging around Kursk in southern Russia and swivelled south. As for Joseph Goebbels, he noted in his diary that while the English were still concentrating on the Ruhr, the northern skies were so quiet that the anti-aircraft commander had taken some heavy flak guns away from Hamburg to send to Italy, along with some mobile batteries mounted on specially converted trains.

Sent wherever they were needed, civilian cynics said of the latter, '*Die Flak läuft den Bomben nach*' – the flak runs around after the bombs.

In the briefing rooms of 42 bomber bases back in England, a message from Butch Harris was read out to his crews. "The Battle of Hamburg cannot be won in a single night ... at least 10,000 tons of bombs will have to be dropped to complete the process of elimination. To achieve the maximum effect of air bombardment, this city should be subjected to sustained attack."

As the crews filed out to their aircraft the weather was calm and clear, and when the first bomber climbed into the air at 9.45pm it wasn't quite dark. By a few minutes after 11pm all the bombers – half being Lancasters – were in the air. Forty-five turned back due to mechanical difficulty before reaching the coast of Europe – average for a raid this size – the rest pressed on.

Several hours earlier, Germany's *Nachtrichtentruppen* – Signals troops – heard a mass of test transmissions from the bombers on the ground, which they knew was a precursor to a raid. The message went out that an attack was to be expected. The long-range Freya radar stations along the European coast picked the bombers up as they began to climb away from their airfields, relaying approximate numbers, heading and course details to Kammhuber's 'battle opera houses'. On airfields across northern Europe the Nachtjagd prepared itself. Waiting for the bombers were five night fighter geschwader with 301 trained crews and 371 serviceable aircraft, mainly Bf 110s and Ju 88s, with a few assorted Dorniers. There was still no clear indication of where the bombers were heading, but they were coming, and they were coming in numbers.

In Hamburg it had been a hot, sunny day – as it had been for the last fortnight – and as the afternoon turned to evening people were out and about relaxing and enjoying the weather. As on so many other nights the sirens sounded a general alarm and everyone tensed, waiting for the second alarm which would send them scurrying for their shelters. But, again as on so many other nights, it didn't come and instead, ten minutes later at 9.30pm, the All Clear was sounded. The city breathed a collective sigh of relief.

Over the North Sea the bomber stream was nearing the German coast and would soon enter the Himmelbett system. Among the Nachtjagd the safe money was on the British entering Himmelbett over the Netherlands as they usually did. The experienced and skilled crews of NJG 1 readied themselves for a busy night. They would be disappointed. The bomber stream did not turn inland but stayed out at sea, shadowing the coast and heading northeast. In *Generalleutnant* Walter Schwabedissen's 'opera house' at Stade on the lower Elbe, female auxiliaries connected to the coastal radar stations continuously updated their colleagues, who plotted the course of the bombers on the enormous, frosted glass map superimposed with Himmelbett boxes. Where were the bombers heading? Kiel, or maybe Lübeck or Rostock for a second time? Wherever it was, it was clear that Stade would be the nerve centre of the German night fighter defence this time and the long rows of ground control officers in the operations room immediately began to contact their respective fighter bases to get the crews of NJG 3 in the air. Those crews were less experienced than their comrades in the Netherlands but were still confident of giving a good account of themselves as they climbed to their patrol positions and awaited further instructions.

Then came the first contact. A lone Mosquito – one of four sent out on a decoy nuisance raid – had not received the recall signal that took all three of his compatriots back to base and, instead, saw a Ju 88 night fighter taxi to take off from its field at Westerland on the island of Sylt. It was a prefect target. The Mosquito pilot dived into the attack, shooting up the helpless Junkers before it knew what hit it. The riddled German aircraft crashed into the sea with the loss of its crew, *Leutnant* Wilhelm Töpfer and his radio op, *Obergefreiter* Reinhold Hostmann. They were the first Germans to die that night.

The bomber stream had now turned southeast just north of the Heligoland Bight. It seemed that Kiel, Lübeck or even Hamburg would be the target. Liaison officers at Stade called their counterparts in the air raid warning service, gave them the information – and then everything went crazy. "It's impossible, there are too many hostiles ... the enemy are reproducing themselves ... Apparatus put out of action by jamming." Every German radar screen was now showing the same thing – an unimaginable mass of reflected signals as if there were hundreds of thousands of aircraft in the sky all at once – what had happened? The answer was *Düppel*. Thirty-five miles out from German territory the bombers had unleashed a secret weapon; strips of black paper 27cm long and 2cm wide with aluminium foil stuck to one side, pre-packaged into bundles of 2,200 strips, with one bundle dropped every minute. As they dropped, the strips would separate out to form vast clouds, reflecting the radar beams to simulate uncountable numbers of bombers as they slowly descended to earth at 3-400 feet per minute. The British codename for the strips was *Window*, and War Cabinet approval had been given for its use two days earlier. The Germans had also been experimenting with its use at a location in the Berlin suburb of Düppel, hence their name for it, and knew what it could do, but high command hadn't authorised work on any possible countermeasures.

Its use that night came as a total surprise. Josef Kammhuber was in his Berlin control centre at the time and exclaimed, "*Die gesamte Abwehr war mit einem Schlag blind!*" "With one shot the whole defence was blind!" The Nachtjagd had lost its eyes. The Germans scrambled to react. *Oberleutnant* Joachim Wendtland – an experienced fighter control officer in Stade – described it as "like trying to find a ball of glass in a barrel of peas". Up in the air, Otto Kutzner, a Bf 110 pilot from NJG 3, reported that his radar operator "suddenly had more targets than could have been possible … I was picking up targets everywhere that didn't exist. We kept finishing up behind a target, but it was never the slipstream of a bomber." A fellow flyer declared, "We were all helpless and bewildered." Peter Spoden was airborne and patrolling his Himmelbett box when "Suddenly we were blind, all our radar equipment just twinkled. Ground control could no longer tell us anything." The Himmelbett system was effectively taken out and, in desperation, the Stade controllers turned to the volunteer observers stationed on rooftops. Their reports were clear; the bombers were pouring through the Himmelbett boxes unimpeded and flying parallel with the River Elbe. They were heading for Hamburg.

In the city the sirens went off again. Many Hamburgers thought it another false alarm, but then came the *Luftgefahr 30* (Air Warning 30) – the 30-minute warning for all flak and civil defence organisations. At a gun battery in the northern suburbs a teenaged flak helper described how he and his comrades "staggered from our beds when the loudspeakers woke us with the order". One of his friends complained that this was yet another false alarm but "some of us had only been there [at the flak station] for a few days and our excitement was feverish. Some boys behaved very dramatically and said our eardrums would burst when we opened fire but the old hands calmed them down ... we soon heard the humming of engines, like a thousand bees." Albert Hartung was a teenaged auxiliary with a searchlight battery: "Our radar was hopelessly confused ... the master searchlight was useless and the ordinary searchlights had to try on their own. It was like going round with a torch in a dark room trying to find a fly." Düppel had not only nullified the night fighters, it did the same for radar-controlled flak and searchlights – Hamburg was effectively defenceless.

Across the city, people huddled around their radios listening in to the official State emergency channel as all the other regular stations went off-air. Through the airwaves came the soothing tones of *Onkel Baldrian* (Uncle Valerian – brand name of a herbal indigestion remedy) – Hamburgers' nickname for *Staatsekretär* (clerk to the State Council) Georg Ahrens. Irmgard Burmeister remembered he had "a particularly calming voice and was generally referred to as '*Herr Tranquilizer.*'" Broadcasting from Gauleiter Kaufmann's personal bunker, he tried to reassure an anxious city, and then came the dreaded words. "The first bombs will fall in a few minutes. Everyone must go to their shelters."

Walter Luth, a doctor with the Kriegsmarine stationed on a patrol boat in the harbour, recalled: "The engine noise above us became louder and every flak gun in Hamburg and on the ships opened fire, but still no bombs! It was so bright you could have read the *Hamburger Tageblatt* (Hamburger Daily News) without difficulty. And then it all started!" A hausfrau in the northern suburb of Winterhude was on the roof of her apartment block with some of her neighbours and saw, "these things burning in the sky – like burning gold – not actually burning but glowing". No-one was sure what this was, and after the raid "people in the street were talking about the golden colours we'd seen. They said it was *Phosphorregen* – phosphor-rain."[1] It wasn't. They were target indicators dropped by the Pathfinders over the western side of the residential areas north of the Elbe.

The first bombers reached the markers at just after 1am on 25 July. Below them, Frau Otti Schwarz and her husband "ran to the public shelter, not down the middle of the street but along the side … we didn't want the men in the planes to see us." On reaching the shelter the Schwarz's "showed the shelter warden our place cards which gave each person's room and seat number".[2] With space at a premium, the general rule was that each person was allowed one small suitcase for their most important documents and personal effects, but people flouted it. "[They] had brought in all their pets … cats, dogs and rabbits. One woman had brought in her canary in its cage." Others had even taken in "chickens, brought in baskets but now running round the shelter". The journalist Ben Witter recalled how "It was no longer night, it was as light as day after the first bombs fell and I took my parents into the cellar, which wasn't reinforced, and it seemed as if its walls were moving all the time."

Claus Fuhrmann – a former merchant seaman – was now working in a tyre factory in the city. "At first there was nothing unusual about it [the bombing]; people sat cowering in their damp cellars, children wept, the whistle of falling bombs, dull thudding hits, blasts of air which blew out windows and doors … this was nothing new, but what was new was the way in which it went on."[3] This was no ordinary raid, as Ines Lyss soon realised as she sat helpless "on a small wooden bench in the basement … when it didn't seem it was going to stop, people began to pray, some started to scream." The teenaged Polish forced labourer Irena Chmiel and a fellow Ostarbeiter nearly didn't make it. They were locked in their accommodation by their female German warder who promptly went and took shelter, leaving the terrified girls to their fate. As they screamed for help, "A policeman and another man came along and kicked our door down." The two men then took the girls into a shelter as their erstwhile prison burnt down.

Being in a shelter was no guarantee of safety. A direct hit could blow one to pieces, and if the building above caught fire and collapsed the unfortunate occupants could be buried alive. Their only way out then was "to break down the wall into the basement next door and clamber through". Otti Schwarz's husband was a policeman, and in between the waves of bombers he left the safety of the bunker to look around, to see if there was anyone who needed help and check their own second-floor flat nearby. After the first foray, he returned to the shelter and told Otti that he'd seen "a piece of blackout material in our window burst into flames … burning pieces of the house were coming through the ceiling of our flat and falling on our furniture … we were losing everything we had." After the next, "His face was all black and his whole body was trembling. *'Es ist alles aus.'* It's all gone."

The raid lasted 58 minutes, and then it was over. Claus Fuhrmann left his bunker, "Red flames still stood above the houses and the air was black with dust and dirt as the fire engines were clanging through the streets." Otto Mahncke went out in search of his sister, mother and aunt, and "on the Schaarmarkt we [he was with a neighbour] saw sailors rescuing people from a burning house, passing them from balcony to balcony. Some people were saved, then, suddenly, the house collapsed like a pack of cards. Everybody fell into the ruins, it was dreadful." Stumbling on, he saw an old lady trapped on the third floor of a burning house and stopped to try and help her. "It was too hot. I had to retreat … I saw the woman looking down with wild eyes and then fall back to her death among the flames."[4]

The city's emergency services went into action, led by the *Schnellkommandos* (Fast squads) – motorised teams of four Hitler Youth teenagers commanded by a reserve policeman – whose job it was to put out small fires before they took hold, but there were so many fires and so many roads were blocked by fallen masonry it was proving impossible. They couldn't even report back as to the most badly hit parts of the city, the telephone lines between the central Control Room in Gauleiter Kaufmann's bunker and the epicentre of the bombing in the city's Western sector had been destroyed, so follow-up fire teams were mistakenly directed to the Eastern and Harbour sectors instead. People did the best they could, but all around was chaos. Daybreak brought little comfort. The war correspondent, Erich Andres, described how "the day after, it was still dark by noontime due to the smoke and dust. Altona district had been particularly hard hit." Returning home, he recalled that "the heat was still intense, the walls of the houses still burning hot." He found people lying on the beds in his blackened house: "Their skin had been roasted dark brown, and their faces and bodies were bloated beyond recognition from the intense heat." They were a handful of the 1,500 residents killed in the raid. Thousands more were injured and another 200,000 were left homeless.

The cost to Bomber Command was 12 aircraft lost; three to flak and nine who had strayed out of the Window umbrella and fallen prey to night fighters. To claim those three solitary bombers, the anti-aircraft batteries had fired an astonishing 50,000 rounds. The attack had been a stunning success for the British. The much-feared Nachtjagd had been rendered powerless to intervene and spent most of the night flying in circles. Wim Johnen and his radio operator had been scrambled that night from their base at Parchim, and then flown all the way to northern Holland to intercept the bombers, only to be caught in the Düppel deception.

> Facius [his radio op] proceeded to report three or four targets on his screen. I hoped that I had enough ammo to deal with them! Then Facius shouted, 'Tommy flying towards us at great speed. Distance decreasing … 2km … 1500m … 1km … 500m…' I was speechless. Perhaps it was a German night fighter … Then Facius had a new target … it was not long before he shouted again; 'Bomber coming for us at a hell of a speed' … 'You're crackers Facius' I said jokingly, but I soon lost my sense of humour as this crazy performance was repeated a score of times.

Then a ground station came through: "Hamburg, Hamburg … calling all night fighters … full speed for Hamburg." Enraged, Johnen opened his throttles and headed northeast, but arrived only in time to find the city "blazing like a furnace, it was a horrifying sight."

The Schwarz's, Erich Andres, Otto Mahncke and Claus Fuhrmann, had little reprieve. As they gazed out across a city still obscured by the smoke from hundreds of fires, once again they heard the drone of massed aircraft engines. It was the Americans. The previous morning, Brigadier Fred Anderson – the commander of the Eighth Army Air Force – left Harris's daily conference and had been driven the three miles back to his own headquarters at Wycombe Abbey Girls' School. It was still early days for the Americans in the air war, and he could only muster some 300 bombers in total, less than half Bomber Command's fleet. Nevertheless, Anderson had agreed to Harris's request to join in the offensive against Hamburg – calling it 'Blitz Week' – and pretty much every serviceable aircraft was put in the air to strike the Hamburg shipyards, the Focke-Wulf factory at Warnemünde near Rostock, and Kiel. It would be the biggest American attack of the war so far.

Some 123 Flying Fortresses were assigned to attack the Hamburg yards, but with dense smoke still obscuring the city, only 100 positively identified the target and released their payloads. The Warnemünde attack didn't even happen, cloud cover forcing the bombers to switch to their secondary target. German day fighters from JG 1 and JG 11 were scrambled to intercept and tore gleefully into the unescorted Fortresses. One B-17 pilot recalled that "It was the first real battle we had gotten into and I thought the German [an attacking Bf 109 pilot] was quite a daredevil ... he was firing but I don't know which plane he was firing at, he certainly didn't hit us." Jack Owen wasn't as lucky. His B-17 had been damaged by flak over Hamburg and as his formation headed home, he and his crew "were falling behind and losing height fast. The rest of the group flew on, just like we were standing still, and I thought; 'My God, you're all going back to England and here I am.' Then the fighters started coming in at us. I saw several on each side, just queuing up to have a go at us." Left with little choice, Owen ordered his crew to bale out before they were blown apart. Another straggler "lowered the landing gear and rang the bale-out bell". Recognising this was a signal the struggle was over, "When the gear was lowered the fighters ceased firing and circled our B-17 as we baled out."[5]

Fifteen bombers were shot down, and another five were so badly beaten up they had to be scrapped on return. Dozens more bore the scars of battle and had to be patched up by their ground crews. The American gunners claimed to have shot down 44 German fighters over Hamburg and Kiel, with another six probables and 27 damaged. The real tally was seven fighters lost, one of which was an NJG 1 Bf 110 night fighter whose crew were forced to ditch in the North Sea before being rescued by a Royal Navy torpedo boat and taken prisoner. Five pilots were wounded, and Major Karl-Heinz Leesman, Kommandeur of III./JG 11, was killed. His body washed ashore on the Dutch coast over a fortnight later on 16 August. The US raid on Hamburg lasted 12 minutes, killed 20 people and did little damage.

That same morning of the American attack, at his usual daily conference, Harris decided to hit Hamburg for a second successive night. However, reconnaissance reported that the dense smoke still hanging over the city would make a successful raid nigh on impossible. With great regret Harris switched that night's raid to his old favourite, Essen. The ensuing attack killed 486 people and caused heavy damage to the Krupp's works. Düppel was used once again. Joseph Goebbels wrote that "the raid caused a complete stoppage of production in the Krupp works. Speer is much concerned and worried." Hamburg didn't get off scot-free. Six Mosquito fast bombers sent on a nuisance raid caused a city-wide alarm and wrecked another night's sleep for the hapless population. The RAF crews spotted the still-burning city from 70 miles away. One pilot said, "I remember fire, smoke and cloud, but no flak."

A few short hours after the Mosquitoes landed back at their home airfields, the engines of some 300 Fortresses began their warm-up for the next American phase of the offensive. Their main target would be synthetic rubber manufacturing sites in Hannover, but around 120 bombers would once more look to hit Hamburg's shipyards. This time the German day fighters used a different tactic. On their way in, the bombers were mainly left in peace, with only a few half-hearted attacks made, of which none were pressed home. Over the city the smoke generator units had done a fine job and target identification was extremely hard. To the credit of the American crews, they bombed accurately and, despite the heavy flak, put one of Hamburg's two main power stations out of action. Underneath the falling bombs was 12-year-old Irmgard Burmeister: "We sought refuge in our basement, which wasn't totally underground, and we even had shell fragments on our basement stairs … My grandmother knew how to tell fortunes with playing cards and she'd tell us 'No, nothing is going to happen to us. Everything is going to be all right.'" Gertrude Löhr had a 4-year-old son: "I was terrified … I felt like a rat being smoked out of a hole. I remember sitting in the basement with my son on my lap, clinging to him for dear life."

As the bombers turned for home it was time for the fighters to strike, focusing their efforts on any stragglers damaged by anti-aircraft fire. It proved hard going for the German pilots. American formation discipline was good and only two of the Hamburg bombers fell to their guns. The Hannover force was not so fortunate. With the Fortresses having to fly a far greater distance to their target and back, the German pilots were almost all able to fly two sorties each; one as the bombers flew in, and a second as they made for home. The newly instituted German policy of encouraging pilots running low on fuel and ammunition to put down on the nearest airfield to restock and then get back in the fight, instead of having to return to their base, proved a success. The result was 22 bombers shot down from the Hannover force, with damage to four times that number. *Leutnant* Eberhard Burath of JG 1 was flying an Fw 190 that day and, not for the first time, ended up separated from his own gruppe in the vastness of the sky:

> I caught a straggling B-17 with the last of my fuel. There wasn't enough left for overtaking and an attack from ahead. Flying at the same level I did a steep turn to starboard and fired a well-aimed burst at him down from the cockpit right through to the tail. I wouldn't have liked to be on the receiving end of that.

Forced to break off his attack and flying on fumes, he managed to get

... an emergency bearing from Borkum – everyone was shouting for bearings – and with God's help, and my brakes, I managed to stop my 190 at the field's edge on the perimeter track. That's how I imagined a landing on an aircraft carrier. The take-off afterwards [for his home airfield] was equally hair-raising, just clearing the hangar roofs with the tailwheel almost touching the tops.

That evening, after two straight nights of 'maximum effort' raids; the first on Hamburg, the second on Essen, and with bad weather forecast, Bomber Command stood down and Hamburgers could get a few hours of desperately needed sleep. The next day, Tuesday 27 July, smoke still hung over the city, but a semblance of order was back in the streets, and water and electricity were being reconnected. Everyone looked fearfully to the skies, waiting to hear the drone of engines as the Americans returned for the third day in a row, but the sky stayed quiet. Just as with the British, the Americans had called a rest day for their aircrews. The ground teams, meanwhile, had no such luck and were kept busy patching up their battered aircraft.

In Hamburg, people began to say to each other that it was over. Their city had taken a battering but was still standing – they'd made it through. Butch Harris had other ideas. At his morning conference that same day he announced a maximum effort raid for that night, and its target would once again be Hamburg. Fred Anderson asked if he could go along as an observer – which given his rank and intelligence value to the Germans if captured – was strictly against the rules. Harris agreed. The time on target for the main bomber force was set at 1am on the morning of Wednesday 28 July.

Hamburg's citizens may have thought the worst was over, but among the upper echelons of the Luftwaffe there was near panic. Nazi Germany's second city had been hit hard. Residential areas had been heavily bombed, particularly in the northwest, 2,000 of its citizens had been killed, thousands more injured and hundreds of thousands rendered homeless. This was bad enough, but what made it infinitely worse for the Luftwaffe was the way that its entire defensive structure, which had taken it over two years to perfect, had been rendered impotent in minutes. Huge resources of men, machines and money had been poured into the Himmelbett system – and the corresponding radar-controlled flak and searchlight network – and it had all been undone by strips of black paper and aluminium that cost pfennigs. The British use of Düppel had ruthlessly exposed the limitations of radar-directed flak and searchlights, but most especially Himmelbett and the Nachtjagd.

After his Führer conference disaster, Kammhuber's personal standing in the Nazi hierarchy now dropped to a new low. Goebbels angrily noted in his diary, "We shot down remarkably few of the enemy bombers … this raid has finally blown apart the illusions that many people still had about future enemy aerial operations." The Germans didn't know when the bombers would come again, but come they would, and that made time of the essence. Innovation was desperately required, and some among the Luftwaffe were bursting with ideas.

One such 'idea meister' was the tall, stern-faced bomber pilot turned staff officer, Hajo Herrmann. Having had his plan to radically increase fighter production and convert large numbers of bomber and Stuka crews into fighter jocks shot down as "a naïve fallacy", he had refused to give up, and instead had focused his thinking on how to maximise the use of what fighter resources the Luftwaffe *did* have, rather than what it *could* have. On 25 March 1943, he had sent out a memo, classified SECRET, where he stated – among other things – that "The huge shortfall in night fighters into 1944 can be remedied by operating day fighters at night.'" His argument ran that hundreds of single engine day fighters, fighting the Americans by day, could then be used at night instead of sitting around idle. Herrmann even tested the idea himself. Borrowing a fighter from a friend, he began to carry out trial flights from Berlin-Staaken, first against "an He 111 [German medium bomber] which was acting as a target so that I could latch on behind and carry out flying and target practice", and then attempting to intercept a British Mosquito on a nuisance raid. Herrmann's idea was to attack the bombers visually right over their city targets by using the light from the flames below and from the searchlights. When a bomber was highlighted or coned there would be enough light for the day fighter pilot to attack.

Their own flak was an occupational hazard. That night he saw three searchlights cone the Mosquito, "There's my bright fellow! I turned in. Too late, stupid fool, I'd miscalculated and was 800 metres behind him." Opening the throttle to try and catch him, he eventually got close enough to fire. "Flashes appeared before my eyes! My tracer was blinding me. The belts should have been loaded with night tracer. Bad planning, stupidity, inexperience!" The Mosquito escaped into the night.

Nevertheless, he was allowed to carry on trialling the idea and used volunteers to further develop the technique, including using bomber pilots, as *Major* Wilhelm Herget, a successful night fighter pilot recalled. "Hajo Hermann had the idea of using bomber pilots on Messerschmitt 109s to fly at night because they knew about instrument flying, but a bomber pilot is not a fighter pilot and when he is looking at his instruments he isn't looking outside." Herget himself tried out the idea and wasn't convinced. "I watched the instruments when I was taking off and when I was landing, but during the whole flight I only looked at them to see if I was flying in the right direction." Herrmann persevered, and on the night of 3 July 1943 a Battle of the Ruhr raid by Bomber Command provided him and his disciples the opportunity to test the concept for real.

Flying right into the heart of the attack he described "the intoxication of that summer night's battle" and how "we forgot the countless flak splinters and other dangers that faced us ... we tore into the witch's cauldron, hot with anger and spurred with enthusiasm. This was *Wilde Sau*, pure and simple." *Wilde Sau* translates as Wild Boar, but perhaps better translated as 'wild blood rush' – this was Herrmann's name for his new night flying tactic, and it fitted the bill perfectly. At the end of that first night's action, "Twelve four-engine bombers had been downed, and the flak ... were congratulating themselves on the result – until I claimed the 12 as having been destroyed by my pilots.

The horse-trading began." The horse-trading ended with each side credited with six, much to Herrmann's annoyance. However, Goering was so impressed with the new tactic that Herrmann was immediately promoted to *Kommodore* and asked to set up an entire geschwader of Wilde Sau – JG 300. He agreed and set a target of having his men ready by mid-September.

On the evening of 27 July, 787 Bomber Command aircraft were readied for that night's attack on Hamburg. The day's weather reports stated that northern Germany had been baking in the summer sun all day with temperatures in Hamburg itself hitting 30°C – the city was tinder dry. As a result, the decision was made to increase the number of lighter weight incendiaries in the payloads. Once again, the German signals service picked up the mass of radio chatter that presaged an attack and the word went out. Hajo Herrmann was at his training field near Bonn preparing for another day's hard work with his new Wilde Sau unit. Called to the phone, he found himself talking to Bernd von Brauchitsch, Goering's adjutant and member of his infamous 'Kitchen Cabinet'. "How near to being operational are you?" to which he replied "Mid-September at the earliest." Goering himself came on the phone. Referring to the recent attacks on Hamburg, the Luftwaffe supremo said, "Herrmann, Hamburg has been attacked and it has never been so bad. The whole night fighter force has been put out of action. You are now the only person I can rely on. You must start operations at once – even if it is only with a few machines." Herrmann took 25 aircraft of his command and flew north.

With the Wilde Sau airborne, the long-range Freya stations picked the bombers up as they took off and climbed into the darkening sky. German ground control knew it was likely that the British would once again deploy the dreaded Düppel and they'd be blinded, so they had adapted. The concept was called *laufende Reportage* – running commentary – and the idea was to substitute reliance on the vulnerable Würzburg radars with the controllers providing exactly that, a running commentary on the bomber stream using a host of information sources, some more accurate than others, but in the hope of providing enough direction to bring the night fighters into the stream so they could attack in any way they could. As the bombers neared the German coast, the controllers were broadcasting reports from the Freyas, roof and ground observers, sound detector stations and searchlight batteries, all to try and build a picture for the night fighters while they still could.

In Hamburg, fire crews were still busy dealing with the aftermath of the previous raids, damping down the piles of smouldering bricks and timbers that used to be houses and demolishing buildings considered unsafe – they'd been at it for three days and more and were exhausted. In another part of the city a woman remembered standing in front of her house in the still warm summer air. "It was completely quiet. No planes. No flak. It was an enchantingly beautiful night."

The bomber stream had now passed north of the city, with the intention of then turning and coming in from the east. This was partly done to bypass and confuse the defenders, but also because the target for that night was Hamburg's residential eastern zone. That part of the city was home to predominantly working-class Hamburgers living in standard six-storey apartment blocks. The blocks – each of which typically housed 18 families – weren't slums, but were low-rent, cheaply made and densely packed, with few open spaces between them to act as potential fire breaks. Back among the bombers there had been the usual few turn-backs due to mechanical issues, leaving some 735 bombers to begin their approach as the Pathfinders dropped their target markers. On the ground, Hamburgers' hopes that Bomber Command was finished with them were shattered as the sirens sounded and Onkel Baldrian came on air once more. People flocked into the shelters. Settling themselves in they prayed for a short raid, and then the bombs started to fall.

"The earth shook, the walls cracked and the plaster came down like flour until the whole basement was one cloud of dust. We thought it was like an earthquake and no-one spoke a word." The supplicants' prayers were answered in part, the raid was brief, as the first night's was, but in less than an hour 2,417 tons of bombs were dropped, with the Hammerbrook, Hamm and Borgfelde districts particularly hard hit. With the whole city so dry, fires started to burn immediately, swiftly taking hold. As the last bombers flew over, one RAF crewman described Hamburg as "a sea of flame". Decorated panzer officer Hans von Luck was visiting his old friend Boos just outside the city at the time and "from Boos's garden we could see Hamburg on fire."

Herbert Brecht was a 15-year-old member of a Schnellkommando tasked as first responders, but "the heat from the surrounding houses – which were on fire – was unbearable, we whimpered and cried from the pain of it." Brecht and his team were some of the only emergency workers in the eastern part of the city at the time, all the rest were still over in the west, and as they tried to reach the east they found the streets blocked with rubble, barring their path. In their absence the thousands of small fires began to coalesce, at first into hundreds of bigger fires, then dozens of huge fires, and finally into one all-consuming *Feuersturm*.

The firestorm sucked in air from around it, feeding on the oxygen and growing stronger all the time, and as it grew stronger it sucked in ever more air in a whirlwind of terrific force; trees were uprooted, cars and buses flung into the sky, and any human being above ground was torn screaming upwards as they burst into flames in the furnace-like heat. The journalist Ben Witter "saw people running away, they were burning like torches", and in panic "people tried to leap down into them [the canals] but the water was on fire. It was burning because lots of small boats had exploded and oil had been released into the water and people, who themselves were on fire, jumped into it … they burned, swam, burned and went under." The firestorm began to spread out, expanding faster than a man could run, and soon four square-miles of the city were in its grip; equivalent to an area from Euston station to the Thames, across to Hyde Park and then over to the Tower of London.

By now, Hajo Herrmann and his fellow Wilde Sau had arrived over Hamburg. "The clouds of smoke over Hamburg were so dense it made you shudder … I even smelt it." Using the light from the flames below, as well as the swinging beams of the searchlights, the fighter pilots tried to find the bombers. The tail gunner of a Lancaster bomber remembered seeing one of them.

"I knew he was weighing us up before coming in on his curve ... suddenly he dropped his nose and came in, I screamed [to the pilot] 'Corkscrew port!' and at the same time opened up with my four Browning machine-guns ... he broke to starboard and shot beneath us in the dark ... we didn't see him again." Herrmann himself was more successful than his comrade. "I saw this bomber in the searchlights ... the attack was very simple, I went into the searchlights – I wasn't very experienced, another pilot would have kept in the dark." Then the German's luck was in: "I could see the rear gunner, he was looking downwards, probably at the inferno below ... I fired and he burned ... I watched him burst on the ground." Unlike the Wilde Sau, Peter Spoden was tied to a Himmelbett box east of the city and was ordered to remain there. "I asked ground control if I could fly to the bombers ... but control said it was impossible." On landing, and seething with frustration, he and half his gruppe went straight to their boss, Rudi Schönert: "We told him it was crazy. We had had to watch helplessly as they destroyed a German city."[6]

Helplessness was a common feeling that night. A neighbour of Erich Andres had been on air raid duty at his factory earlier in the evening, but with the bombers gone he'd rushed home to try and find his wife in the basement shelter of their building. On arrival he found terror. Falling masonry had blocked the only exit, and "as the wall of fire had steadily moved closer, the cellar had got hotter and hotter." The only possible exit was a small iron-barred window at street level. From inside the shelter he heard "women sobbing, men screaming and children whimpering". Quickly searching around he found an iron rod which he used as a lever to bend the iron bars in the window. Slowly forcing the bars apart, he managed to make an opening that was just big enough for someone to squeeze through: "A woman, crying uncontrollably, grabbed my arm, I reached for her and tugged until finally she squeezed her way through." He pulled out a child, and then "a man's head appeared next, I pulled and pulled, he was screaming, begging me not to let him fall back." With one final yank the man came out like a cork from a bottle. The next moment the cellar roof collapsed.

Devastated, he would later tell Andres that "during the clean-up, 72 bodies were counted [in the cellar], I had been able to rescue three of them."

Herbert Brecht and the other members of his Schnellkommando had given up all attempts at firefighting and were just trying to stay alive. They attempted to drive away from the flames, threading their way through the burning streets, until they found the road totally blocked by a burning tram. "Our car caught fire immediately. We all managed to get out and just stood there in those fires of hell." The power of the wind was at hurricane force and blew the teenager and most of his comrades into a large bomb crater. "Those of us who didn't get into the crater had no chance ... one of my group was never seen again." As the firestorm raged, most of the people who lived in the blocks now being turned into ash were huddled in their shelters below. They could hear the firestorm above – "it was like an old organ in a church when someone is playing all the notes at once" – but they had been told over and over by the RLB and the city authorities that the safest thing to do was to stay in their shelters until the all-clear sounded, no matter what. Inside, people could feel the temperature rise and rise, the air stifling, and the smoke was making people cough and wheeze as their eyes watered. Outside, the heart of the firestorm was now above 800 degrees Celsius.

Traute Koch's mother had had enough. Sitting in a shelter with her 15-year-old daughter she made a decision – they would brave the outside. Wrapping Traute in a wet sheet she stood by the door telling her that when she opened it, she wasn't to look back but was to run as fast as she could. Crying with fear, the young girl hesitated at the door: "In front of me I could see only fire – everything red, like the door to a furnace. An intense heat struck me. A burning beam fell in front of me ... but then it was whirled away by a ghostly hand ... I had the feeling I was being carried away by the storm."

Another young Hamburg teenager faced the same dilemma. "The door [of her shelter] was burning just like a ring in a circus through which a lion has to jump. Someone in front of me hesitated and I pushed her out with my foot ... it was no use staying in that place." Trying to find somewhere safe she saw the asphalt melt on the street she was running down, "There were people on the roadway, some already dead, some still alive but stuck in the asphalt ... their feet had got stuck and they had put out their hands to try to get out again. They were on their hands and knees screaming." She lost her father, an aunt and two uncles that night.

Ben Witter was trying to flee the flames too. "Our car was jolting over dead people. Because of the heat the bodies had shrunk and we thought they were children but they were adults."[7] Witter and the Kochs were fortunate – and in a minority. Across six entire city districts the almost innate German deference to authority had condemned thousands to remain in their shelters even as the firestorm killed them – not by engulfing them with flames or crushing them with falling masonry – but silently and stealthily. As the fiery hurricane consumed the oxygen around them, Hamburg's citizens died from carbon monoxide poisoning. They were later found fully clothed, still sitting on their benches in serried ranks, as if asleep.

As the bomber stream headed home the Nachtjagd tried to gain a measure of revenge. Joachim Wendtland had asked to take a break from his desk job as a ground controller and take part in the fight at the sharp end. His request had been granted and he found himself sharing a Bf 110 cockpit with Egmont Prinz zur Lippe-Weissenfeld. Having already missed one possible target as it disappeared into the dark, Wendtland realised his pilot was onto another: "It was a visual sighting with no radar. The exhaust flames were so small and weak." Lippe got underneath it: "It was a Lancaster." Opening fire, he "hit its left wing and burning pieces of it flew off". The bomber flew on, and the aristocratic night hunter had to make repeated attacks until "his wing started burning." The bomber went down. There were no survivors. It was Lippe-Weissenfeld's forty-third victory. The Lancaster was one of just 17 bombers lost that night – four of them shot down by Herrmann and his Wilde Sau.

Back in Hamburg the firestorm passed its peak, and by 7am had burnt itself out. The city's police president and Air Protection

Leader, Karl Kehrl, described the destruction it left behind as "so radical that literally nothing is left". Almost 40,000 Hamburgers died in the attack.

Otto Müller was a policeman in the emergency motorcycle messenger service and was driving through the shattered streets after the raid. A young girl came running towards him. "She was dragging her little dead brother behind her, the right side of his face was already scraped smooth ... she put her arm round my neck and said, 'Dear soldiers, please take us with you.'" Müller hadn't seen his own family since the attack began and was overcome by rage. "I was so angry that I would have shot any enemy airman who'd parachuted down. I think any English or American person would have felt the same way. Thank God I didn't find myself in that position."

Despite the damage, the authorities somehow began a clear-up process. The teenaged Uwe Köster had survived and was roped in to help. "We cleared out the corpses, sometimes the burned bodies of people in cellars as well as those on the streets. We stacked the bodies in layers on top of each other ... The air was absolutely still. We didn't have any sun at all for three or four days." Helmut Schmidt, a young *leutnant* in the flak arm, would later describe his own experience: "The worst thing was the stench – like being in the kitchen of McDonalds ... a smell of beef ... but the beef were people." Schmidt would survive the war and go on to become the Chancellor of West Germany from 1974 to 1982.

Terrified of further raids, Gauleiter Kaufmann made a public broadcast that morning advising all non-essential inhabitants to leave for their own safety – people didn't need much urging, and by nightfall almost 1.2 million people had left the city. It was the largest and quickest mass evacuation in Germany during the war. Hans von Luck saw them stream by. "Thousands of refugees arrived in the suburbs on foot, many with phosphorous burns ... they were given shelter in emergency reception camps ... I can still see those poor people today, some had barely escaped with their lives." Irmgard Burmeister was deeply affected by the sight. "An almost endless number of refugees began to pass by our house ... The thing that impressed me the most was the total silence. They just kept passing by, not uttering a word." A friend of her grandfather's arrived at their house, "I will never forget the frightened look in his eyes. He had witnessed the inferno. 'It's all in ruins, everything is gone. Hamburg no longer exists.' That was all he said."

Kaufmann's fear of more raids was totally understandable. What was happening to Hamburg had not been visited on any German city in the war so far, including Essen, and Harris was still determined to press on; his own instinct, and aerial reconnaissance, telling him the plan was working – Hamburg was on its knees, it was time to pile on the pressure. The Americans though, had other ideas. Their Blitz Week had seen them bomb Hamburg's port and shipyards, but that was in line with their own strategy of hitting precise military-industrial targets, and now it was time to carry that fight to the German aircraft industry.

That day, just over 300 American bombers took off and headed for the Fieseler aircraft factory at Kassel-Bettenhausen and the AGO Flugzeugwerke (aircraft works) at Oschersleben. Both factories produced Focke-Wulf Fw 190 fighters. Hamburg would get a brief respite. As it happened, bad weather over Germany and concerted attacks by up to 350 fighters resulted in only a third dropping their bombs on target and little damage was done.

That day's poor weather also forced Harris to stand his men down that night, and then it was the Americans turn again the following day. Their targets this time were the U-boat yards in Kiel and another Fw 190 factory at Warnemünde. Hamburg had now had two days and a night without a bomb falling – surely this time it was over? The answer was no.

At his morning conference on Thursday 29 July, Harris was clear; Hamburg would be bombed again that night in another maximum effort. The northwestern districts of the city were the epicentre of the bomb path, with Barmbek taking the brunt. Once again, fires took hold and burned out of control. One of the returning bomber crew remembered, "We could see the fire from 150 miles away, we could see Hamburg burning. It was just awful, a terrible sight." On hearing the all-clear, 17-year-old Helmut Wilkens left his shelter to witness horror.

Our block of flats, on the other side of the street, had collapsed and the house next door was fully ablaze. Someone stood at a second-floor window calling for help. It was Herr Schwarz, who never went down to the shelter. There was no way to save him and two sailors said 'shoot him, he won't suffer anymore, he's burning already.' They started to fire with their pistols. He fell forward and smashed onto the pavement.

Eight hundred of Helmut Wilken's neighbours joined Herr Schwarz in death.

Düppel was deployed once more, and while still effective, the Germans were adapting, this time by using large numbers of additional searchlights sent from across northern Germany to act without radar control and create walls of light the bombers would have to fly through. Any bomber picked up would then be coned for the flak and fighters to go at. Sergeant Joe Weldon – a radio operator in a Halifax – recalled how immediately after their bombing run "the mid-upper shouted, 'Fighter!' and he opened up … we were hit by cannon fire straight away … he hit the starboard outer engine which was set on fire."[8] Ordered to bale out, Joe Weldon was one of only two crewmen to escape the burning plane alive. Bomber Command lost 28 aircraft that night – their worst loss so far.

The 29/30 July raid was the last great burst of the offensive against Hamburg. Harris wanted to carry on but could not persuade the Americans, who hit the Fieseler works at Kassel-Bettenhausen once more on 30 July instead. Frustrated, Harris was then ordered by the Air Ministry to forget Hamburg and attack the three northern Italian cities of Milan, Turin and Genoa, to help push Italy out of the war. When that raid was called off, Harris turned to western Germany, and in the last act of the battle of the Ruhr the bombers attacked Remscheid, which was more or less wiped off the map. Two more attacks on Hamburg were planned, but thunderstorms across England forced the cancellation of the 31 July/1 August raid, and an electrical storm on the night of Monday 2 August scattered the bombers and only half reached the city. Casualties on the ground were few, but the damage had already been done.

The battle of Hamburg was finally over after ten days and nine nights. The RAF had dropped 8,344 tons of bombs on the city – the Americans dropped another 306 tons – reducing fully half of the city's houses and apartments to ash and making 900,000 residents homeless. Its industrial base was crushed, with all four shipbuilding yards badly damaged and more than a third of its large factories destroyed. British-born Countess Bridget von Bernstoff, wrote to her husband Count Hugo after the battle in an effort to describe what it was like.

> You can't imagine, there is nothing, nothing, nothing left ... the sky is black with smoke and the garden is black with ash ... streets littered with blackened corpses, and the heat is appalling, typhus has broken out because there's no water and the people have drunk from the Elbe. There are about 90,000 wounded and a quarter of a million dead.[9]

In those last statistics the countess was, at least, mistaken. At over 45,000 dead, and the same number injured, the butcher's bill was bad enough, but the quarter million figure was passed by word of mouth and soon became accepted wisdom among a bewildered and frightened German public. As Adolf Galland commented, "In every large town people said, 'what happened to Hamburg yesterday can happen to us tomorrow.' A wave of terror radiated from the suffering city and spread throughout Germany." That terror was helped to proliferate by the Hamburg diaspora across Germany. At first, the homeless took shelter in the villages and woodland just outside the city where the authorities did their best to support them, and then those with family or friends elsewhere gathered what few possessions they had left and took to the road. On arrival at their destinations, "[they] spread panic throughout Germany."

As the tide of misery rippled out from the stricken city, the upper echelons of the Nazi hierarchy were gripped with fear and a sense of foreboding as they realised there was no way even their strict control of information was going to stop the German people finding out what had happened. Goebbels – almost always willing to write down uncomfortable truths in his diary – called the bombing a "catastrophe, the extent of which simply staggers the imagination", although within a few short days he himself banned all media from using the word 'catastrophe' to describe it. Gauleiter Kaufmann implored Hitler to visit the city so he could see the destruction for himself and lift the people's spirits, but the dictator refused. Unlike the British Prime Minister Winston Churchill, he would not look upon the appalling human cost of the war because he did not want to – or he decided it would be politically ill-advised for him to appear in person at the scene of devastation. Albert Speer – who also tried to persuade the dictator to go see for himself – said Hitler "gave no reason for his refusals", and then in a perverse kind of way excused him: "You couldn't expect him to be any different when he was in a bad temper." In an ironic twist, it was the man who had left the city so open to attack by halting the development of countermeasures for Düppel who went and faced the people.

On 6 August Hermann Goering arrived in Hamburg. Walking through the shattered streets he was heckled and abused with cries of "Hey Meier, what have you got to say now?" At his insistence the police and SS did not respond and no one was arrested. At a meeting later that same day with local leaders at the Party headquarters, he candidly admitted the Government couldn't guarantee to prevent such attacks in the future. What Goering did not admit was that the Nazi leadership did not fear the deaths of tens of thousands more German civilians – or even the damage to the country's war machine – but the threat of insurrection. Nazism had been birthed in the violence of the streets and its leaders feared it would die the same way.

Erhard Milch was no diehard Nazi, rather he was a ruthlessly ambitious schemer and his concerns post-Hamburg were less apocalyptic, but worrying nonetheless. He told colleagues in the Air Ministry that "another five or six attacks like those on Hamburg and the German people will just give up, no matter how strong willed they are. The people will say, 'We've had enough, we simply can't take anymore.'" Warming to his theme he went on to say that the attacks "strike deep at our nation's morale. If we don't succeed in smashing these terror attacks … very soon, then we must expect a very difficult situation to arise for Germany." Milch – like the rest of the Nazi leadership – looked to his Führer for an answer, and his response was clear: "Terror can only be broken with terror."

Hitler ordered the Luftwaffe to prepare a bombing blitz against British cities. Milch fawningly concurred, declaring "Our entire armaments effort … is dependent on whether we can clear our own skies by carrying out raids at such a level that the British will call off their own attacks." The result was yet another pointless frittering away of the Luftwaffe's limited strength in a mini-bombing offensive against Britain that achieved nothing.

Apart from the renewed bombing of Britain, Hamburg's impact on the Luftwaffe was significant but not revolutionary. Hajo Herrmann's Wilde Sau had proven themselves a useful addition to Germany's night defence and were set to expand to three full geschwader – albeit with no new aircraft or pilots. To show they were now an accepted part of the Luftwaffe they were given their own nickname; *Herrmann Knaben* – Herrmann's Lads. Of far greater import for the Nachtjagd, Josef Kammhuber was forced to alter his beloved Himmelbett system. At a conference he presided over on 30 July, attended by Milch, Galland and Nachtjagd luminaries such as Werner Streib, he reluctantly conceded that his fighters would not be strictly held in their boxes and instead would use them as a starting point. From then on, they would be guided into the bomber stream by whatever method worked best, including running commentary. Once into the stream they were released to hunt freelance, aided by their Lichtensteins or the new SN-2 airborne radar. This was officially named the *Zahme Sau* tactic – Tame Boar. Kammhuber's concession was no great shock after the failures over Hamburg. As the decorated ground controller Walter Knickmeier noted, "Düppel was the death sentence for controlled night fighting in boxes."

As the Luftwaffe and the Nazi leadership busied themselves with the aftermath of the bombing, the citizens of Hamburg had other concerns. Gauleiter Kaufmann appealed to Joseph Goebbels as chair of the Inter-Ministerial Bomb Damage Committee: "Food must be found for ... a million people. Shelter must be secured...They must be given clothing." His calls did not go unanswered. Remarkably quickly, the Nazi authorities sprang into action; registering the homeless, organising temporary shelters and distributing food brought in from across the Reich. Life began to return to a semblance of normality with a big emphasis being on getting people back to work in Hamburg's war industries. Wilma Rathjens went back to her job in a U-boat yard and received "244 Reichsmarks [about £24 or $100 equivalent at the time] and a large box of sweets", whilst male workers got "beer, cigarettes and butter for their families, all free".[10]

There was also the 'Blitz phenomenon' among Hamburg's inhabitants. Just as in Britain during the Luftwaffe's bombing campaign of 1940-41, some people – but by no means all – found the experience bound them together more tightly than was the case before. Anne-Lies Schmidt recalled it being "really extraordinary", with "the population becoming *Kumpels* [mates]. We shared everything. Everyone helped each other." For those that left the city, their experience was mixed – again as it was in Britain during the huge wartime evacuations – some hosts in the countryside found their guests' hygiene somewhat lacking, with lice being a common problem, and they were shocked at Hamburgers' acceptance of bad language and petty theft. Southern Germany's Catholics in particular were not enamoured of the new arrivals, derisively nicknaming them *Bombenpack Preussen* – a pack of bombed out Prussians. About half the refugees returned to Hamburg over the next year.

The battle cost Bomber Command 87 aircraft destroyed – 33 of them on the last night – with 59 of those shot down by night fighters, despite the use of Window. Without it the blood price would, without doubt, have been far heavier. Hamburg was a major success for Harris and Bomber Command. Coming as it did in the dying embers of the battle of the Ruhr, it caused all Germans a shock almost as seismic as the calamity at Stalingrad earlier that same year. With excellent foresight Joseph Goebbels noted in his diary that "The air war is a sword of Damocles hanging over our heads."

# 6

# 1943

# BATTLE OF BERLIN
# AND SCHWEINFURT

The Nazis never had a high opinion of the American fighting man on pretty much any level. Goering infamously went as far as saying Americans were good at making razor blades but little else. Unsurprisingly given this opinion, the German response to the Americans entry into the air war over Europe was rather lacklustre, with only a single new geschwader activated as Dolfo Galland explained. "When, in January 1943, the daylight attacks by the Americans began to traverse north-western Germany ... a new geschwader, JG 11, was set up near Bremen." The Germans clearly were not taking the Americans very seriously, but Galland was gracious enough to admit they had underestimated their new opponent, and especially the B-17 bomber. "First attacked from the rear, this resulted in heavy losses for the German fighters, and it was quickly realised that the fighters' armour and armaments must be increased."[2] The Americans continued to be infrequent visitors over the Continent during the next few months, but the German fighter pilots who faced them soon realised how different they were from anything they had seen before.

Not since 1939 had enemy bombers flown raids during daylight, and now the Americans were doing exactly that. They also flew differently, in tightly structured aerial boxes – optimally of at least one hundred bombers each – with interlocking zones of fire from their on-board machine guns. That meant 1,300 machine-guns protecting a 100-plane box. The Germans would christen these formations *Pulks*, or 'herds'. At the time – as Galland described – the accepted practice in the Luftwaffe's day fighter force when attacking a bomber was to do so from behind and slightly above, but against the massed guns of a Pulk this put the fighter in harm's way for a considerable amount of time as they closed with the bombers, hence the losses. So the Germans had adapted.

Starting in November 1942, the likes of Egon Mayer had been trialling the head on attack – von Schnauze auf Schnauze – and by the summer of 1943 it had become the preferred option, as Otto Schmid explained: "We realised very soon that conventional methods of attack wouldn't achieve any measurable success ... there was no alternative but to attack from head-on and slightly above." Georg-Peter Eder had come to much the same conclusion and employed the tactic against an American bomber force hitting several targets across northern France on 14 July.

We were doing about 450km per hour now and were coming down slightly, aiming for their noses. There were about 200 of us attacking 200 bombers, but there was also the fighter escort above them. We were going for the bombers. When we made our move the P-47s began to dive on us and it was a race to get to the bombers before being intercepted. I was already close and about 600 feet above and coming straight on. I opened fire with the twenties [20mm cannon] at 500 yards. At 300 yards I opened fire with the 30s [30mm cannon]. It was a short burst, maybe 10 shells from each cannon but I saw the bomber explode and begin to burn.

With a combined closing speed of 500mph the German pilots were reducing their own firing time to a second or less, but also minimising their exposure time to the American gunners. Nevertheless, it took a determined flyer to carry out a '12 o'clock high' attack as it was known. "You could count on incoming fire from 30 to 40 machine-guns simultaneously, it was like flying through a blizzard." The same pilot also admitted it took him some time to get used to the method. "I used to fire far too early … but later I learned to grit my teeth and swallow my fear until I was within range." Having fired, the fighter pilot then had another decision to make; to dive on through the bombers or pull up and skim over the top of his target and through the formation. The former was the easiest in straight flying terms, but it took the fighter out of the battle as the pilot had little chance of getting into position for a second attack before the bombers had flown on, whereas the latter exposed the fighter's belly to any willing turret gunner. Alfred Grislawski – one quarter of the famous Luftwaffe fighter *Karaya Quartet* – advocated the riskier option. "Attack from exactly head on at the same height, firing with all weapons from a distance of 200 metres, then pass over the bombers 20 metres above them."

The Americans didn't only bring with them new bombers and new tactics, but also a new phenomenon – the day fighter escort. The most common escort in the early summer of 1943 was the P-47. The American P-47 Thunderbolt, to give it its proper name, was not a handsome fighter. It didn't have the Bf 109's classically sleek lines, indeed it was dubbed the 'seven-ton milk bottle', and it was – in point of fact – the largest and heaviest single engine propeller-driven fighter ever built. Its weight did not help its range, and when it arrived in England old 'Thunderjugs' could only just reach Antwerp from its bases in east Anglia. At that point the fighter boys had to peel away from their bomber charges and head for home. On refuelling they would head east again and pick the bombers up on the last leg of their homeward journey. In between, the bombers fought it out alone with the Germans.

Most of those battles had been fought out over France as the Americans built up their strength and focused on hitting U-boat pens on the French Atlantic coast, or French factories making engines and parts for the Nazi aircraft industry. As their experience grew, the Americans moved on, following the British example and attacking Kriegsmarine naval bases on the North Sea, and little else. The outcome was that by the summer of 1943 the vast majority of the German people had never seen an American warplane, nor heard an air raid siren during the day. As far as most Germans were concerned, the war in the skies above their heads was against the British and no-one else. Fred Anderson's Blitz Week was the first major step in radically changing that reality.

On the 28 July raid against the aircraft factories at Kassel-Bettenhausen and Oschersleben, the bombers were escorted by 123 Thunderbolts. Then, to the complete surprise of the stalking German fighters, the 'Thunderjugs' didn't turn back at their normal point, but flew straight on, reaching as far as Germany's western border. The increase in range was due to the addition of a 75-gallon belly tank, which made the fighters ungainly but kept them in the air. The German fighter pilots attacked anyway, only to be fended off by the well-trained American fighter jocks. In the end, the Germans downed 27 bombers and a single P-47, but their own casualties were high; 23 fighters and 8 pilots lost, and another 13 fliers wounded.

Two days later on 30 July, the Kassel raid was repeated, but this time the Germans did not sheer off when the bombers reached their escort on their way home, choosing instead to fight it out with the American escorts. The result was the largest air battle to date between German and American fighters. In the ensuing melee Major Eugene Roberts became the first US pilot to shoot down three German aircraft in one dogfight, as the Germans lost 31 fighters in total, with 14 pilots killed and many more injured. The battle was a profound shock for the German day fighter arm.

For the preceding two years the greater part of the Luftwaffe day fighter force had been in Russia, with the fighting in the west resting on the shoulders of relatively few – not quite 'We happy few' perhaps – but their jousts with RAF Fighter Command were infrequent and on a relatively small scale. The arrival in strength of the American Eighth Army Air Force would now irrevocably change that dynamic. From the 30 July Kassel raid onwards the Luftwaffe's day fighter force in the west would be faced by an enemy forever growing in strength, whose aim was the progressive destruction of Nazi Germany's vital war industries by precision, daylight bombing. As the Germans recognised this new challenge, they began to understand that the best way to combat it was to inflict so many losses on the Americans that they would be forced to call off their offensive. So began what the Eighth Army Air Force would come to call 'the bloody summer of 1943'.

On the morning of Tuesday 17 August 1943 in the Franconian city of Schweinfurt in southern Germany, 10,000 workers drank their morning ersatz coffee and headed off to the Kugelfischer-Werke factory over on the western edge of town. They were joined by 8,000 more employees of Vereinigte Kugellager Fabrik (VKF), split between the VKF I and VKF II works, plus those from Fichtel und Sachs AG and Deutsche Star Kugelhalter. The five factories were the city's lifeblood, and they all specialised in one thing – the manufacture of industrial ball bearings. These anti-friction bearings were a vital component in vast swathes of the Wehrmacht's equipment roster, including everything from searchlights (each of the new 200cm searchlights required 90 bearings) to airframes (a Ju 88 minus its engines needed 1,056). In fact, the German aircraft industry as a whole consumed 2,395,000 a month. The Reich had 38 ball bearing factories within its borders, but Schweinfurt was the key, with just over half of all production centred in the five plants grouped around the city's railway station just north of the River Main.

Albert Speer recognised ball bearing production – and Schweinfurt – as a major vulnerability in the Nazi war machine, and he had pestered Goering to do more to protect it. His warnings were not misplaced. As late as the previous August, a senior RAF commander described the city's flak as being composed of "only a few light gun batteries".[1] Those days were now long gone. By the summer of 1943, Schweinfurt's defences included over a hundred anti-aircraft guns supported by a large number of smoke generators. There were also no fewer than 49 searchlights and three complete decoy sites, as the Germans believed the main threat was at night from Bomber Command. They thought Schweinfurt far too deep inside Germany for unescorted American bombers to pose a danger during daylight.

The Americans disagreed. Their plan was to hit Schweinfurt on the afternoon of Tuesday 17 August, and hit it with the largest attack the Americans had launched in the war so far. On bases scattered across the wide-open flatlands of East Anglia, 376 Flying Fortresses and 240 Thunderbolts were being armed, bombed up, fuelled and readied for the raid.

The plan was complex. The bombers would be arranged into two completely separate waves. The leading wave of 146 Fortresses would head for the huge Messerschmitt factory in Regensburg. The Regensburg plant was a juicy target, producing 200 Bf 109s a month – a quarter of Germany's entire single-engine fighter output. After dropping their payloads, the bombers would fool the German fighters by not turning around and heading for home, but fly on southwards, touching down in American-held Tunisia instead. It appeared to be an excellent idea. The Germans would be denied a second bite of the cherry, and many American lives would be saved. The problem was that Regensburg was the secondary target that day. The main aim of the attack was to deluge the ball bearing factories of Schweinfurt with high explosive from the second wave of 230 bombers. But designed as it was, with this plan there would now be no surprise, the Regensburg bombers effectively acting as a wake-up call. The Schweinfurt defenders would be well and truly alert as the second wave bore down on them, and with the Regensburg wave disappearing south to Africa the Luftwaffe would be free to concentrate all its might on the Schweinfurt force.

Meanwhile, on Bomber Command's bases, the RAF was preparing for a very special raid of their own planned for that night – the British were going to attack Peenemünde. Peenemünde was a small fishing port on the isolated island of Usedom off Germany's Baltic coast – it was also home to the Nazis secret research and testing facility for the V-weapon programme. Having discovered its whereabouts and purpose, Bomber Command intended to wipe it off the map. Nazi Germany would be attacked by day and night.

On the day itself, dense ground mist shrouded the airfields of the bombers destined for Schweinfurt, while the Regensburg-bound crews looked up into clear skies. This posed a major problem. To sit and wait until the mist cleared could well mean the Regensburg force would reach its intended landing fields in Africa in darkness – and that was considered too big a risk. The alternative was simply to attack Regensburg and scrap the Schweinfurt raid, but that was seen as being too big a hit to morale. The decision was made for the Regensburg force to take off immediately, and for the Schweinfurt crews to wait until the mist cleared and then go. It was a compromise that would magnify the inherent flaws in the overall plan.

For the Germans that morning, the huge amount of American radio chatter clearly signalled a major operation was on the cards, and Luftwaffe ground control readied no fewer than seven fighter groups for action from as far as 200 miles away from the predicted bomber route.

As the Regensburg bombers reached the Dutch islands, the Americans' bad luck continued. They were supposed to be met by 87 Thunderbolts who would escort them to Eupen on the German border, but some of the fighters didn't make the rendezvous and most of those that did clustered around the front of the formation, leaving the combat wing at the back unprotected. The waiting Germans went into near frenzy. As many as 200 German fighters were involved at any one time, as they attacked in pairs, in staffeln and in entire gruppen, focusing their attention in particular on the rear wing. When the escorts turned back at Eupen, it just got worse. From that point it was 90 minutes flying time to Regensburg, and for the American crews involved it was like running the gauntlet. One American co-pilot saw a B-17 "completely disappear in a brilliant explosion, from which the only remains were four small balls of fire – the fuel tanks – which were quickly consumed as they fell earthwards." Exhausting their fuel and ammunition, most of the fighters landed at any air strip they could find and readied themselves for the bombers' return leg, only to watch in amazement as the B-17s carried on flying serenely south after hitting their target. They'd done their work though. Twenty-four bombers had been shot down with another 51 damaged. One would land in Tunis in such a state it was scrapped.

With their enemy having flown the coop, over 400 German fighters were now fuelled and armed and sitting on airfields along the expected return route of the Regensburg bombers, their pilots kicking themselves in frustration at what they saw as a lost opportunity. Then the Schweinfurt-bound force appeared in the skies above them. Having waited two hours for the mist to clear, the 230 B-17s detailed to hit Nazi Germany's ball bearing industry were flying into a bear pit. Waves of 109s and Fw 190s attacked from head on, abeam, from astern, from underneath, from above, as singles, pairs, fours and more. Whole staffeln bore in wing tip to wing tip, with lone Ju 88s and Bf 110s standing off out of range and radioing instructions to their comrades. Bomber after bomber was hit. *Leutnant* Heinz Schwarz of JG 1 attacked a B-17. "I fired at the left-most Boeing in the fourth Pulk with such effectiveness that the left inner engine showed a black smoke plume. As I pulled out I saw the Boeing quickly drop some 4-500 metres behind and 100 metres below the formation." Turning to finish off his victim, Schwarz saw the Boeing he had shot from formation "was under attack by an Fw 190 and two Bf 109s and was spinning down".

Other Bf 109s from JG 11 attacked from the rear, firing a new weapon; the *Werfer-Granate* 21 – a 21cm rocket launcher based on the dreaded *Nebelwerfer* system and slung under the fighter's wings. Designed to be fired from outside the range of the bomber's machine-guns, the warhead would explode at a pre-set distance, which if nothing else would break up the enemy formation and make each bomber much more vulnerable. To maximise just such an outcome, whole staffeln would fire them in volleys, as if they were musketeers in the eighteenth century. When it worked, the effect was dramatic, as a German fighter pilot recalled on seeing two bombers "literally burst asunder in the air". A B-17 pilot saw a rocket "hitting the side of [a B-17] just behind the cockpit, it ripped open the fuselage, blew off one wing and gave a brief glimpse of the two pilots at the controls before the whole plane disintegrated." Gustav Rödel was one of the attacking pilots that day and saw "the burning planes and crash fires, as well as some of our own fighters going down". It wasn't just the usual suspects from the single-engine fighter geschwader that were involved either; Me-210s, Dornier 217s and even a few Fw 189 reconnaissance planes joined in, anything that could fly and fight was thrown at the bombers.

That included Bf 110s from the Nachtjagd. *Unteroffizier* Otto Fries and his radio op, Fred Staffa, were scrambled from their base at Sint-Truiden in Flanders and joined the fray. Having already engaged one B-17, Fries saw three Bf 109s circling another bomber with its port wing undercarriage lowered. None of the German fighters was attacking and the young NCO assumed they had run out of ammunition. He went straight in and fired a long burst into its starboard wing, which burst into flames. Crew members baled out, and the doomed aircraft exploded before hitting the ground. Fries was later told that it was common for bombers to lower their undercarriage when crippled as a sign the aircraft was finished and the crew were preparing to bale out. He felt ashamed for weeks afterwards.

Finally, the returning bombers reached the German-Dutch border where they were due to rendezvous with their fighter escort – only it wasn't there. Instead, there was an entire German fighter group led by Dolfo Galland's younger brother, Wilhelm-Ferdinand. 'Wutz' Galland already had 55 victories to his credit and was determined to add to that tally, but as he manoeuvred his men into position they were jumped by the missing escorts. They had overflown the rendezvous point by 15 miles before realising their mistake and turning back. The error now worked in their favour, as it brought them behind the unsuspecting Germans. Galland went down in a ball of flames west of Maastricht.

Thirty-six bombers were lost from the Schweinfurt force, making a total for the day of 60 B-17s shot down from 376 sent up. It was a huge success for the Germans. Capitalising on a litany of American errors, the Germans had managed to concentrate a large number of fighters and make it count. Pilot morale soared, especially when they heard that in the aftermath of the raid the American bomber crews were "shocked, they couldn't get their pilots to fly, there was almost a mutiny." True or not, there was no doubt the Schweinfurt debacle had a major impact on the Eighth Army Air Force. In the 19 days after the raid, the Americans only flew six missions, and none were to Germany. Erhard Milch, who carried out a tour of the fighter units involved in the battle, reported that "The morale of our pilots is excellent; their performance … cannot be stressed too much." They were also cheered to hear that damage to Schweinfurt's ball bearing factories was relatively light and repaired in four weeks. Speer claimed production fell by over a third after the raid, but noted with satisfaction that existing stockpiles more than covered the shortfall.

As the surviving Americans limped home, Bomber Command's main force took off for Peenemünde. The Nachtjagd were caught napping. Expecting an attack on a city, when radar picked up aircraft heading for Berlin the night fighters were scrambled to protect the capital, only to discover it was actually a diversionary raid carried out by 20 fast-flying Mosquitoes. With almost all the available fighters drawn south, it was left to a handful of pilots and crews to try and combat the main raid. One such crew were *Oberleutnant* Hans Meissner and his radio op Josef Krinner in their Bf 110. Krinner remembered: "It was a bright moonlit night and the sky was cloudless." He was in contact with *Oberleutnant* Reidel, a fighter control officer. "He told us to give up flying towards Berlin and head for Ameise, a Himmelbett box on the east coast of Denmark. After this we had no further radio contact with the ground. After a short time I picked up a lot of contacts on my Lichtenstein radar." Following instructions from Krinner, Meissner came up on a Lancaster. "I closed in and opened fire from about 150 metres, somewhat to the right and 50 metres below. The No. 3 engine caught fire. As I broke away from him, return fire from the rear gunner passed to my left." Attempting to dive to safety, the Lancaster pilot "came into my sights and I was able to give him a short burst. He went down … crashing a few hundred yards from Ufer." Krinner reported the shoot down. "I then picked up another contact. We closed on the target to about 50 metres below and behind. Meissner opened fire and we shot it down." Meissner remembered that the bomber "went into a dive and crashed at 0301hrs on the shore of the Apenrader Bight." Incredibly, the two Germans then latched onto a third Lancaster and attacked as before, and again "the No. 3 engine caught fire." As the pilot tried to escape, he pulled up and instead flew straight into Meissner's gunsight, "I pulled up to within 20 metres and with a few rounds set the No. 2 engine and fuselage on fire. The aircraft broke up and crashed at 0311hrs." Meissner and Krinner's treble were three of the 41 aircraft Bomber Command lost that night.

Max Mayer was a test pilot at the Peenemünde facility and remembered that evening as "a wonderful night with a full moon". He had just returned from Friedrichshafen and had brought back fresh plums as an after-dinner treat for his mess comrades. "Suddenly the alarm sounded ... 650 four-engine British bombers dropped their bombs on us – an area 500 yards wide and a little over a mile long." Mayer ran for shelter in a bunker in the middle of the administration area and "when the attack was over, everything was on fire ... *Oberstleutnant* Stahms – who'd lost a leg landing a Ju 88 – lost his artificial leg in the fire. Approximately 765 people died during the attack."[3]

Another night fighter pilot, Peter Spoden, engaged the bombers. He had trained for 27 months to be a fighter pilot, but so far had had no luck. "My first mission was Hamburg but I couldn't find anyone because of Düppel." Initially sent to cover Berlin that night, he was re-routed to attack the raiders.

> We flew there very fast and I shot one down ... you have to shoot between the engines and we'd been trained to do that. We were told 'Shoot between the engines, it will cause a fire and they [the crew] will have a chance to bale out.' So I shot between the engines to give them a chance to bale out ... when I shot it down I was so excited, I landed and went to the crash site and spoke to one of the survivors. I felt free, as if I had achieved what I'd been trained to do. How can I explain how I felt? Like an avenger for Essen [Spoden's native city].[4]

Hans Meissner and Josef Krinner also went to the site of one of their victories, as a local youngster, Rasmus Jessen, witnessed:

> The morning after I saw two Luftwaffe crew members visit the site of the crashed bomber. The bodies of the crew members were lined up ready to be taken away in a covered wagon. As Meissner stood by the bodies, a member of the small crowd that had gathered stood on one of the dead crew and called him a 'British pig'. This made Meissner very angry and he spun around and slapped the person about the face.

The 765 engineers, guards, ground staff and production workers were not the only German casualties in the Peenemünde raid. Shortly after 8am the following morning, the Luftwaffe's Chief of Staff, Hans Jeschonnek, walked out of his back door and into the shed in his garden. Taking out his service pistol, he shot himself in the head. He had been under enormous strain for weeks, constantly bearing the brunt of Hitler's anger at the Luftwaffe's inability to stop the Allied bombing raids. The night before he had personally taken charge of the defence, ordering the Nachtjagd to cover Berlin and leaving Peenemünde exposed. To compound his error, he had then ordered the capital's flak batteries to open fire, despite the fact there were almost 150 night fighters flying over the city at the time. When he was told the morning after that the rocket site was almost totally destroyed, it was the final straw. In a bid to try and cover up the link with the Peenemünde attack, the Nazis delayed the announcement of his death until 19 August.

The Americans broke their self-imposed ban on attacks into Germany just over three weeks after Schweinfurt on 6 September, sending 338 B-17s and 176 escorts to hit aircraft manufacturing plants clustered around the southern German city of Stuttgart. There was heavy cloud cover over much of the Continent, but the Americans refused to delay, leading to confusion in the air and a dangerous dispersal of the various bomber groups. A diversionary sweep by an entire wing of B-24s failed to fool the fighter controllers, and just as at Schweinfurt the Germans were able to concentrate a large force of fighters that pounced on the American bombers. *Hauptmann* Werner Schröer and his unit had only recently arrived back in the Reich after six months in the Mediterranean theatre battling away against the Anglo-Americans, where Schröer had already scored a dozen victories against the big Viermots. Now, he and the 20 Bf 109 Gustavs with him saw a Pulk of B-17s and went into the attack. In 30 minutes of savage combat, nine bombers were downed, with Schröer claiming three.

Hermann Graf's JG 50 was also committed, its original mission to hunt down and destroy the fleet-of-foot Mosquitoes all but forgotten in the push to hit the bombers. Graf – a consummate

# THE NIGHT WAR

*Right:* Helmut Lent - one of the *Nachtjagd*'s most successful pilots – plays cards before a mission. (Courtesy of Bundesarchiv, Bild 1011-358-1908-09)

*Below:* Cockpit of a Bf 110 night fighter as seen from the onboard *Funker*'s (radio operator's) seat. (Courtesy of Bundesarchiv, Bild 1011-649-5371)

*Above:* The fighter control room at Döberitz. Nicknamed 'Kammhuber's Cinemas', these control rooms were the nerve centres of the Luftwaffe's campaign. (Author's collection)

*Left:* By 1943 the Luftwaffe's ground defences included thousands of teenaged schoolchildren who were taught school lessons alongside their air defence duties. (Courtesy Georg Gunter)

*Luftwaffehelferinnen* cleaning a 150cm searchlight. These female auxiliaries were central to the Reich's air defences. (Author's collection)

*Above:* Fighting the air war was a national effort in the Third Reich. Civilians like these in the fire service and the RLB were crucial. (Author's collection)

*Below left:* Female auxiliaries in the Luftwaffe took over the roles in signals and communications as able-bodied men were sent to the Front. (Courtesy Georg Gunter)

*Below right:* The Nazis were masters at propaganda. This poster exhorts the population to join the RLB and take part in the war effort. (Author's collection)

*Right:* The head of RAF Bomber Command, Arthur 'Butch' Harris, in his headquarters outside High Wycombe. (Author's collection)

*Below:* The mainstay of RAF Bomber Command from 1943 was the superlative four-engine Avro Lancaster. (Author's collection)

Hermann Goering talks to a *Wilde Sau* pilot. The tactic's originator, Hajo Herrmann, stands over Goering's left shoulder. (Author's collection)

# THE DAY WAR

Heinz Knoke – an enthusiastic Nazi and day fighter pilot in defence of the homeland. (Author's collection)

*Above:* Gordon Gollob – a Luftwaffe Experte and the man chosen by Goering to replace 'Dolfo' Galland after his dismissal. (Author's collection)

*Right:* Hannes Trautloft – one of the Luftwaffe's most successful fighter pilots of the war and a key player in the failed 'Fighter Pilot's Revolt' to try and replace Goering. (Author's collection)

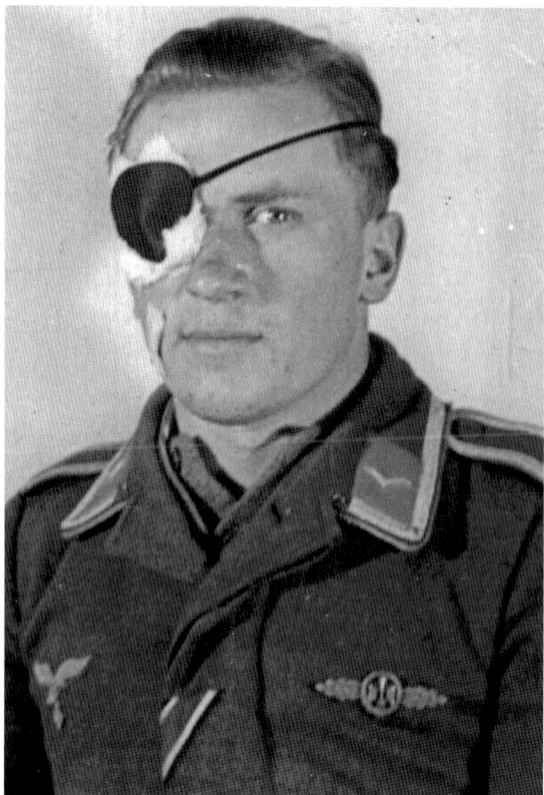

*Unteroffizier* Otto Schmid.
(Courtesy Otto Schmid)

Erhard Milch (right) was
in charge of Nazi aircraft
manufacturing and worked
hand in glove with Albert
Speer to ramp up production.
(Author's collection)

*Above:* Photograph taken by a B-17 Flying Fortress waist gunner showing just how heavy the flak was over Nazi Germany. (Courtesy USAAF)

*Below:* Badly damaged by flak over Leuna in November 1944, this B-17 was finally shot down by German fighters over France on its way home. The cannon shell holes in the cockpit are clearly visible. (Author's collection)

# 'EUROPE IS A FORTRESS WITHOUT A ROOF!'

*Above: 'We can take it'* – Nazi propaganda tried to downplay the devastation of the bombing raids, instead portraying a civilian population unbowed. (*Signal* magazine)

*Below:* Albert Speer, the architect-turned-armaments supremo (right centre, facing the crowd), addresses a gathering of the very industrial workers Bomber Command's goal was to de-house and demoralise. (Author's collection)

A group of *hausfrauen* in Hamburg looking bewildered and scared after yet another bombing raid. (Author's collection)

Following the first big raid on Hamburg on the night of 24 July 1943, survivors were told to report to local Nazi Party headquarters, as the board on the right states, for emergency accommodation, ration cards, food and compensation. (Author's collection)

*Opposite, top:* The Ruhr 1944 – Hermann Goering chats with local people after yet another bombing raid. Unlike so many senior Nazis, Goering had little problem talking to ordinary Germans about the raids. (Author's collection)

*Opposite, bottom:* Hamburg's wrecked *Hauptbahnhof* (main railway station) after the first raids in late July 1943. (Author's collection)

*Right:* Inmates from nearby concentration camps were used for the dirtiest jobs after raids, such as the clearing up and disposing of corpses. (Author's collection)

*Below:* The bomb-ravaged centre of Munich at the end of the war. (Author's collection)

*Above:* Kassel's Untere Königsstrasse in 1945. The rubble has been cleared away for traffic. (Author's collection)

*Left:* Adolf Hitler comes face to face with the reality of the air war in the skies above the Third Reich. (Author's collection)

An exhausted German civilian air raid warden the morning after another devastating raid. (*Signal* magazine)

Galland attending an event in Billericay, Essex in 1975. In that year he was a guest of RAF Museum Hendon for the unveiling of the Battle of Britain Hall, where he was entertained by Prince Charles. (Courtesy Gerhard Granz, from *Alarmstart!* by Patrick G. Eriksson)

Galland's grave in
Oberwinter, Germany.
(Courtesy MisterBee1966)

The memorial statue to
Sir Arthur Harris and the
men and women of Bomber
Command who lost their
lives in the air war over Nazi
Germany, outside St Clement
Danes Church in London.
(Author's collection)

veteran of the Russian Front and the first ever pilot to reach 200 victories – shot down two, and his old pal Alfred Grislawski claimed one.

Walther Dahl's gruppe – like Schröer's – had just returned to the Reich, only for them it was from Taganrog on the Sea of Azov in southern Russia, and now they faced the American bombers. *Oberfeldwebel* Alfred Surau was one of Dahl's veterans. "We reached a B-17 formation flying at about 7,500 metres in the Stuttgart area and immediately attacked. During my first attack from the front, I observed effective hits in the top turret and right inner engine. I had to break away beneath the bomber and received hits in my propeller and wing. When I pulled up I could see that the bomber I'd hit had dropped from the formation in a flat dive, trailing a long white plume of smoke." Dahl's gruppe did even better than Schröer's, destroying ten B-17s in a fight that spanned much of southern Germany and only ended in eastern France.

By the time the bombers reached home they had lost 45 of their number – some forced to ditch in the sea having run out of fuel – and 116 were damaged. Ten more B-17s were so badly shot up they were scrapped after landing in England. US command officially admitted the operation had been a 'costly fiasco', although this didn't do justice to a battle that in many ways was worse than Schweinfurt. It was yet another fillip to German morale, especially as only nine pilots and aircrew were killed and eight more wounded in a fight that saw half the bombing force destroyed or damaged.

Just as after Schweinfurt, the Americans went into shock, imposing a block once more on going back to Germany, this time for another three weeks, before on 27 September dispatching another 300-plus bombers to the North Sea German port of Emden. Alerted early due to a radio intercept, the Luftwaffe controllers were once again able to concentrate a large fighter force, among whom was the highly decorated *Hauptmann* Günther Specht. Specht had lost an eye in 1939 flying a Bf 110 but had managed to get himself back flying. Now, as he led his men directly beneath two Boeing Pulks flying east, he realised a prolonged turn they were making "made a head-on attack impossible", so he manoeuvred his gruppe into position for an attack from the high rear, in which the 5. Staffel would go in first firing its 21cm mortar shells. Force of habit made him look up just before he attacked and to his surprise he spotted "enemy fighters ... Thunderbolts ... 2,000 metres above the Boeing Pulk". He immediately radioed "Kleine Indianer über uns [Small Indians – enemy fighters – above us]". There were 262 P-47s escorting the bombers, and every one of them had auxiliary tanks, allowing them to reach all the way to Emden and back. Specht pressed home his attack regardless, his own wingman being "hit by the Thunderbolt behind me, which was then driven away by a diving Fw 190".

The presence of the American fighters transformed the battle and saved the B-17s from another potential Schweinfurt or Stuttgart. In the end it was the Germans who suffered, losing 28 fighters and 18 pilots and crew – most of whom came down in the sea and drowned. Günther Specht noted in his after-action report that the biggest reason for the mauling they had taken was that their pilots were "inexperienced in fighter versus fighter combat ... and were forced into individual fights without adequate knowledge of tactics or situational awareness". With American fighter strength growing by the day, Specht's analysis was ominous.

October saw a significantly increased level of activity by the Eighth Army Air Force over Germany. Multiple targets were bombed, including the Messerschmitt factory at Wiener Neustadt and the Focke-Wulf plant at Marienburg (modern-day Malbork in Poland), with the latter described as "one of the most accurate raids of the war". The Germans repeatedly managed to bring large numbers of fighters to bear, causing significant losses among the US bombers, the most injurious being against a raid on Münster on 10 October. Close enough to England to allow fighter escort there and back, the Germans rightly guessed that the late take-off time for the bombers meant the objective wasn't deep in Germany, and they scrambled an incredible 476 day and night fighters to meet the threat. Groups of Bf 109s were detailed to keep the Thunderbolts busy while everyone else was told to go for the bombers, and in particular the leading bomb division.

Walter Hoeckner was flying an Fw 190 that day. "I attacked a B-17 from the right, hitting the right wing from the side, dove beneath its right wing and hit the last B-17 on the left flank in a steep bank from beneath ... while diving away beneath the B-17 I was hit in the engine. My cockpit immediately filled with smoke and gasoline fumes and I baled out." Hoeckner's excitement for the day wasn't quite over. "While in my parachute another B-17 dived past me in a steep bank and crashed into pieces 80 to 100 metres away from me." In an attempt to outfox the Germans, US command decided to cluster the P-47s around the trailing division, believing the lead unit would achieve surprise and therefore require less protection. They were wrong. Thirty-three B-17s were lost, 30 of them from the leading wing.

On the morning of 14 October – eight weeks and two days since the Schweinfurt disaster – the crews of all three Eighth Army Air Force bomb divisions shuffled into their briefing rooms across eastern England to find out the target for the day. To their utter dismay it was Schweinfurt, again. The decision had been made at short notice, based on favourable weather reports over the target site, even though conditions in England were poor. With fighter strength now higher than it was back in August, it was decided to attach an entire P-47 group to each of the divisions for the journey out, and to meet them on their return. It was hoped this would help prevent a repeat of the August debacle. The route selected was basically a straight line from East Anglia to the target, and with all three bomb divisions due to take part, radio traffic before the raid was exceptionally heavy – mistake number one. The bombers took off early, signalling to the Germans that the objective was deep inside Germany, and as they climbed the B-24 Liberators of the smallest division struggled to form up. Exasperated, US command told them to carry out a diversionary sweep in the North Sea instead. Inexplicably, their P-47 escort group went with them. Mistake number two.

Walter Grabmann was in charge of the defenders. An experienced and intelligent officer, Grabmann had started his combat career in Spain with the Condor Legion and was the perfect choice for the Germans that day. He scrambled every Luftwaffe fighter unit in western Europe, bar one, to take part in the battle, sending them into the bomber formations in waves that gave the hard-pressed American crews no respite. The only time his fighters were not attacking was when the B-17s were over the target and being peppered by flak. Herbert Zimmer was one of the German fighter pilots, flying a 'gunboat' Bf 109 – a Gustav with 20mm canons mounted under each wing for extra firepower. Attacking near Frankfurt am Main, he "hit the left wing of a Fortress with a long burst, whereupon the enemy plane showed two strong white smoke plumes and sheered away from the formation ... the fuselage burst into flames." His comrade from JG 1, Wolfgang Brunner, was flying an Fw 190 and was forced to join another trio of 190s when his wingman was unable to drop his auxiliary fuel tank and had to break off. Nevertheless, he still attacked, the foursome targeting "five Boeings flying alone in close formation". Making his pass from the front and slightly left, he saw "hits in the fuselage and tail and I saw the vertical tail break up." He watched the stricken bomber drop out of formation but was unable to finish it off, having run out of fuel and ammunition.

The Americans were out of range of their fighter escort for three-and-a-quarter hours and were desperate for the safety of their Thunderbolt umbrella, but on reaching their rendezvous point on the return leg there was no-one to meet them. Bad weather over their airfields had grounded all the fighters. The Germans now had an opportunity to more or less wipe out the remaining bombers. The only reason they didn't was the same weather front that stymied the Thunderbolts also provided cover for the B-17s, who gratefully found shelter in the clouds and limped home.

The Germans had won a resounding victory. They had lost 53 aircraft with 29 airmen killed and another 20 wounded, but they had come within a whisker of smashing the entire bomber force. As it was, they had downed 60 bombers – exactly the same as they had during the first Schweinfurt raid – and damaged 138 more. Losses among the American crews were horrendous, with 605 men killed or missing on the raid and another 43 wounded – little wonder the 14 October raid became known throughout Eighth Army Air Force as 'Black Thursday'. The American commander,

Ira Eaker, described the Luftwaffe's performance as "unprecedented in its magnitude, in the cleverness with which it was planned, and in the severity with which it was executed".

In practical terms, the Americans called a temporary halt to long-range raids into Germany. Only two further attacks were made in the last two weeks of October: one on the German border town of Düren, and the other on Wiener Neustadt. Both were rather tame affairs and little damage was done. As for Schweinfurt and its ball bearing industry, the October raid was more successful for the Americans than its August equivalent, with Albert Speer bemoaning that production was reduced by two-thirds in its aftermath. However, his own policies of dispersing key industries across large numbers of plants – and pursuing technological innovations that did away with the need for bearings in the first place – were beginning to have a dramatic impact. The latter in particular was proving so successful that Speer himself would later jokingly refer to it as the *Kugellagerdämmerung* – the 'twilight of the ball bearings'.

Arthur Harris, by his own admission, had an acid tongue, and wasn't afraid to exercise it. When Churchill – someone else afflicted with the same trait – described a senior American air force commander as "a man of limited intelligence", Butch replied "You pay him too high a compliment." The observation was ungracious and also quite surprising, as Harris, unusually for many of Britain's senior military commanders during the war, got on very well with his American counterparts. A very sociable man, in contrast to his rather austere manner at work, he loved to entertain at home and he and his wife hosted a constant round of dinner parties for all manner of people, with many Americans among the guests. Harris himself felt he had much in common with his American peers, always feeling something of an outsider in the upper echelons of the British establishment, his early years of service in the colonies no doubt influencing his view. Now, having watched in horror as the Americans were decimated in the skies above Schweinfurt and Stuttgart, he thought the time ripe to persuade them to give up their belief in daylight precision bombing – which he believed to be absurd – and join Bomber Command in their night-time offensive.

Specifically, he wanted them to join him in his next big battle, the one he was sure would decide the war in favour of the Allies – the battle of Berlin.

Following the success of Operation Gomorrah, Harris felt the same level of destruction could potentially be visited on the Nazi capital, paralysing the German war effort and causing a collapse in morale and the population's willingness to fight on. In a personal note to Churchill dated 3 November 1943, he bombastically claimed, "We can wreck Berlin from end to end if the Americans will come in on it. It will cost between 400-500 aircraft. It will cost Germany the war." This was heady stuff, and the stakes couldn't have been higher, as Albert Speer later acknowledged "If you [the Allies] had succeeded in destroying Berlin, as you did with Hamburg, it would have been disastrous for Germany, I think that is certain."[5] Speer knew that Berlin – just like every other city in the Reich – didn't have enough purpose-built air raid shelters for its population, and that was even without the 300,000 foreign workers, mostly forced labourers, who were not allowed in what bunkers there were.

What he did not know was that in the aftermath of Hamburg the word had spread among the people about the threat from oxygen starvation in the shelters in case of a firestorm outside. Inside Berlin's packed shelters it was now standard practice to place burning candles around the shelter at ground, chair and head height and keep watching them – if they started to gutter then the oxygen level was getting low and people had to get outside to face death from the bombs or stay inside to risk death by asphyxiation.

With his mind set on Berlin, Harris went all out to bring the Americans on board with his plans, but they refused. Schweinfurt and Stuttgart had indeed been a shock, but the Americans believed the key alteration to their approach was to provide adequate fighter escort for the bomber all the way to the target and back, and they would not abandon daylight bombing itself. Berlin would be a job for Bomber Command, and Bomber Command alone.

The 'Big City', as the RAF crews called Berlin, had already been bombed many times during the war, often heavily, as the Irish nationalist writer, Francis Stuart, saw for himself on 1 March

1943 when he emerged from watching a performance of *Antony and Cleopatra* just as "the worst raid there has yet been on Berlin" began. Afterwards, he walked home "through smoking streets, past blazing houses". After that attack the Ruhr and Hamburg had taken precedence, and a raid carried out on the night of 23/24 August was the first major attack on the city since March. Peter Spoden was defending Berlin against that attack, and for him "it was one of those nights you remember for the rest of your life!" Flak filled the air and *Leichenfinger* – literally 'dead man's fingers', the Luftwaffe term for searchlight beams – criss-crossed the sky, illuminating "between 30 and 40 aircraft all milling around". The overriding impression Spoden got was of chaos, with "everyone firing at everyone else and I was in the middle of it all – it was hell." He wasn't wrong. The capital's defences were second to none and claimed 56 bombers that night – almost as many as the Americans lost over Schweinfurt. Regardless, Butch was determined to go back, and two more main force attacks were made in September.

Ivar Corneliussen was a Danish volunteer in the Nazis' Waffen-SS, and was convalescing after losing an eye in the fighting in Russia:

I was given an assignment to escort another Danish Waffen-SS volunteer from Ellwangen to the Waffen-SS administration centre at the Lützowplatz in Berlin. This guy had had a mental breakdown at the front and wasn't allowed to travel alone. Shortly after we arrived at the Anhalter Bahnhof in Berlin the air raid alarm sounded off and we ran for cover in the nearest shelter, which was in the basement of a large apartment block, but in the chaos I got separated from my comrade. The bombs wrecked the entrance to the shelter and we were buried alive. We had to dig our way out through to an adjoining basement. When we came out above ground it was a total mess. There was rubble everywhere, so many houses had collapsed, the asphalt on the roads had melted in the heat of the fires and they were still digging dead bodies out. Entire neighbourhoods were demolished, but I'd survived. My only thought was to get out of this hellhole and find the nearest Red Cross station to get something to eat and drink.

Herbert Winkleman was in Italy at the time, helping round up former Italian Army soldiers after the country switched sides. A Berliner, he was given compassionate leave after his home was bombed. "I found the house in better condition than I anticipated. The house across the street had been destroyed and the vacuum from the exploding bomb had left the front wall of our house bulging ... to my surprise the electricity as well as the plumbing were still working and most of the furniture was undamaged." Tired from his journey, he went to bed only to be woken by the sound of falling bombs. "I jumped from my bed to witness the horror of an air raid over Berlin." Convinced he had to move the family possessions out of harm's way, he was astonished to be told by the authorities that Berlin was "a safe town". Initially thwarted, he bribed a moving company with some "black-looking and awful tasting Italian and French cigarettes ... within a week the furniture was in Dresden."[6]

Both September raids were costly for Bomber Command, and almost two months would elapse before Butch was ready to start his long-awaited offensive. This time he would keep up the pressure and hit the city repeatedly, although not in the same way as Hamburg was hit. Berlin would be attacked far more times than Hamburg was during Gomorrah – 16 major raids in all – but they would be spread out over four months, and in between Bomber Command would also carry out 19 attacks on 11 other cities, including Schweinfurt of all places, and that old favourite, Essen.

Berlin was the focus though, and the Germans were determined to defend it at all costs. It wasn't just the nation's capital and seat of government, it was also the Reich's largest city by far, and the third largest city in the world by area, with a pre-war population of four million that had been increased by an influx of native Germans to work in all branches of the military and civil authorities, and by huge numbers of Ostarbeiter working in every sector from domestic service to the factory floor. To protect it all a ring of steel had been built around it, with flak batteries concentrated like nowhere else in the Reich. Two hundred searchlights were grouped in the city, and three giant Flaktürme built at the zoo in Friedrichshain and Humboldthain. Several decoy sites were constructed, the most impressive being at Nauen in Brandenburg, 20 miles west of the city. The Nauen site covered a huge nine square miles and had dummy buildings, rail and tram lines and a complex array of purposely dim lighting, combustibles for fires and sparking electrics, all to confuse the bombers.

The battle began with a large-scale attack on the night of 18 November. Much of the Nachtjagd were drawn away by a diversionary raid on Ludwigshafen, including Otto Fries and his radio op, Alfred Staffa. The young pilot ended up engaging a Stirling. "I fired a burst as the starboard wing passed through my sights, then a second into the port wing ... within seconds the whole bomber was aflame, it reared up, fell over on its port wing, then plunged down like a stone." It was Fries's fourth victory. The subterfuge was a success, with only nine bombers lost over Berlin, but poor weather over the city and issues with target making meant the bombing was scattered and ineffective. Four nights later the weather had improved significantly, and Harris ordered a second raid on Berlin. In Berlin's Wannsee district, Wolfgang Falck – the father of Germany's Nachtjagd – was now a senior staff officer helping co-ordinate the Reich's defences from its new operations centre in a specially constructed bunker. Falck was impressed by what he saw. It was a complex job:

> The operations room was the heart of operational control, here all the decisions were made ... An essential task was to maintain liaison with the flak divisions, the fighter divisions, industry, the railways, hospitals, the Gauleiter, the *Organization Todt* [a paramilitary construction and labour corps], the Luftwaffe construction battalions, the Red Cross, the fire brigades, and all organisations responsible for damage repair and assistance to the civilian population.

Bomber Command sent 764 bombers to Berlin that night, flying on a direct route that meant the Germans would know they were coming, but which also meant they could carry a bigger payload, instead of the fuel needed for a more circuitous route. The raid went badly for the Germans. One Lancaster bomb aimer wrote in his diary that on looking down he saw "the capital of the Third Reich at our mercy". He was almost dazed. "Everywhere below us for miles around is burning." The following morning Falck went into town "to get an impression of the damage, fires and casualties among the population. It was a dreadful sight to see … Berlin had become an inferno, entire sections of the city had been destroyed."

The bombers didn't have everything their own way. Peter Spoden had been injured baling out over Berlin in late August and was now back in the air with one leg slightly shorter than the other. Still angry after his near-death experience, he spotted a Lancaster and "didn't aim at the wings, but fired a long continuous burst into the fuselage until the Lancaster exploded and went down to earth in countless flaming pieces." His choice of aiming point meant the crew had no chance to bale out, an act he greatly regretted. "To this very day I am ashamed of doing so." Spoden's victory was one of 26 that night.

Buoyed by what even Falck described as "an RAF success", Harris ordered another attack the next night, but for once his exceptional ground crews were unable to patch up as many bombers as he wanted, and less than 400 took to the skies, causing relatively little damage. The bombers went back on 26 November, and 2 and 16 December, but never managed to reach the 500-aircraft mark, with a raid on the day before Christmas Eve going in with fewer than 400 bombers. The 2 December attack was also notable for German success, with 40 bombers brought down. By now, Schräge Musik was common among Nachtjagd crews and proving deadly. A Ju 88 night fighter pilot described why:

The [bombers] rear gunners found it much more difficult to get at us as we flew under the bomber and fired up into its right side to make it burst into flames, that worked quite well. We were also given a follow-up round which was belted on so we could destroy a bomber's fuel tanks. We used to pierce the tank with an explosive shell, which increased the size of the hole we'd made and then next was an incendiary shell to start a fire. We used to usually fly in a right-hand curve. The thinking was that the pilot sat on the left and we assumed it was the same in the Allied planes, so when a plane caught fire the Allied pilot wasn't going to turn onto the side that was burning, so mainly they would fly away to the left to keep the fire above and not below and that gave the crew a chance to bale out. The way we fired at them was something of a secret weapon, I heard they reported it as shot down by flak because they didn't know how they'd been shot down. I always hoped the crew survived but it was important for us that the plane and its bombs didn't get to their target.[7]

He was right about the confusion Schräge Musik caused among the crews of Bomber Command. The brilliant Cambridge mathematician Freeman Dyson was working in Bomber Command's Operational Research Section at the time, and looked into crew reports claiming they had seen other bombers blow up out of nowhere with no return fire, sign of attack or flak. One of the wilder theories going round was that the Germans were flying captured aircraft into bomber streams and then blowing them up to unnerve the RAF crews. Dyson dismissed such reports as fantasy and thought it far more likely that the Germans had invented upwards firing weaponry allowing a fighter to shoot unseen from below, and to further confuse, the crews weren't using tracer rounds.

Not that using Schräge Musik was simple, as one night fighter pilot explained. "When you got into the bomber stream – which wasn't easy – you saw more aeroplanes, but you had to be very careful. On one raid raid I'd shot down three bombers using Schräge Musik, but after those three victories I was absolutely exhausted. I was trembling hard so I landed very quickly."[8] The British still didn't know about the Luftwaffe's secret tactic for sure, but experienced bomber crews were already carrying out evasive manoeuvres just in case. John Whitely explained: "We did what they call a banking search. The blind spot of a Lancaster is right underneath it … so every five or six minutes you'd tip the aeroplane about 60 degrees to port and half the crew looked up and the other half looked down."[9]

There were six more raids in January, but it was becoming clear that Berlin was a very different proposition to Hamburg. Its sheer size made it far more difficult to seriously damage, while its wide streets, open spaces and predominantly brick and concrete construction made it less vulnerable to fires. As Albert Speer explained, "Berlin did suffer heavy raids but Berlin is a large area, much larger than any other town in Germany." The tinder-dry nature of Hamburg at the time wasn't replicated either. Berlin in winter is a pretty wet place, and so it proved, reducing the effect of the 14,000-odd tons of incendiaries dropped on the city, as well as covering it in protective cloud for much of the time. The battle limped on, with the last major attack going in on the night of 24 March 1944. Over 800 bombers made a concerted effort to blast the city but lost a dreadful 72 of their number to the increasingly efficient night fighters.

Reluctantly, Harris ended the offensive. The 'Big City' hadn't become another Hamburg and Butch was forced to eat humble pie, his grandiose claims the battle would win the war defeated by the weather and a German defensive effort that downed 500 bombers, with another hundred so badly damaged as to be scrapped on their return. Some 9,390 civilians were killed in the battle, mostly Berliners, but also several hundred Ostarbeiter. Over 800,000 were made homeless, forcing the authorities to build temporary shelters in many of Berlin's parks until more suitable accommodation could be found.

Joseph Goebbels – Gauleiter of Berlin as well as Reich Minister for Propaganda – stayed in the city throughout the bombing, touring the worst hit areas and eating with ordinary citizens at 'public meals' set up in the wake of a raid to ensure everyone was fed. He was horrified at what he saw: "The misery you see is indescribable, it breaks your heart to see it." Goebbels admitted surprise at how he was received by Berliners, with little sign of bitterness or anger towards the regime, even in the Wedding, "once the reddest [most communist supporting] part of the city ... I would never have believed it possible for such a change in attitude to take place." A teenaged flak auxiliary echoed Goebbels' thoughts:

I was constantly surprised again and again how people still had the discipline to go about their daily work after the heavy attacks. I'm talking about the young woman or mother who

worked on the trams in Berlin. She went to her depot and
worked. The factory workers went back to their factories,
if the factories had been hit they'd clear the rubble and then
went back to work ... Herr Harris deluded himself that he
could demoralise the population.

Not all the city's residents felt the same. Erich Dressler was a
soldier serving in the élite *Grossdeutschland Division* and a native
Berliner. Home on leave he was shocked to find that "My parents
had aged ... as soon as Berlin received its first heavy air attacks
their belief in ultimate victory had just faded away."[10] In truth,
morale in the city was a mixed bag, although Goebbels would have
been relieved, and Harris annoyed, to hear Ursula von Kardoff's
opinion. "If the English believe they can undermine morale, then
that's a miscalculation."

Through 1943, the flak arm and Nachtjagd had grown
substantially and were taking a heavy toll of British bombers –
some 3,028 in the year – but they had not stopped coming, night
after night, in the end dropping 148,457 tons of high explosives
and incendiaries on Germany's cities, killing a hundred thousand
of her citizens and dislocating her war production, despite the best
efforts of the likes of Wilhelm Herget:

Usually I only had two successes in any one night and then
I landed, but that night I was in the middle of the bomber
stream ... I dived on the first plane in front, the next to the
right, the next to the left. I was shooting between the engines,
it was a Lancaster, and to the left another Lancaster, I shot
again between two engines, only a short burst, sometimes
I only needed four to eight rounds before the plane was
burning. I had five successes against aircraft on their way to
Frankfurt, and on their return leg I shot down another three.
The last one was the hardest because the Lancaster saw me
as I came from the direction of Frankfurt, which was one big
fire. I came from right underneath and was firing into the
fuselage until it crashed to earth ... I wasn't able to climb out
of the aircraft myself, they had to lift me out.[11]

Herget's spectacular feat of shooting down five Halifaxes and three Lancasters in just 45 minutes on the night of 20 December, made him an ace-in-a-day.

For the majority of Germans however, 1943 would be remembered for one thing: Hamburg. In the worst failure of its kind in the war, the Germans had been unable to stop the annihilation of the country's second city. Not even the cities of the Ruhr came close to seeing the levels of destruction visited on the old Hanseatic port. Leipzig's President of Police, Wilhelm von Grolman, was a veteran of the trenches of the First World War, but when his fire chief told him what he'd seen in Hamburg after being sent there to help out, he exclaimed in horror, "For God's sake what kind of war is this!' To which his subordinate replied, "General, this isn't war, this is sheer madness." Hamburg was also the end of the line for Josef Kammhuber. After such a disaster, heads had to roll, and Wurzelsepp's fitted the bill. Stripped of his responsibilities he was eventually packed off to Norway to command the handful of aircraft marooned up there.

It was the arrival in force of the Americans and their doctrine of daylight precision bombing that made 1943 such a pivotal year in the battle in the sky. Throughout the war, it was the Russian front that absorbed the lion's share of Nazi Germany's military resources, but just when the Army in the east needed all the help it could get from the Luftwaffe, more and more of its strength was diverted instead to defending the homeland. The numbers tell their own story: in March 1943, the day fighter force protecting Germany could count on 120 serviceable aircraft. By August that number was 485. Alongside that growth were the losses. In the first three months of the year the Germans lost 42 Bf 109s and Fw 190s, with 17 pilots killed. In the last three months of the year those figures were 421 and 189 respectively – a ten-fold increase.

True, the day fighters had made the Americans pay a heavy blood price, shooting down 517 bombers and 123 escorts in those last three months, but the number of men and machines coming off the conveyor belts back in the States more than made up for them, and the close of the year saw the Americans able to field more bombers than the Luftwaffe had day fighters. Already the Germans had been forced into using night fighters to try and combat the US bombers, with disastrous results for the specially trained crews, as *Oberleutnant* Martin Drewes of NJG 3 recalled: "Alarm! A strong formation of Viermots was flying in the direction of Kiel. We climbed to a height of 7,000 metres ... Leschnik came into shooting distance of the last Pulk of B-17s. I watched the exchange of fire, then Leschnik's machine plunged steeply – no parachutes."[12]

Losses among the so-called *Zerstörer* (Destroyer) units were high as well, the German belief in the usefulness of twin-engine fighters like the Bf 110 for day fighting being consigned to the rubbish heap. Johannes Kaufmann, a Bf 110 pilot, saw it for himself. "In the daylight defensive role the Bf 110's shortcomings were apparent. It could fly long distances to intercept approaching US heavy bombers and was sturdy enough to carry extra-large calibre cannons and rockets, but these heavy anti-bomber weapons impaired its already marginal manoeuvrability ... making it easy prey." He was equally scathing about the Bf 110's long awaited replacement, describing it as "the disastrous Messerschmitt 210".

Unlike the Americans and the British, the Germans were struggling to replace their human losses. Lack of fuel for flight schools was severely impairing training, meaning "the new crews being drafted in to replace the casualties were becoming ever younger, less experienced and less adequately trained to survive the horrendous aerial battles being fought in defence of the *Heimat* [Homeland]." Inexperience also meant changes in tactics, as Dolfo Galland lamented. "Initially, most German fighter formations flew attacks from head on. This type of attack required very good flying and shooting ability ... it was harder from a flying and gunnery standpoint, especially for the young pilots, and because of the progressive decline of formation flying skills the attack from the rear became standard instead."

To try and bridge the experience gap, Luftwaffe high command turned to Russia, siphoning off men and machines and throwing them into battle with the American bombers. *Leutnant* Gerhard Thyben and his unit were transferred out of Russia after Hamburg "as a kind of 'flying fire brigade'" and he wasn't particularly pleased about it: "What confronted us in the West was a combination of material quality, flying skill and numbers. In short it meant 'biting into wholemeal bread.'" His comrade, Uwe Micheels, agreed: "Flying here [in the West] is completely different than the enjoyable days we had in Russia, and all of us would readily go back ... I'd managed a few kills in Russia whereas over here you get shot down." Micheels found facing the bombers unnerving at first: "The first time I saw these beasts I was flabbergasted ... we poor little devils can achieve so little against them." He bemoaned the dramatic differences from Russia, where he was used to seeking out combat and having more tactical freedom. Against the bombers he and his fellow fliers "fly here the way infantrymen attack. Unwaveringly we commit to the attack in our birds, despite the defensive fire that is hurled at us in great quantity and might." Thyben agreed.

> In Russia we'd been accustomed to throwing ourselves with gusto at the rear of any formation of Ivans and helping ourselves as independent hunters – *freie Jagd* [free hunt] – and we thought it would be similar in the West [but the] Dicke Autos fly in formation, making their firepower almost impenetrable ... soon we only attacked them from head on, which of course meant the chances of scoring hits was considerably reduced for both sides.

New aircraft did not even things up. "We went up from the 109 G2 to the G4 and G6 which instead of the 7.65 'light squirters' [machine-guns] now had 13mm guns mounted over the engine, which didn't improve the flying quality due to the bulges on the fuselage." The Russian veterans were used to being the hunter, better trained than their Soviet enemies and usually flying better machines, and while they were also used to taking casualties, the losses in the West were of an altogether different magnitude. Thyben was shocked to see how his "stout Gruppe had soon shrunk to the size of a strong Staffel", with sorties becoming "sacrificial journeys". Micheels was more prosaic: "In the few weeks we've been here in the West we've suffered severe losses. My chief has been shot down twice already." The shift in strength from Russia to the homeland meant that by the end of 1943 only 20 per cent of the Luftwaffe's fighters were facing the Soviets.

There were now two distinct types of battle going on in the skies above Germany. The night-time battle was one of cat-and-mouse, with bombers hiding in the darkness and seeking to evade the predators, who hunted alone. The only signs of the life and death struggle going on were the occasional explosions of aircraft in mid-air or a fiery trail as one plunged earthwards. Not so in the daytime. Those were more and more becoming set-piece battles involving hundreds of aircraft from both sides, all engaged in a whirlwind of combat, with fighters twisting and turning and bombers spitting out fire or rearing upwards before going belly up and crashing in a ball of flame. So large were the battles that people on the ground described seeing masses of condensation trails in the sky like giant white string, while up in the air pilots would see so many parachutes floating down it looked like confetti. Big battles meant numerous casualties. The Nachtjagd could lose three, four, maybe even five crews on any one night against a main force attack, whereas the day fighter force could lose five times that number every time they went up, and the Luftwaffe simply couldn't afford those sorts of losses.

To make matters worse for the Germans, on 1 November Washington formally activated the establishment of the Fifteenth Air Force based in Italy's south, with its main base at Foggia. From now on the Reich would be bombed by day from two separate directions.

The Eighth Army Air Force raid on 5 December against Luftwaffe airfields at Bordeaux, Cognac and in the Paris region was not a success, but it was significant. A total of 548 bombers took off, with only three dropping their payloads due to terrible weather over much of western France. Nine B-17s and one Thunderbolt were lost, and two Luftwaffe pilots were wounded. But what made the raid so portentous was that among the cloud of escorting P-47s and P-38 Lightnings were 36 brand-new P-51 Mustangs – the fighter that would overwhelmingly tip the balance of the air war in the Allies' favour had made its debut.

Overall, any German's views on the state of the war in their skies depended as much on how it was personally affecting them as anything else. Mausi von Westerode was a German aristocrat whose life was usually characterised by a never-ending round of social engagements. Moving between houses, she was living in Berlin when Hamburg was destroyed. "There were more dead than ever before and many of the terrified survivors arrived in Berlin in their nightdresses ... everyone had to help with the building of shelters and attend lectures about poison gas. Even the children were trained as air raid helpers." She was still in Berlin when Bomber Command began its offensive against the city.

The whole thing was over in half an hour [raid of 22 November], but while it was on it was like nothing ever before. I was dining with friends in Lichterfelde that night, and although the main attack was on the Hansviertel, about 15 kilometres away, the noise was so great that we literally couldn't hear ourselves speak ... from then on we'd get routine warnings on the radio 'Planes coming over western Germany' ... the best thing to do was turn off the wireless and forget about it till it happened ... it was dreary.[13]

Claus Fuhrmann was not in Baroness von Westerode's privileged position. Part-Jewish – what the Nazis called a *Mischling* – Fuhrmann and his girlfriend Bunny were viciously persecuted and lived in perpetual fear of being arrested by the Gestapo and shipped to the East for 'resettlement'. The couple lived in "one of those old Berlin houses in Alexanderplatz which had been built at the time of Frederick the Great". When Bomber Command began its attacks on the city, they would take shelter in the cellar – "small, angular, damp and uncomfortable". On hearing the all-clear Claus went upstairs to find the flat "badly damaged; doors and windows were smashed, furniture ruined, around us whole blocks of houses were in flames. It was as light as day and there was a scorching heat ... screaming people were running through the streets, houses were blazing and ruins collapsed with a reverberating thunder." Hating the Nazis, he "did nothing to help, I was sorry that every bomb wasn't a hit."

For the men fighting it out in the skies, there were still instances when simple human compassion overcame the brutal violence that was part and parcel of their existence. Franz Stigler was a Bf 109 fighter pilot defending Bremen against an American raid, a few hours before Wilhelm Herget would claim his extraordinary eight bombers in one night. After the B-17s had made their bomb run and turned for home, Stigler noticed one which had been badly damaged by flak and was struggling to keep in formation. Diving down he saw the bomber's nose section was almost shot away, and one engine was out. It had also clearly been subjected to several attacks by Stigler's fellow fighter pilots. "It was like a sieve and there was blood everywhere. I could see the crew were having a terrible time dealing with their wounded and struggling to stay in the air. I was amazed that the aircraft could fly … it was one thing to shoot an airplane, but in this case I saw the men. I just couldn't do it … I cannot kill these half-dead people. It would be like shooting at a parachute."

The B-17 pilot was Lieutenant Charlie Brown, and it was his and the crew's first mission. He remembered a Bf 109 suddenly appearing a few feet from his wing tip and flying alongside the stricken bomber. The B-17 only had one machine-gun still working but almost the entire crew were wounded and no-one was in a fit state to man it. Brown just sat and waited for the end. Instead – to his utter amazement – the German pilot looked straight at him, saluted, and dived away without firing. Brown thought he must have run out of ammunition. Somehow the B-17 made it back to England. He and Stigler would meet after the war and become friends.

Back on the ground in the Netherlands, the NJG 2 pilot Karl-Georg Pfeiffer passed judgement on the year: "The Ami bomber attacks on Germany in '43 were really the end of the best times in Leeuwarden…"

# 7

# 1944

# D-DAY AND OIL

Human beings are creatures of habit. By 1944, air raids over Germany were commonplace, and both the authorities and the population had developed a routine to deal with them in an attempt to reduce the trauma. Firstly, in a change from the general siren and then the all-clear of the early war years, there was now a tiered system with an initial 'Raid Possible' alarm to warn of a potential attack. At that point it was time to turn off the gas and switch on the radio. If you had a bathtub you filled it with cold water. If you didn't, then you'd fill up any large buckets or containers instead. If air defence command then believed your city was the target, the radio announcer would warn listeners and the general alarm would sound. On hearing the general alarm, you would grab your flashlight and your pre-packed valuables box or case and get to your shelter. If your shelter was outside your house or apartment building, you would make sure you were wearing your coat with its issued fluorescent badge on it to avoid colliding with others in the black-out, and then follow the fluorescent paint on the kerb to your designated bunker. When the bombers were on their final approach a six-minute warning would sound and everyone was expected to be under cover at that point.

Those taking shelter were instructed to observe some simple rules of common courtesy to try and make the experience as endurable as possible, so there was meant to be no smoking or drinking of alcohol, and the only animals allowed in were meant to be guide dogs for the visually impaired – although as Frau Otti Schwarz saw in Hamburg, this rule was often disregarded by anxious German pet lovers. Despite these measures, conditions in many shelters were dreadful, as one female munitions worker in Bremen remembered: "The air raid shelters were too few and too small. The one which I used was built for 800 people but was actually used by three to four thousand. We were so crowded and hot that people used to vomit and that made the air even worse. We just took off our clothes without shame because of the unbearable heat."[1]

With so few purpose-built bunkers, most people used their cellar as their shelter – as long as they had one – and would sit for hours on a bench or a blanket, trying to snatch some sleep or take their mind off things by reading a book or newspaper in the dimly lit space, even though "the walls would shake and shudder from the explosions." With cellars lacking reinforcement, a near miss could blow out people's eardrums, or start a fire that would see smoke pour in. People traded tips on how best to deal with it all; some would wrap themselves in wet blankets and put strips of wet gauze on their eyelids, while keeping their mouths open to protect their eardrums, and breathing in shallow breaths to minimise smoke inhalation.

Understandably, people were desperate for some distraction, and cinemas were wildly popular, with people flocking to see whatever was showing to try and take their minds off what was happening around them. Cinemas, however, were just as likely to be hit as anywhere else, so when the sirens started the film would be stopped and *Flieger Alarme* would flash up on the screen as everyone's cue to get to shelter. Patrons didn't have the option of ignoring the alarm as – unlike in any other European state during the war – it was illegal in Nazi Germany not to seek shelter when instructed to do so.

The day routine was similar, but with most civilians at work, they would usually follow their employer's instructions and make do with whatever arrangements they had made. Psychologically, most Germans could handle the night-time raids better than the daylight attacks. At night they couldn't see the bombers but could see the flashes of the anti-aircraft guns, which provided some sort of reassurance. During the day the scale of what Germany faced was all too apparent in the masses of con trails in the air, as Wolfgang Falck – by now in charge of much of the Luftwaffe's night fighter defence – admitted himself. "It was on a beautifully clear day … The US Air Force attacked in broad daylight with B-17s. I saw the bombs being dropped on the centre of Berlin, and there wasn't a single German fighter. Hundreds of Flying Fortresses. On that day I thought, poor old Germany." General Hap Arnold – having taken command of the Eighth Army Air Force away from Ira Eaker and given it to Tooey Spaatz – echoed Falck's opinion, if not his sentiment: "For us the beginning has ended; for our enemies the end has begun."

Spaatz now led a force that from its first mission on 17 August 1942 until the end of 1943 had lost 1,187 aircraft either shot down or scrapped, with another 6,940 damaged. The human cost of America's involvement in the air war was even starker, with almost 10,000 pilots and crew killed or missing, and thousands more wounded – and yet. And yet Spaatz's command was now bigger than ever. He had 4,242 aircraft based in England, organised into 26 bomber and 12 fighter escort groups, and by the end of January '44 the Fifteenth Air Force in Italy could field another 12 bomber and four fighter groups. The American genius for scale had created a leviathan, with the United States now in control of the largest air force in the world with 2,385,000 men and women in its ranks. Its flight schools in the cloudless blue skies of the American South were churning out remarkable numbers of trained crew; 65,700 pilots, 16,000 bombardiers and 15,900 navigators would graduate in 1944, without sacrificing quality. In particular, the American fighter pilots now arriving in theatre were of such a standard as to be qualitatively superior to all but the best the Luftwaffe could put in the air.

The Germans weren't about to give up however, even as their skies became slaughter yards and their cities charnel houses.

The Nachtjagd, in particular, battled on, believing – quite rightly – that for them the campaign was not yet lost. They were now at their largest, too, their technology was better than it had ever been, and their ranks were filled with capable crews. At the apex of their operations were their *Experten* (literally Experts, usually translated as Aces), men like Werner Streib and Helmut Lent, who had been flying against the British for more than three years, and who had become poster boys among the German public for their exploits. First among equals at the time was a 27-year-old aristocrat, born in Denmark when his father was on diplomatic service in Copenhagen, and mainly raised and educated in Switzerland – Heinrich Prinz zu Sayn-Wittgenstein. The Nachtjagd's other prince, alongside Lippe-Weissenfeld, zu Sayn-Wittgenstein had traversed from the pre-war German cavalry to the Luftwaffe as a bomber observer, before switching to the night fighters in August 1941. An eccentric, he was driven by ambition, even his obituary acknowledging his burning desire to be 'head of the night fighter élite'. Wim Johnen remembered his arrival at the Gilze air base in 1943: "'What's going on? Where is there something to shoot down?' He's in a hurry I thought." Indeed he was.

On 1 January 1944 the lanky airman took command of NJG 2 and claimed six bombers that same night to take his score to 74 in total. His regular radio op, Herbert Kümmritz, told his comrades: "There's no holding back the Prince once he's in the air, he takes off like a maniac and only lands when he hasn't a drop of juice left."

Wittgenstein's eccentricity could be somewhat alarming at times, he once made Kümmritz "stand to attention in the plane and confined him to his quarters for three days because he'd lost the picture in his screen during a mission". Luckily for Kümmritz, "He [Wittgenstein] shot down three bombers shortly afterwards, pardoned the man and awarded him the Iron Cross First Class. All this took place at 15,000 feet and right in the middle of the bomber stream."[2]

Less than three weeks after taking command of NJG 2, Wittgenstein took off for another mission, accompanied this time by Friedrich Ostheimer as radio op, as Kümmritz was home on some well-earned leave. He had already shot down two bombers and lined up a third: "A burst from our Schräge Musik blew a big hole in the wing and started a blazing fire." To Ostheimer's surprise, "The British pilot reacted unusually, he remained at the controls of his burning machine and dived down on top of us." Wittgenstein immediately threw the Ju 88 into its own dive to get away, but to his dismay "the blazing monster came closer and closer … a heavy blow staggered our aircraft, the Prinz lost control of the machine and we went into a spin, plunging down into the night." Somehow Wittgenstein managed to recover and belly land the Junkers. Shaken but unhurt, both men were shocked to find almost two metres of one wing shorn off by the burning Lancaster's propeller. The *Prince of Darkness* – as Wittgenstein was nicknamed – was now on 78 victories.

The following night, Wittgenstein managed to get into a bomber stream bound for Magdeburg. The Prince tore through the bombers, shooting down four in less than 40 minutes. Attacking a fifth, his victim burst into flames only for his own Junkers to be hit on the left wing – probably from an escorting British night fighter. Ordering his crew to bale out, Wittgenstein stayed with the aircraft. He was found dead the next morning, a short distance from the wreckage of the Junkers. His unopened parachute beside him. His death sent shockwaves through the Nachtjagd. He was a relative latecomer to the ranks of the night fighters, but his reputation was already legendary, and his tally of 83 aerial victories made him the highest scoring night fighter pilot in the Luftwaffe at the time. In the Luftwaffe, things like that mattered.

More than in any other air force in the world, scoring victories was fundamental to how German fliers viewed themselves and others. To become an *Experte* was the goal of each and every pilot; to be respected, admired, even idolised, and to earn all the plaudits that came with it. Such men were adorned with every award the Nazi state could dream up – Wittgenstein himself had the Honor Goblet of the Luftwaffe, the Front Flying Clasp in Gold, both classes of the Iron Cross and the Knight's Cross of the Iron Cross with Oakleaves and Swords – it was a miracle he had room for them all on his uniform jacket. What this all meant was that, with the system around them designed to help build their score, a relatively small number of fighter pilots were the heart of the Luftwaffe's killing machine – in 1943 just 12 Experten were responsible for shooting down a staggering 1,160 enemy aircraft. The loss of even one of these men mattered.

Bomber crews feared flak more than German night fighters – despite it downing fewer aircraft – because it could be seen and heard, whereas the night fighter was the silent killer, sneaking up and blowing them out of the sky before they even knew what was happening. To help the crews, Bomber Command brought in a whole series of countermeasures to try and disrupt the Nachtjagd, as Peter Spoden recalled. "The British were very clever and had German immigrants [mostly German Jews] … they gave their orders over the radio using our German code words, we'd land only to find out that the order hadn't come from Germany, it had come from some other broadcasting station." It was the Germans' turn to counter, and they did so by switching to female controllers. "We were told to only obey the codes given in women's voices … we complied, but on that particular night the British even succeeded in using female operators. We were absolutely baffled." Next, the Luftwaffe "used different types of music to pinpoint the area where the British had massed. If they were positioned over Vienna we played Strauss, for Berlin we played Brandenburg marches."

The bomber crews themselves used differing tactics to try and survive; some would blast away at anything they saw as soon as they saw it, while others would resist firing in almost every circumstance, certain it would do more harm than good by giving away their position to any stalking fighter. Being in a bomber under attack from a night fighter was truly terrifying, as one young bomb aimer explained. "The sound in the aircraft when you're being attacked is terrifically loud … the noise of the German shells from the fighters is quite horrific. It's the noise of absolute mayhem … some of this mayhem is actually doing your aeroplane damage and there's a little fire coming up here and another fire there."[3]

The bombers weren't helpless though, as one crewman remembered. "Jim, the mid-upper gunner just arced [his fire] from front to rear. The cockpit cover [of the German fighter] came off and the pilot came out. His parachute streamed and he hit our port wing and we actually brought his flying boot back, it was stuck in the wing. I don't suppose he survived, he hit the wing and disappeared into the dark."

As the Nachtjagd and Bomber Command played cat and mouse in the darkness, the daytime battle over Germany was going up through the gears. The veteran Experte Heinz Bär described how the German fighter pilots prepared for an American attack:

> The briefing always took place in the unit's briefing room with the *Gruppe Kommandeur* presiding. Present were the pilots, Staffe, COs, the Technical Officer, the weatherman and the Operations Officer ... around 6.45am the pilots assemble and strength is reported. At 7am some physical training is done, including body bends, twisting exercises, knee bends and a short run. Around 7.15 the briefing begins.

The weather report was read out, then the tech-officer covered the number of serviceable aircraft and the signals officer detailed frequencies to be used, then the actual briefing by the Gruppe CO began. He set out where each staffel will be in the formation and ordered "attacks from head on are to be flown. Remember, approach from the same altitude as the bombers, aim well, don't shoot from long range and remember to pull up and slip away after the attack." Details of other airfields that can be used to refuel and rearm are given out so pilots can get airborne for a second sortie if possible. "Then comes the check on pilots; papers, their emergency packets with burn bandages and salve, and rubber tourniquets for arterial bleeding ... At the conclusion of the briefing the pilots go to the unit dispersal areas where their aircraft are standing ready for take-off." Those dispersal areas were often kitted out with "a small kitchen, sports facilities and washing facilities improvised out of drop tanks. Until take-off everyone stays in the dispersal areas."

Twenty-two-year-old Austrian Rüdiger von Kirchmayr had been flying against the Viermots since their arrival in Europe. On

11 January 1944 he found himself attacking a 300-strong raid by B-17s on the Fw 190-producing AGO Flugzeugwerke site at Oschersleben. "Coming out of the sun I fired at the right outside B-17 from the front ... the canopy and other pieces flew off the Boeing's fuselage and wing, its landing gear dropped and it fell away to the right in a steep spiral." He went on to down another B-17 and was credited with one victory. The German fighters shot down 65 bombers and eight fighter escorts during the raid – more than in either of the Schweinfurt attacks the previous year – but unlike then, there was no pullback from missions into Germany, and the Eighth Army Air Force would quickly replace both aircraft and men. For the Germans, the 38 pilots killed and 28 wounded that day were a significant loss.

A week before the Oschersleben raid, Hap Arnold signalled a change in American strategy that would take some time to have an impact on the air war, but when it did it would lead to the destruction of Nazi Germany's day fighter force and the achievement of Allied air supremacy over Europe. Arnold now confirmed to Tooey Spaatz that his mission was to "Destroy the Enemy Air Force wherever you find them, in the air, on the ground and in the factories." Spaatz was to achieve this goal by bombing Nazi Germany's aircraft industry into rubble, and – critically – by using his fighters to hunt down any and all German aircraft and destroy them. With the number of American fighters in theatre now reaching seven, eight or even 900 serviceable aircraft on any one day, there were enough of them to not only escort the bombers but to sweep out around the bomber formations and actively go after the Luftwaffe.

From then on, groups of four or more American escorts, previously tied to close protection of their bomber comrades, were now expected to range as far as eight miles, or even further, away from the bomber boxes and engage German aircraft wherever they found them. On the homeward leg of a mission the American fighters were also tasked to fly at low level and strafe German airfields, destroying their enemy on the ground, or as they attempted to land or take-off. It would prove effective but unpopular, with the fighter pilots fearing the wall of light flak surrounding the Luftwaffe's bases and improvised defensive measures such as *Drahtsperren* (literally 'wire locks'), thick steel hawsers strung across any narrow approaches to airfields which would slice an incoming fighter to pieces. Overall, this switch of the American fighter arm from the defensive to the offensive would have dramatic consequences for the Germans.

Even before Arnold's directive began to feed through to the fighter groups, the increasing size and tempo of the American offensive in the air was already forcing the Luftwaffe to radically alter the way it was fighting the battle, or concede it was powerless to stop it. As a stopgap measure to try and bring more fighters to bear on the American formations, the decision was made to once again use night fighters to help combat the daylight attacks. Peter Spoden was one of those selected to fly these additional sorties. "Only crews with few night victories were selected for these missions, as the Experten were too valuable for the powers that be … those daylight missions were quite exhausting, as we were also at readiness at night."

Spoden was dubious as to how effective he and his fellow Nachtjagd would be during the day. "We were too slow in daylight with our Bf 110s equipped with Lichtenstein and flame-dampers … the losses among our night fighters were horrendous." He was scrambled in early January to intercept an American formation bound for Ludwigshafen:

> We night fighters arrived on the scene too late and all I could see were pieces of wreckage and between seven and ten Ami airmen in life jackets floating in the sea. They signalled us … we immediately alerted the German coast guard and stayed with the Americans who kept waving at us. And now the terrible thing happened, by the minute the movements of the men in the water became slower and in the end they didn't move anymore at all. We could see the German marine craft approaching and flew as low as we dared in an effort to keep the men awake.

Spoden and his comrades' honourable efforts were in vain. "We were later told that no-one survived and they all died of hypothermia. From that day on I always flew with a one-man dinghy firmly attached to my body."

Spoden was now facing both the Americans and the British, and he was thus in a unique position to contrast and compare their different approaches.

> The American tactics were completely different to the British.
> The British flew in a stream, by night – it was an effective way
> of bombing, though as Adolf Galland eloquently described it,
> it was like 'many small raindrops which used to unite over
> the target area into a cloudburst bombing effect', but the
> Americans flew in a kind of box so there would be about 25
> B-17s grouped together like a swarm of bees ... When they
> fired it was like a shower. They had many more machine-guns
> on board.

A fighter's speed was its best defence against the bomber's defensive firepower, but much of that speed was bought at the price of carrying limited armament; not a major problem when facing other fighters or even light bombers, but against the Viermots it was akin to throwing pebbles at a wall. The answer was bigger guns, hence the Bf 109G and the 20mm gondola guns many were fitted with, but that slowed the fighters and made them less manoeuvrable. The German engineers also realised that no matter how skilled their own pilots were, the sheer volume of fire the US crews could put into the air was going to strike home at some point, making it imperative to protect the pilots and their machines far more than was hitherto the case. The answer to that problem was more armour plating. The inevitable result was a decisive shift away from the original sleek-lined Bf 109F and Fw 190A-2 models to the steroid enhanced bulk of the Gustav and Fw 190A-6 versions. Now, the German fighter pilots could tear bombers apart while taking a lot more punishment themselves, but it came at a high price in lost speed and agility.

As their aircraft evolved, so did their fighter tactics. Hans-Günter von Kornatzki, an East Prussian from Liegnitz, had fought in the French campaign and the battle of Britain, before taking up a number of staff appointments in the Luftwaffe. As the American bomber force grew through 1943, he began to explore ways of combating the threat, and spent time with an experimental unit in the latter half of the year looking at new weapons and tactics. On the basis of that experience, he proposed what he called his *Sturmtaktik*; an attack on the bombers from the rear, not the front, using specially armoured fighters to absorb the inevitable defensive fire. The fighters would literally fly straight and true through the massed American machine-guns and deliver a blast of concentrated firepower at close range that would send the big bombers spiralling earthwards – that was the theory.

To test it out, Kornatzki was allocated a staffel, *Sturmstaffel 1*, with its own Focke-Wulf variant – the Fw 190A-8/R7. As well as having an armoured air cooler for the engine, a protective shell surrounded the pilot, a thickened windshield, 6mm fire-proof plates and cabin sides and 8mm armour plate on the back of his seat – all designed to stop the US bomber's standard .50 calibre round. Armed with an impressive array of two 30mm cannon and four 20mm machine-guns, the aircraft was hugely heavy, ungainly in flight and drank fuel at a prodigious rate. The second part of Kornatzki's proposal was that the new units that would carry out these attacks should do so en masse and not in penny packets – hundreds would be met by hundreds. Kornatzki was swimming with the tide in that regard, with no less a figure than Erhard Milch agreeing with the concept. "To achieve any decisive success against American formations ... the fighter forces must outnumber the enemy by four to one."

To try and achieve those sorts of numbers, Milch and Speer were revolutionising Germany's aviation industry. In the autumn of 1941, Germany was producing 360 fighters a month, roughly equivalent to what it was losing in combat and accidents. The following spring Milch met with Goering and Jeschonnek and proposed upping that number to a thousand a month, at which point the Luftwaffe Chief of Staff dismissed the idea out of hand. His plan rejected, Milch had gone ahead anyway, his ambition cloaked in secrecy, and by the summer of 1943 had almost achieved the 1,000 fighters per month target. It was this manufacturing success that helped underpin the German victories over Schweinfurt and Stuttgart and prompted Ira Eaker to declare that "If the growth of the German fighter strength is not arrested quickly, it may become literally impossible to carry out the destruction as planned." Eaker's hasty dispatch to the Mediterranean, and his replacement with Tooey Spaatz, didn't change the underlying truth of his comments. The American response was Operation *Argument*.

*Argument* – or 'Big Week' as it became known – was a plan to launch a large-scale, sustained aerial offensive against the Third Reich's aircraft industry and deal it a crippling blow that would starve the Luftwaffe of new aircraft and help the Allies achieve air supremacy over Europe. It would mainly be an American operation, but Bomber Command would play its part, launching attacks on five separate nights, starting on the night of 19/20 February 1944. Gerhard Wollnik was a gunner in *Hauptmann* Heinz Reschke's Bf 110 that night, as his unit was scrambled against a "strong RAF bomber formation, an estimated 300 aircraft ... heading on a course towards Berlin and Leipzig". After several unsuccessful attempts to get into a good firing position, they finally lined up what they believed to be a Lancaster, "judging from its green exhaust flames ... if it were a Halifax the flames would have been more reddish." Opting to use his Schräge Musik, Reschke "slowly approached the enemy bomber from below ... then a short burst from the guns; in all *Hauptmann* Reschke only fired nine 2cm rounds. The shells struck home between the two engines in the right wing, and immediately the bomber started burning fiercely."[4]

A few hours later it was the Americans' turn, when more than a thousand B-17s and B-24 Liberators were escorted by over 800 fighters to attack a dozen aviation targets in Germany and western Poland. The Hollywood star Jimmy Stewart was flying that day, piloting his bomber towards the Bf 110 assembly plant in Braunschweig. Waiting for him on the ground was Helmut Biederbeck, a Russian front veteran in JG 1.

Loudspeakers blared out military marches. We would gather near our aircraft, accompanied by the music, which was sometimes interrupted by news concerning the advance of the dicke Autos or Indianer, we followed their progress on a map. Each Staffelkapitän had a telephone on the wing of his aircraft linked to the stag section. The music was interrupted – *Sitzbereitschaft* – cockpit readiness. At any moment we could be taking off. A green flare was the signal; engines would be started and we'd take off.

Inexplicably, the German reaction that day was slow and indecisive, and the bomber crews couldn't believe their luck when they were hardly touched on the way to their bomb runs. John Howland was a B-17 navigator heading to the Junkers factory at Bernberg:

> I was looking out the right-side window when I saw an Fw 190 climb out of the cloud and pass under our right wing and over our elevator and vertical stabiliser. He had us dead to rights but his guns never fired a shot. Either his guns were jammed or he forgot to turn on his arming switches, or he was too busy trying to avoid a mid-air collision and didn't have time to fire.

By the time the German fighters were airborne in any strength, the bombers were on their way home. Helmut Biederbeck and 20 of his comrades did manage to catch up with one bomber group, and they prepared to attack. "For several seconds we flew parallel to the formation to assess its strength and direction ... we picked up speed, swept wide of the target and carried out a 180-degree turn. We were then head on and opened fire while traversing through the bomber stream." But the attack went wrong. "We lost cohesion and that was what the enemy fighters were waiting for. They then picked us off at the rear of the Viermots." Four JG 1 pilots were killed and two others wounded.

The actual results of the bombing were mixed. More than a few reports stated only light damage was done, but a few were more severe. The raid on Leipzig and its ATG Maschinenbau GmbH plant, for example, was rated a success, with one eyewitness recalling "the gigantic hall [of the Plagwitz station] was just a mass of tumbled down girders and splintered glass." The German defenders paid a heavy price, losing 79 aircraft and 51 aircrew killed. With only 26 bombers and six fighters to show for their sacrifices, it was a bad day for the German fighter force. The next day was a similar story, although poor weather over Germany made bombing difficult and hindered the German response. Another 27 German pilots and crew were killed.

Day Three of the operation was a combined attack by both the Eighth and Italian-based Fifteenth Air Forces, with more than 1,300 American bombers and escorts due to hit targets across Germany and Austria. The young Heinrich Freiherr von Podewils' unit had just received their new Bf 109s "and wanted to give them a run out, but it turned out differently." Scrambled to intercept the Liberators and B-17s of the Fifteenth Air Force, on finding the bombers, "We attacked from behind with all guns firing and the American bullets came at us like out of a watering can." Podewils damaged a B-17 and continued with further attacks and finally shot it down 15 kilometres southwest of Straubing. Three men baled out. The joy of his success rapidly evaporated when he returned to base and found it had been bombed: "My quarters and the mess [were] completely destroyed." Far worse was the fate of a downed American airman who "had come down by parachute, and dropped onto a metal structure which had cut him into two halves from between the legs to his head."

More attacks were launched on 23 February, although bad weather grounded the Eighth Army Air Force, forcing the Fifteenth to go it alone. Better weather the following day allowed a full-strength attack to be launched on three separate targets in Gotha, Rostock and Schweinfurt. The views of the crews detailed to hit Schweinfurt can only be imagined. The good weather worked in the Germans' favour, with the bombers flying ahead of schedule and so missing linking up with their escorts on the way out. Bf 110 pilot Johann Kogler reported seeing "eight Pulks, each of about 15 Liberators ... we attacked near Holzminden at 1330 hours from the left and above ... several Liberators were observed flaming brightly, and others were seen to crash." Fifty-one US bombers and 10 escorts were downed or scrapped on return, but once more the German fighter pilots were decimated, 41 killed and another 18 wounded. By now morale among the German fliers was beginning to suffer, as Eberhard Burath remembered. "Before take-off you risked getting lost in the cigarette smoke. The majority of pilots were withdrawn, unapproachable. There was only *Major* Bär who didn't change."

Burath himself had been flying against the Viermots for almost 18 months, scoring his first victory – a B-17 – in May 1943. Hit by return fire from a bomber during a raid two months later, he had been forced to crash land in a potato field and was lucky to walk away unhurt. Just over a week before Argument began, he was on a sortie near Braunschweig and had made a pass at a B-17, when he was once more hit by return fire. "Like lightning flashes, the bullets ripped into the fuselage. Soon there was no response from my joystick or from the other controls. I had to get out. I'd already jettisoned the canopy, but like a stamp on an envelope I remained stuck to the armour plate in my cockpit." Terrified he would go down with his plane, he struggled for all he was worth and eventually managed to get out of the aircraft and fall through the sky. Once he was clear of the wreckage, he opened his parachute and drifted down. Landing in a snow-covered field he found himself on all fours with his parachute all bundled round him looking like "a pig trying to find a truffle".

The last day of Big Week saw the Fifteenth Air Force launch a relatively small 300-bomber raid on Regensburg, while the Eighth attacked the same target – an hour after the Fifteenth had hit it – as well as Augsburg and Stuttgart. Willi Hofmann was a plant manager for the Bosch manufacturing company in Stuttgart, where his factory made aircraft components. "The main plant, a building 350 feet by 350 feet, was set ablaze. You had to hold on tight to avoid being dragged into the roaring flames by the tremendous air suction. The plant was precision bombed ... and it broke the old factory's back." Hofmann was consoled by the fact that production had already been dispersed, so by the time his place was bombed out, "The original factory was operating at 16 different locations, including two prisons in the Stuttgart area."[5]

By the time it was over, the offensive had dropped just under 20,000 tons of bombs on Nazi Germany's aviation industry, with almost half of that coming from Bomber Command's five night-time raids. It cost the British over a thousand crewmen killed, missing or wounded, and 157 aircraft. The Americans lost far more; 266 bombers, 28 fighters, and over 2,600 aircrew, and the German aircraft sector was far from destroyed. But that – according to the cruel audit of total war – was beside the point. What the Germans had lost was more than 320 fighters and over 180 pilots and aircrew, including a number of specialist night fighter personnel. Another 118 men were wounded, and many of those would either never fly again or spend months in hospital and convalescence. All this in just five days and nights. It was a battle of attrition the Germans were beginning to lose.

The key was the American fighter escorts. By the advent of Argument, the Thunderbolts no longer had a single extra belly tank, but two additional 108-gallon fuel tanks slung under their wings, allowing them to fly deep into western Germany. The window of opportunity for the German fighters to attack the bombers without having to worry about their escorts was fast closing. Very shortly it would shut altogether.

The dual nature of Operation Argument, with the Americans bombing by day and the British returning by night, necessitated further changes to daily life for the mass of Germany's people who were themselves increasingly *becoming* the battleground. Wilhelm von Grolman's Leipzig had already suffered multiple raids, but Bomber Command's attack during Big Week had been the heaviest yet. The grizzled old Nazi implemented a constant stream of air defence directives, including ensuring that "the children, old men and women in the [apartment] blocks were systematically trained to take prompt and courageous action to treat injured people and especially to handle incendiary bombs." Like so many after Hamburg, fire was his greatest fear:

> Children, who can run up and down stairs quickly, and who know every corner of the house from their games, have prevented many catastrophes by throwing burning incendiary bombs out into the street and by putting out smouldering fires. If several smaller fires are allowed to develop there is

the danger of an area conflagration and several such large blazes can cause a firestorm. Once this happens the situation is hopeless. Those who manage to escape death by burning, or being crushed under the masses of debris, simply asphyxiate.[6]

For the pilots battling to defend them, being brought face to face with the tragedy of what was happening in Germany's cities was an unnerving experience, as Gustav Rödel knew only too well: "Seeing the destruction and the wounded, you couldn't help but feel guilty and think that maybe you could have done more."

The Luftwaffe's pilots and aircrew might only see the impact of the bombing on the relatively rare occasions they went home on leave, but for the huge numbers of Germans directly involved in their own defence in the anti-aircraft branch, it was a fact of life. Hannah Ritau served in a light flak battery north of the capital.

Our job was to protect the Heinkel aircraft factory in Oranienburg, a suburb in the north of Berlin ... we couldn't fire higher than 3,500 metres but the planes usually came over at twice that height, around 6,000 metres, and only the heavy anti-aircraft guns could reach them. Berlin was bombed almost every night, well, perhaps not every night but very regularly. The worst of it came in 1944 ... the sky filled with planes and during these raids I was on the range finder. I had to pick up the planes, get all the data and transfer it to the guns so they could fire. There was no time for training, we learnt on the job ... the raids usually started at around 2200hrs. We were alerted by radio and told where the bombers were, and we were then in action for three or four hours ... Our battery had four guns, one range finder and one radar. There were about six people operating each gun, another six to operate the range finder and five on the radar.

Hannah was part and parcel of what was increasingly a national effort, with huge numbers of ordinary Germans involved. Hannah's battery was just one of over 250 grouped around the 'Big City', most on the outskirts, except for those on the immense flak towers. Across the Reich in January 1944 there were some 20,625 anti-aircraft guns, up from 15,000 a year earlier. Depending on what service elements you included, there were around 1 million Luftwaffe personnel involved in Germany's air defence, plus an additional 400,000 auxiliaries, which included 80,000 teenaged schoolboys and around 60,000 prisoners-of-war, mostly former Red Army men. The usual practice on batteries like Hannah's was to use the POWs to do the heavy lifting and carry the shells, while the boys acted as gun layers. The relatively few trained soldiers in the battery's complement would act as master gunners. Seventeen-year-old Hans Ring's battery was typical for the time, with 20 Russian POWs, 90 schoolboys like him, and 36 regular Luftwaffe personnel, almost all of them middle-aged. He remembered the ambivalent nature of it all. "We were expected to shoot down enemy planes with our 105mm guns, but we weren't considered old enough to be issued rifles when we went to round up enemy aircrew who'd come down by parachute."

The flak arm didn't just require huge numbers of people, it also required guns and ammunition in prodigious quantities; three-quarters of the country's superb 88mm guns were deployed at home, and fully 12 per cent of total German ammunition production was assigned to home defence – twice as much as was allocated for the Army's vital field guns at the battle front. In terms of aircraft shot down, that ammunition expenditure evinced poor returns, with the Luftwaffe estimating that only one bomber was shot down for every 16,000 rounds fired. Indeed, the German people themselves were pretty cynical about how effective the guns were. A current joke was that a soldier was condemned to death and given a choice as to the manner of his execution. He opted to die by anti-aircraft fire, so a tower was constructed and he was tied to the top, then three flak batteries blasted away at him for three weeks, but didn't hit him. They stopped and went to cut him down, only to find he'd starved to death.

As for Hannah, she had no illusions about her own battery's efficiency. "Unfortunately our flak wasn't very effective, our battery shot down a total of eight planes which wasn't much considering how many there were. We put a ring on our guns for every plane we shot down … we used to think of the pilots above us and wondered how they felt, I don't suppose it felt good to sit in an aircraft and know the next shell might hit you, but we were the ones being bombed so we were very glad when we shot down an Allied plane … we were scared, no question, all of us."[7]

While flak may not have shot down vast numbers of bombers, it damaged a very large number indeed. As many as 27,000 suffered flak damage in 1944, and although the majority were repaired and sent back into action – often on more than one occasion – it required a huge maintenance and logistical effort to do so and significantly reduced the number of bombers available at any one time.[8] American flak-damaged bombers were also more likely to drop out of formation and hence out of the defensive fire umbrella the formation provided. Such stragglers were invariably pounced on by German fighters and finished off. US high command had a healthy respect for German flak, calculating that it played a major part in the downing of half of all their bomber losses over Europe during the war, and causing damage to 66,000 of their four-engine heavies in total.[9] The B-17 pilot Ed Herron, described the type of damage flak inflicted during a raid to hit V-weapons sites in northern France: "Firecrackers broke loose in the cockpit. My co-pilot was hit in the back of the neck and badly wounded. The instrument panel was a mass of shattered glass and small flak had hit me in the hands. The No. 4 engine suddenly spluttered and cut out."[10]

Despite the growing barrages from Nazi Germany's ground-based air defences, the forces ranged against it continued to increase, especially the Eighth Army Air Force, which was well on the way to earning its sobriquet of 'The Mighty Eighth'. While not quite able simply to shrug off the losses from Argument, the through-flow of new aircraft and crews from the States was now so great that the Americans were able to continue the pressure from Big Week onwards into March. Now, the target they most wanted to hit was the Big City – Berlin. Bomber Command's night offensive against the Nazi capital was still rumbling on, and while the Americans hadn't changed their minds about Harris's request back in November to join the battle, they were willing to attack specific industrial targets in the city that fitted their own strategy.

Bad weather initially plagued the Americans, with raids planned for 3 and 4 March redirected to other targets, and it wasn't until Monday 6 March that the full force was able to make for Berlin. The Germans countered with their new large formation tactics, forming two *Gefechtsverbände* (Battle groups) with six fighter groups in one and eight in the other. The Germans fought a running battle with the Americans, with over 130 fighters involved at any one time, only leaving the bombers alone when it was the flak's turn to take over. Refuelling and re-arming while the gunners blasted away, the Luftwaffe's pilots and crews took off once more and made attack after attack on the American formations. Hans Weik was flying a Bf 109G that day. "After the first attack, we caught up to the enemy again … I attacked an aircraft on the left outside of the formation from exactly in front and began firing at 500 metres." Hitting the bomber on the right side, Weik "pulled away over the bomber and saw that the outer part of the right wing was totally shot up". He saw his victim drop out of formation and "spiral to the right. I saw two men bale out. The bomber crashed west of Brandenburg."[11]

In what should have been a stunning success for the Germans, 75 bombers and 14 escorts were downed – the highest total from any one raid in the war so far. But the cost was equally dramatic. Thirty-two pilots and crew were wounded and 37 killed, among them *Hauptmann* Hugo Frey, one of the Luftwaffe's foremost Viermot victors with 32 bombers to his name. Frey had shot down four that very day before his luck ran out. Seventy-five German aircraft were lost, including large numbers of twin-engine fighters, whose usefulness against escorted bombers was now in major doubt.

Two days later the Americans headed back to Berlin, their targets being the Robert Bosch vehicle and aircraft ignition manufacturing works in the Klein Machnow district, and the Vereinigte Kugellager Fabriken (VKF) ball bearing plant in Erkner. As on 6 March, the Germans guessed correctly as to the raid's likely target and were able to concentrate a large number of fighters to defend the capital.

Heinz Knoke was one of them. A staffel commander now, he had given up dropping bombs on the American formations and now focused on shooting down as many as possible in an almost maniacal frenzy. "In the first frontal attack I shoot down a Fortress just north of the airfield and leave a second in flames ... On our second mission I succeed in shooting down yet another Fortress." He then became embroiled in a dog fight with the Thunderbolts, where his engine, left wing and undercarriage were badly shot up. Somehow managing to land, he ordered a reserve aircraft be prepared for him to take off on a third mission, only for it to be destroyed itself minutes later, during a "low-level strafing attack" that also seriously wounded two mechanics.

Refusing to stand down, Knoke was allocated another aircraft, and along with two wingmen and his boss, the one-eyed Günther Specht, took to the skies again, this time to attack a formation of Liberators over Lüneburg Heath. Bounced by "approximately 40 Thunderbolts, in the ensuing dog fight our two wingmen are both shot down." It seemed that Knoke was not the only German fighter pilot spurred to extraordinary endeavour that day, and for once, the Germans managed to overwhelm the escorts, shooting down an unprecedented 34 of them, before plundering the bomber formations for 40 Liberators and Fortresses.

Bob Thornton was a crewman in a B-17 that was damaged by flak and then finished off by fighters. He managed to bale out, pull his parachute rip cord and drift earthwards. "As I came through the clouds a Bf 109 almost hit me. He was using cloud cover to get to the formations. When he saw me, he banked around and throttled back. I thought he was going to shoot me as I hung in my parachute. He came up alongside, took a good look, saluted and went back after the formation."[12]

The next day – 9 March – the Americans came again. There was no attempt to try and deceive the Germans as to the target, no diversionary raids to draw the defenders away, it was just straight and true to Berlin with maximum force. To the disbelief of the American crews, there was no sign of German fighters. What had happened? Heinz Knoke knew exactly what had happened. "In a telephone conversation with Division during the night, the

CO [Specht] requests that we be withdrawn temporarily from operations. We cannot continue." In his memoir, Knoke noted that "The request was refused, we are to continue flying to the last aircraft and the last pilot." However, Luftwaffe high command, justifiably concerned about the exhausted state of their men and machines used the weather as an excuse to keep their fighters grounded and left battling the raid to the flak alone. Hannah Rittau and her fellow gunners did their best – and shot down nine aircraft while damaging another 221 – but there was no hiding the fact that the Americans had won a victory. Hannah herself said that "Berlin looked very, very damaged, houses came down and collapsed in ruins."

One of the things that makes the air battle over Germany special – and different – from the other theatres of the Second World War, was that there was no decisive turning point, no battle that can be pointed to with a flourish and pronounced as 'the one'. The campaign had no Battle of Britain, no Midway or Stalingrad, no El Alamein or Kohima. The balance between the combatants seemed to shift from one side to the other, often influenced by relatively small events in the grand scheme of things; the Heligoland Bight battle back in December 1939 that convinced Bomber Command to abandon daylight bombing and switch to a night-time campaign being perhaps the best example.

The American raid on Augsburg on Thursday 16 March 1944 was arguably another. Overtly, the attack was nothing special. Some 740 US bombers set out on a deep-penetration raid that was scuppered by cloud cover over the target, which meant the bombing was inaccurate and ineffective. The weather affected the German response too, with the fighters unable to mass effectively and only attacking in dribs and drabs. Victories for the Germans were hard to come by, and only 24 bombers and half that number of escorts were downed.

What made Augsburg special however, and a landmark in the air war, was what happened to a newly formed gruppe of Bf 110s. The unit in question – III./ZG 76 – was based in southwestern Germany and had been ordered to attack the American bombers in force. Given what had happened previously to other Bf 110 units at the hands of American fighters, it was decided to provide them with an escort, comprising Bf 109s from JG 7. Those same Messerschmitts found themselves in a battle all of their own before they could rendezvous with their charges. The 43 Bf 110s of III./ZG 76 found themselves all alone as they slowly ploughed on towards the bombers. Suddenly, a swarm of American fighters appeared and fell on the cumbersome Bf 110s with glee. It was a slaughter. In a matter of minutes, 23 of the German fighters were blown out of the sky, as the rest desperately scrambled to safety. Most of the downed crews were casualties, inflating German personnel losses for the day to 39 dead and 32 wounded. Not a single American fighter was lost. This would have been bad enough, but what made the day so significant was that the victors were flying an aircraft that would swing the balance of the day campaign decisively in the Allies favour, and spell doom to the Luftwaffe fighter force – the P-51 Mustang.

The Mustang was an extraordinary aircraft. Originally commissioned from the North American Aircraft company by the RAF as a long-range fighter in 1940, the prototype was designed and built in just 117 days. Fitted with an American-built Allison engine, it did well in testing, but performance fell off at high altitude. The assistant Air Attaché in the US Embassy in London, Major Thomas Hitchcock, suggested that the problem could be solved by fitting the aircraft with the British Rolls-Royce Merlin engine instead. So was born arguably the finest fighter of the war. There were teething problems for the new plane, and the Thunderbolt would remain the dominant American fighter in terms of numbers for some time yet, but in combination the two fighter types were easily good enough to destroy any lingering hope the Germans might have had that twin-engine fighters could battle the bombers and survive, and Augsburg proved that.

After Augsburg, the Americans kept on coming – ten times more by the end of March. Not every raid was into Germany; airfields and V-weapon sites in France were hit, too. On at least two of the raid days the Luftwaffe kept its fighters on the ground, blaming poor weather, whereas in reality it was more to do with pilot exhaustion and attrition. By month's end the Luftwaffe day fighter force defending the homeland had been decimated. The experience of JG 3's III. Gruppe was typical. On 15 March they were scrambled to intercept a large force of American bombers targeting Braunschweig. All twenty serviceable fighters in the group took off and attacked. In a furious battle, four were shot down, with two pilots killed. Two others were badly damaged and had to crash land. In all, six aircraft – almost a third of the group – were lost in just one day. That same day Heinz Knoke and his group were also in action. "Several hundred Thunderbolts and Lightnings [P-38 fighters] came over with more than 1,000 heavy bombers [It was actually 330]." It was a bad day for Knoke's JG 11 as well. "Six aircraft take off to intercept. Four return ... Jonny [Wilhelm 'Jonny' Fest] and I landed sweating like pigs. Both our aircraft were shot up ... This is the end."

February had been a bad month for the Germans, with one third of its single-engine force written off. March was worse. Fully half its fighters were destroyed and one in five of its pilots – some 265 – were killed, with another 121 wounded. Dolfo Galland reported to Luftwaffe high command that the losses "included our best staffel and geschwader commanders ... the time has come when our force is within sight of collapse." New pilots were arriving to fill the gaps but were ill-prepared for what awaited them. One senior pilot despaired of the new boys, declaring that they were "scared of their own aircraft" and, as a consequence, "would be shot down within three to four missions and that was, in practical terms, within two to three days of arriving with us". Little wonder, when those same recruits were typically only receiving between 10-15 hours flying time in frontline aircraft before arriving at their staffeln – with maybe 110 hours flying time in all types in total, a huge drop from the early war years.

The renowned Experte, Alfred Grislawski, concurred with his fellow veteran about the state of the replacements. "Mostly they could hardly even fly their aircraft properly. For them it was about getting their aircraft into the air, and then, if they survived, to get it down on the ground again. In most cases they were shot down after at most three to four missions, or crashed on their own." Heinz Knoke saw that for himself, noting in his diary that on taking a new pilot for a short test flight to help him acclimatize,

"He ran into the ground and was killed while practising low-level flying." As a direct result, more and more responsibility was heaped on the small number of veteran fliers in the frontline units. One of those self-same veterans – Otto Stammberger – described the effect on his comrades: "Many of our older pilots suffered from stomach cramps; they hardly ate any more, just chocolate, coffee and cigarettes. When the loudspeakers blared out 'Alarm!' they often threw up." Anton Hackl, briefly commander of JG 11, had his younger pilots fly with the more experienced ones and he told them to stay close to their leaders. "Of course, if the leader was shot down the inexperienced pilot was almost helpless." Hackl wasn't all mother hen though, he also recommended to Galland that any new pilot who refused to press home their attacks on the bombers to point blank range be threatened with court martial. As Stammberger grimly pointed out, "Fighting against the Viermots was always a matter of life and death."

As for the Americans, the first three months of 1944 had cost them over 800 heavies shot down and many, many more damaged or scrapped, but reinforcements meant they could still field more aircraft than they could back in January. As one Luftwaffe fighter pilot recalled, "As the years of war passed by, we all tended to lose our sense of humour; there was nothing more to laugh about." Heinz Knoke and Jonny Fest were slouched dejectedly in their armchairs following another harrowing sortie, when their commander entered the room and said quietly, "The unit will be withdrawn from operations for six weeks ... I think we've earned the rest." Knoke could have cried with relief.

For Bomber Command, meanwhile, the battle of Berlin was winding down. D-Day was only just over two months away and Harris knew his bombers would be ordered to help pave the way for the landings by attacking targets across northern France and back to western Germany as part of the agreed Allied transportation plan. That plan called for the progressive destruction of the rail network – trains were still by far the most important method of transporting men and equipment across the Continent – to isolate the proposed beachhead in Normandy. But that was for tomorrow. In the meantime, Harris was determined to continue his immolation of the cities of the Third Reich. Harris's faith in Bomber Command's ability to break German morale is mired in controversy, but the despair and shock felt by so many of the Reich's citizens as a result of the bombing is indisputable. Bridget von Bernstoff spoke for many in a letter she wrote to a friend after her home city of Frankfurt was raided, along with one rather specific detail. "The town just doesn't exist anymore. In fact it is a Hamburg, Berlin or Kassel. A great many killed ... everything one touches is black with soot and ashes and the garden is full of odd pages of English, German and Spanish books from the paper factory which got hit."[13]

Having hit Berlin on the night of 24/25 March, it was Essen's turn again two nights later in what turned out to be a defeat for the Nachtjagd, who were almost all deployed to intercept a deep penetration raid and were miles away when the bombers dropped their payloads on the Ruhr city. With negligible losses over Essen, Harris felt confident to order a maximum effort four nights later to attack the Bavarian city of Nuremburg. It was an interesting choice for such a large raid. Deep in southern Germany, it wasn't a big industrial target, having a relatively small manufacturing base, and whilst possessing good transport links, its position meant it wasn't a main thoroughfare between Germany and the Russian front. What it did have though was huge symbolic significance. Goebbels had made the city the centre for a host of pre-war rallies that were beamed out across the world for millions to gawk at Adolf Hitler delivering his fire-breathing oratory to tens of thousands of enraptured Germans, with black-clad ranks of SS men vying with masses of brownshirts carrying a forest of swastika flags. It was all spectacle, and brilliant propaganda. Now, Harris had the opportunity to deal that symbolism a powerful blow – if the Nazis couldn't protect Nuremburg went the thinking, what could they protect?

Some 795 bombers – mostly Lancasters – took off for the long flight, having been told that cloud would shield them from the almost full moon, and that Window would be dropped to swamp German radar, just as over Hamburg the previous year. Once again, the volume of radio traffic in the morning and the early take-off time tipped off the Germans that a deep penetration, large scale raid was in the offing. Beppo Schmid was the senior German commander on the ground. A crony of Goering's, he'd been in charge of Luftwaffe intelligence during the Battle of Britain and had made a prize fool of himself. Prone to bouts of drinking, he had rehabilitated himself in north Africa as commander of the Luftwaffe-manned Hermann Goering Panzer Division. His reward had been a flight out of the Tunis pocket and appointment as head of the 1st Fighter Corps. Unsure as to the bombers' real target, Schmid ordered about 200 night fighters into the air and had them congregate loosely over the 'Ida' radio beacon near Bonn, and the 'Otto' beacon close to Frankfurt-am-Main. As luck, or fate, would have it, the bomber stream's route took them right to the beacons – the British were flying straight into the lion's den.

*Hauptmann* Martin Drewes was airborne that night, piloting his Bf 110 alongside his radio op Erich Handke and rear gunner *Feldwebel* Georg Petz. Handke had previously flown with Sepp Kraft before joining Drewes and Petz, and the three had become a formidable team with 15 victories to Drewes' credit. The addition of a rear gunner had become necessary back in late '43 when the RAF had begun to send more night escort fighters out with the bombers – no night fighter wanted to be caught by surprise by a Mosquito or Beaufighter hitting them from behind. Drewes was making for 'Ida' when Petz called out "Hold hard! A four-engine plane just crossed over us. There, to the left!" Drewes turned east and tried to follow, but lost it. Handke turned on his SN-2 on-board radar and was shocked to see aircraft plots all over both of his tube screens. "We are right in the middle of the bomber stream." Concentrating fully on his controls, Handke directed Drewes to climb to the nearest target. "He must be dead ahead of us and a bit higher." Drewes saw the tell-tale exhaust flames from the engines and then the outline of the bomber. "Range 600 yards," relayed Handke, and then went quiet – SN-2 was blind this close in. Now, beneath the bomber, Drewes matched its speed and climbed. When he was just 50 yards away he opened fire with his Schräge Musik, setting the left wing ablaze. Pulling away port to safety, they watched as the bomber took five minutes to die, at first flying on and then falling away steeply and exploding in a huge pyre as it hit the ground. The Lancaster was the first Bomber Command casualty of the night.

Alerted to the presence of the bomber stream, night fighter after night fighter made contact, helped enormously by ideal atmospheric conditions that silhouetted the bombers against the moon and created undisturbed condensation trails that drew the fighters in like bees. Helmuth Schulte was one of those bees. "I sighted a Lancaster, got underneath it and fired my Schräge Musik, unfortunately they jammed." However, his short burst had knocked out an engine, and having caught the damaged Lancaster up, Schulte tried a second attack. "I tried the Schräge Musik again and after another burst the bomber fell in flames." Delighted with his success, Schulte went hunting for more. He shot down another three before coming across a Lancaster south of Nuremburg. By now his Schräge Musik were well and truly jammed, so he went into the attack firing his forward guns. "As soon as I opened fire he dived away and my shells passed over him. I thought that this guy must have nerves of steel. He'd watched me form up on him and then dived at just the right moment." Schulte decided "that was enough" and headed for home. His four victories were a great success, but he wasn't alone. Three other night fighter pilots scored four victories that night, and one – *Oberleutnant* Martin 'Tino' Becker -- somehow managed to shoot down an incredible seven bombers, his last being a Halifax near the German/French border.

In what had been a disastrous night for Bomber Command, the Nachtjagd had capitalised on all its advantages and downed 79 bombers. With flak accounting for another 16, total losses stood at 95. Ten more were scrapped on their return and 59 were salvageable only after major repairs. It was the Nachtjagd's greatest success of the war. If the Germans could continue to inflict losses at that level, Bomber Command would be forced to re-think its entire strategy. For Harris it was a bad night. When the weather conditions changed, he'd had a chance to call it all off, but had not. However, he wasn't 'Butch' Harris for nothing. Casualties were a source of deep personal regret, but he accepted them as the price of victory. As he later pointed out, a defeat such as the one over Nuremburg could have happened on many a night, but it didn't – Bomber Command would plough on.

Five days before the Nuremburg raid, at an invasion planning meeting in England, Tooey Spaatz proposed a major change to Allied air strategy in the run up to D-Day. "We believe attacks on transportation will not force the German fighters into action. We believe they will defend oil to their last fighter plane." Spaatz had been tasked to achieve air supremacy over Europe by destroying the Luftwaffe, and while he understood the focus on transportation – in military parlance it was and is described as 'isolating the battlefield' – he thought the best way to destroy the Luftwaffe was to hit Nazi Germany's oil supplies. He had proposed the exact same thing at the beginning of the month and been rebuffed by Eisenhower as Supreme Commander, and this time was no different. Ike turned him down flat and told him to stick with transport.

As a dutiful subordinate, Spaatz did as he was told, and in conjunction with Bomber Command the mass of Anglo-American bombers concentrated on German and French rail marshalling yards, repair facilities and transport hubs; the impact of which would be crucial to the landings and cripple the Nazi response to *Overlord* (Allied codename for D-Day). Spaatz, however, saw Ike's refusal as purely temporary and was determined to revisit the subject when the time was right.

For the German soldiers who would face D-Day and the long-awaited opening of the Allies' 'Second Front' in France, the bombing of their homeland was something deeply affecting. By this stage in the war there was hardly a family in Germany who hadn't been touched by the bombing, and on every front there were German soldiers who had lost family or friends. Indeed, it was so common that the men left enraged by their loss were given their own nickname – *Crazy Helmuts*.

Gustav Winter was serving in the 716th Infantry Division at the time, a so-called Fortress unit tasked with defending the Normandy coastline and mostly composed of older and medically unfit men. Winter had lost several fingers and toes to frostbite in

Russia but had not been released from service. "I'd lost several relatives in the day and night bombing of Berlin and I was angry, I was very bitter. Many of my comrades felt the same way." One of his officers – *Leutnant* Wergens – echoed Winter's view. "The bombing had hardened the men's anger at the Allies. Everyone had lost relatives, friends, and neighbours to the bombing, almost without exception." Like most of his fellow officers, Wergens kept a wary eye out for any of his men who received the terrible news in mail from home.

Luftwaffe personnel were naturally just as likely to be affected as their comrades in the Army. Fighter pilot Johannes Kaufmann was in a training role in southern Germany in the spring of 1944, and on occasions, "One of our number might receive official notification that his entire family had been killed in an air raid. The rest of us would then do everything we could to help alleviate our comrades' suffering." Wolfgang Falck, in charge as he was of the Luftwaffe's night defences, wasn't immune. "My mother was killed and so was my brother. My father was bombed at home and buried in the basement, but they dug him out and saved him." Looking back, he tried to be philosophical. "You could get angry, not hatred, but rage, and not against the crews. They are soldiers and they are carrying out orders ... we tried to protect the German people and the towns and civilian population of Germany. The [German] pilots saw the cities burning and knew that down there their parents or relatives lived. When the bombers attacked their hometowns they were very bitter."[14]

Those on whom the bombs were falling were angry too, not only at the enemy but at their own leadership. After the 16 March raid on Augsburg, Party officials reported to Berlin that many locals were saying "If we didn't have this Government we would have had peace long ago. With the stubbornness of our leadership an end to the war can only be hoped for after Germany's complete annihilation." Such reports set alarm bells ringing in the corridors of power, and the Nazis stepped up their efforts to control the population and support the regime. The work of the Air Protection League was increasingly supplemented by that of the National Socialist People's Welfare organisation – the *Nationalsozialistische*

*Volkswohlfahrt* or NSV. Originally a small Nazi-affiliated charity operating in Berlin, after Hitler took power it expanded across the country, using funds stolen from Germany's Jewish citizens to deliver social programmes for the poor. Eventually absorbing all other welfare organisations in the Reich, the NSV established local reception centres in areas that had been bombed. There, NSV volunteers provided hot drinks, sandwiches, first aid, emergency camp beds and so on, as well as providing the opportunity for citizens to log their losses and file compensation claims.

Unless those bombed out were needed for essential war work, the NSV would encourage them to leave and head for safer environs, with relatives or friends if at all possible. The local Party authorities would issue a departure permit – without which they couldn't claim ration cards in their new home – and provide help with travel. So many people sought safety in the more rural provinces of eastern and southern Germany that they were often jokingly referred to as the 'Reich's air raid shelters'.

This mass internal migration wasn't without its problems. Many God-fearing Catholics in southern Germany resented the arrival of northern Protestants, and country folk often thought the refugees from the cities to be lazy and morally loose, while for their part many urbanites thought their hosts rude and unfriendly, and their living conditions basic. One hausfrau evacuated east to Silesia made no bones about telling her reluctant host that "If I [knew] I'd have to come to a nest like this then I'd rather go back to a heap of ruins." Joseph Goebbels – far more attuned to the public mood than the majority of the Nazi leadership – attempted to use propaganda to keep the peace and bind the people together. As usual, he sought a common external enemy against whom he could focus public anger, and he found it without much of an investigation in the Allied aircrews themselves. Poster campaigns that depicted American aircrew as gangsters were increased, with reports circulated in newspapers that the US air force recruited convicts straight out of prison to fly in its ranks.

Going one giant step further, Goebbels himself began to incite ordinary Germans to take revenge on downed aircrew, claiming that "American attacks over Germany are no longer warfare but murder, pure and simple." He circulated instructions to local Party and police services that "Fighter and bomber pilots who are shot down are not to be protected against the fury of the people." Bill Davidson was a B-17 pilot from Texas, shot down near Berlin in late April 1944. On safely landing in his parachute a crowd of locals gathered with one old man furiously hitting him with his walking stick. "I was tempted to grab the stick ... but [he was] beating me because I'd been bombing some of their cities. So I just stood there and took it." Taken to a nearby town, he was paraded up and down the main street with "people jeering at me and spitting at me".[15] Put in a cell in the town hall with another captured airman, he was eventually taken to a Luftwaffe interrogation centre where he was well treated.

Some were not as lucky as Bill Davidson. Rumours spread that captured airmen were being strung up from lampposts in bombed-out cities, and in August 1944 six aircrew who had baled out of their B-24 Liberator over Rüsselsheim in central Germany were beaten to death by an angry mob as they were marched through the town to the local railway station. It was estimated that at least 350 Allied airmen were murdered in such a way in the last two years of the war, although it should be remembered that this was just 1 per cent of the total number who baled out and were taken prisoner.

With the Anglo-American bomber fleets focusing on transportation targets in the run-up to D-Day, Dolfo Galland was given a measure of respite after the hard spring battles, and he used it to try and bolster his day fighter force and adapt its tactics to increase effectiveness. "In May 1944 the first planned enlargement of gruppen in the defence of the Reich happened, this included increasing each staffel from 12 to 16 planes, and more significantly each gruppe received a fourth staffel – drawing these staffeln from geschwader in the East."[16] Galland hoped that this reorganisation of the homeland defence units would be enough to at least maintain parity with the growing American threat, but he also knew that the Russian well was in danger of running dry. Ever since the near destruction of the Soviet air force in 1941, the Germans had had air superiority in Russia, but that advantage was fast disappearing. Nazi Germany's most important battle front was being rapidly stripped of its fighter cover and there were no plans to stop the trend, let alone reverse it.

Additional staffeln were also taken from the Wilde Sau units, whose usefulness had more or less come to an end, as losses among the pilots mounted. "Wilde Sau was fine if the weather was good, but it was wrong to order them to fly when the weather was bad, they'd land in the wrong place or they baled out. They baled out because they didn't know where they were or didn't know how deep the clouds were. Very many pilots died."[17] According to the renowned historian Richard Holmes, as many as half of all Wilde Sau pilots had been killed by the time their operations were called off in April 1944.

On tactics, Galland turned to Kornatzki and his *Sturmböcke* – Billy goats or Battering rams – as his Staffel 1 had proven something of a success, and the young Luftwaffe general was keen to expand on the concept. But there was a problem. At altitude the Fw 190 was slow and cumbersome. "The Fw 190s performance fell off severely above 21,000 feet, and as the B-17 usually came in at that height it was, of course, handicapped in combating the American fighter escort." The addition of more armour plating protected the pilots and their aircraft's vitals, but slowed them down even further. This made their approach from behind a slow process and kept them in the tail gunner's sights for longer. The fitting of heavier firepower exacerbated the problem. It tested a pilot's nerve to the utmost to form up in line behind a bomber Pulk and then gradually close the gap, leaning into a hail of massed machine-gun fire. But there was a balance between the combatants. That balance was shattered by the presence of escort fighters. To a prowling Thunderbolt, a Sturm fighter was a big, fat, waddling duck – easy meat. As Alfred Grislawski phrased it, the German fighters "were forced to 'dance at two weddings'". How could one reach and shoot down bombers without falling victim to the escorting fighters?

In the summer of 1940, an exasperated Hermann Goering had insisted that to counter Germany's own mounting bomber casualties his fighters had to stick to them like limpets, and his pilots were refused permission to actively hunt the Spitfires and Hurricanes of Fighter Command. Understandable as Goering's demand was, it frustrated the fighters and did little if anything to stem bomber losses. Now, faced with the same challenge, the American air force leadership had opted for a completely different tack. The straitjacket of rigid escort duties had been thrown out the window by Tooey Spaatz, and the American fighter wings were on the offensive, aggressively seeking out combat with the German fighters, and sweeping the skies clear of their enemy. The response to this dramatic operational change by Galland and Luftwaffe high command was simply to ignore it. The bombers were the main target, their escorts were secondary and were to be avoided and distracted. In practical terms, that meant fast, lightweight Bf 109 fighters would now act as escorts for their cumbersome brethren, tasked with little more than shielding the heavy Sturm fighters while they tried to reach the bombers. German fighters would now protect German fighters. The old days of the Luftwaffe eagles were truly gone.

What the Luftwaffe really needed was a game changer, something that, at a stroke, would decisively tip the scales in their favour – and they had possessed it all along – the world's very first jet fighter. *Project 1065* had been under development since before the war and had taken its first jet powered flight on 18 July 1942. Dolfo Galland, a major supporter of the programme, had test flown the prototype himself, blissfully declaring afterwards: "It was as though angels were pushing." The aircraft he had described so rapturously was the Messerschmitt Me 262 – *die Schwalbe* – the Swallow. In the spring of 1944, it was the fastest thing in the air by quite a margin, outstripping the Thunderbolt, Lightning, and even the Mustang, by almost a hundred miles an hour, while carrying enough armament to blow the Viermots apart.

Her revolutionary design, however, required certain raw materials that weren't readily available to Nazi Germany, and that had created significant delays to her development. Secondly, Hitler himself had thrown a large spanner in the works. Back on 26 November 1943, the Nazi dictator had attended a secret demonstration of the new fighter, hosted by Willi Messerschmitt

at the Insterburg airfield in East Prussia. The renowned test pilot
Gerd Linter was at the controls, and he put the aircraft through
a punishing series of aerial manoeuvres to showcase her abilities.
Hitler was impressed, and casually turned to ask Messerschmitt
if the aircraft could carry bombs. Without thinking, the designer
replied in the affirmative. Two weeks later Hitler sent Goering
a message proclaiming "the tremendous importance of the
production of jet-propelled aircraft for employment as fighter
bombers ... It is imperative that the Luftwaffe have a number
of jet fighter bombers ready for front commitment by the spring
of 1944.' Hitler clearly had the Me 262 in mind as a significant
countermeasure to the anticipated Allied landings in France
and, given just how important the Allies' own use of fighter
bombers was in the Normandy fighting, it was not without
justification, but in doing so he deprived the Luftwaffe of the
potential answer to the punishing American daylight bombing
campaign.

With the Me 262 having to undergo a significant re-design to
become a fighter bomber, on the other side of the Channel the
Americans were busy converting their fighter groups to the new
version of the Mustang – the P-51D. The D-variant was fast,
nimble, handled extremely well, and its range was jaw-dropping –
it could escort the bombers from East Anglia all the way to Vienna
and back. There was nowhere in the Reich it couldn't reach. Its
appearance over Germany itself caused near panic in Luftwaffe
high command, and after Dolfo Galland reported to Hitler that a
Mustang downed over the Reich was being examined, the young
general was summoned post haste for a furious dressing down by
his master. Goering demanded on what basis Galland had told the
Führer "that American fighters have penetrated into the territory
of the Reich ... That's nonsense Galland, what gives you these
fantasies?"

"Those are the facts Herr *Reichsmarschall* ... American fighters
have been shot down over Aachen, there is no doubt about it!"

"That is simply not true Galland, it's impossible."

"You might go and check it yourself, the downed planes are
there at Aachen."

"What must have happened is that they were shot down much further to the west ... they could have glided quite a distance further before they crashed."

"Glided to the east, sir?"

The arrival of the new fighter was a boon for the Americans, and a disaster for the Germans. The Luftwaffe had drawn up a plan for its response to any landings in occupied France. Christened *Drohende Gefahr West* – Threatening Danger West – the idea was rapidly to switch all available forces from every other front – including Russia and defence of the Reich – to support the Army in throwing the Allies back into the sea. The plan would become popularly known to the officers and men of the Wehrmacht as the '1,000 fighters' promise. Goering was clear as to his intentions. "The moment the British try and invade France to establish a second front, I will not leave a single fighter aircraft defending the Reich. Every single fighter which is air-worthy will be sent forward, and the Reich itself will not have an aircraft to its name – come hell or high water."

Erwin Rommel, the Desert Fox charged by Hitler with defeating the anticipated landings, had little confidence. He thought they might defeat the landings "if enough fighters are in the air which can be thrown against the powerful Allied air forces, but I don't believe in the '1,000 fighters' Göring means to send here ... Göring has let us down before in Africa, and at Stalingrad." Rommel was wrong. Goering kept to his word, as Galland attested: "The invasion on 6 June 1944 forced the transfer of almost all fighter units to the West." Three hundred fighters left the Russian front in under a week, and the Reich's own defensive network was stripped. The timing couldn't have been worse for the Germans.

The Mustang had been coming on stream in large numbers since May, and when the Allies landed in Normandy on 6 June 1944 the Mustang was fast becoming the dominant fighter among the American fighter groups. A gruppe from JG 1 based in the Reich were some of the first to be ordered west to encounter the new American wonder-fighter. *Oberleutnant* Georg-Peter Eder led 32 Fw 190s west and headed for Essay in Normandy. En route, they heard that their original destination had been bombed, so diverted to Le Mans. On changing course, they were bounced by Mustangs and *Leutnant* Johann Brünnler became their first casualty of the new campaign. Their second followed the next day when *Hauptmann* Karl-Heinz Weber was shot down and killed – again by Mustangs. Deployed on ground-attack missions, for which the Viermot hunters had no training, *Oberfeldwebel* Herbert Kaiser, a veteran senior NCO with nine victories against the Allies in North Africa and a further forty in Russia, was shaken by what he and his comrades now faced in Normandy.

> If the missions we had undertaken as fighters in the defence of the Reich until then had been tough and tested our nerves, the missions on the invasion front were giving us an insight into hell. I will never forget our first mission ... skimming over the landing beaches at Caen. The surface of the sea was saturated with hundreds of boats of all sizes, while the sky was filled with bomber formations going to attack our front, accompanied by countless fighters. Lost in the middle of all that, a handful of Messerschmitts – us!

Two nights later, Bomber Command hit Le Mans airbase and the gruppe lost seven fighters destroyed on the ground and five more damaged. With their original destination airfield at Essay now repaired, the gruppe went to fly in and were duly bounced once more by Mustangs; this time five 190s were lost, with three pilots and a hitch-hiking mechanic killed. Later that same day American Liberators raided Essay and it was made unusable again. Transferred once more, this time to Semallé, south-east of Alençon, the Mustangs found them again. Shooting up the airfield, the American fighters destroyed some 26 Fw 190s, and the gruppe was rendered combat ineffective. In ten weeks, Eder and his comrades lost a total of 106 aircraft – more than three times its original strength – along with 30 pilots killed or missing and two others wounded. *Ausgeblutet* – 'bled out' as the Germans called it – the remnants were transferred back home to Reinsehlen in northwestern Germany.

The Russian front veterans fared no better. Men described by the noted Swedish historian and Luftwaffe expert, Christer Bergström, as 'flying war machines', were killed in droves: Friedrich Wachowiak – 86 victories, Eugen-Ludwig Zweigart, 69, Herbert Huppertz, 68, Karl Kempf, 65, August Mors, 60, Siegfried Sinsch, 54, and Emil 'Bully' Lang, 173 victories and the record holder for a single day's tally with a remarkable 17 victories over Kiev back in November 1943. Dolfo Galland watched his ranks haemorrhage pilots as flocks of Anglo-American fighters were given free rein to sweep the skies over northern France clear of German aircraft. He personally visited the invasion front and was dismayed at what he found.

> My impressions were shattering. In addition to the appalling conditions, there was a far-reaching decline in morale. This feeling of irrevocable inferiority, the heavy losses, the hopelessness of the fighting, the reproaches from above, the disrepute into which the Luftwaffe had fallen among the other arms of the Wehrmacht through no fault of the individual ... were the most severe test ever experienced by the Luftwaffe.

In that final judgement the young Luftwaffe general was most assuredly wrong. Back in the summer of 1941 the United States Air Force Air War Plans Division had identified three major industrial sectors in the Nazi economy which, if targeted, had the potential to cripple the Reich's war effort. Foremost was the electricity supply system and infrastructure, power stations, the electricity grid and so on. The second sector was transportation, and primarily the railways, without which the large-scale movement of everything from troops to tanks to food and guns would be paralysed. The final sector selected was the oil industry. As the United States wasn't at war with Nazi Germany at the time, it was decided that further work was required on what was then nothing more than a preliminary study. After Hitler's declaration of war on America in the wake of the Pearl Harbor attack, the Plans Division's efforts were stepped up, and by early 1943 a committee of top analysts delivered their findings in a report that would have immensely important repercussions for Germany and the Luftwaffe.

The report had broadened out the initial three target sectors to six and placed them in order of priority, including the practicality of their destruction. They had concluded that the original primary objective; the electricity system, was not a suitable target given Germany's reliance on a mass of relatively small power plants spread across the country. Their very dispersal made it difficult to seriously degrade the system as a whole. Transportation was much the same and considered far too general a target to be viable – it dropped from second to sixth on the list. The new No. 1 was oil.

Not far below it was the manufacture of low friction ball bearings, and given the concentration of that particular industry in one district of one city, the raids on Schweinfurt in August and October 1943 can be seen as almost inevitable. The German aircraft industry had also figured on the list – hence Big Week and the lengthy campaign against aviation plants – but the very length of the campaign showed just how difficult a sector it was to shatter, and the growing number of aircraft being churned out, despite the raids, proved the point. So, with the electricity system deemed unsuitable, transportation downgraded to a tactical rather than a strategic option, and ball bearing and aircraft manufacturing both proven to not be the keys to the kingdom as hoped, the Americans decided to try again, and this time it would be oil. More specifically Germany's refineries and the 24 plants that processed abundant German brown coal and coal tar into precious synthetic fuel and provided a full third of Nazi Germany's daily needs.

Those plants were so important because Germany didn't have any oil of her own and was shut out of access to the world's oil markets. A senior insider in Luftwaffe high command before the war was clear as to the issue's importance. "The oil problem was, of course, the most urgent one [for the Reich] from the start."[18] With Germany not possessing a single oil well it had no choice but to import its entire need, and after Hitler announced the Reich's rearmament, American and British producers were loath to support Berlin's growing aggression. All that could be relied on were the handful of wells in Austria – *Ostmark* as it became after the 1938 *Anschluss* – the small fields in Axis-aligned Hungary, and above all the Romanian wells grouped around the city of Ploieşti.

As the irascible French Prime Minister Georges Clemenceau had remarked to the US President Woodrow Wilson back in 1917, in war, gasoline was as important as blood, and the increasing mechanization of warfare only made it more so. Hitler was acutely aware of the issue and from the moment he took power Germany's oil problem was never far from his mind. Indeed, so pressing was the Reich's need that the importation of oil from the Soviet Union and its large fields in the Soviet Caucasus was made a cornerstone of the 1939 Nazi-Soviet Non-Aggression Pact that shocked the world.

In total, some 600,000 tons of Soviet oil would reach the Reich before the Nazis cast off the agreement and invaded the Soviet Union in June 1941. Another 600,000 tons was looted from occupied western Europe, leading to massive petrol shortages across France, Belgium and the Netherlands in particular. Under pressure from its German ally, Romania continued to export large quantities of oil to the Reich – some 2million tons in 1943 – even to the detriment of its own fragile economy. But with annual wartime consumption more than three times that figure, a huge tranche of the Wehrmacht's needs was met by the ruinously expensive hydrogenation process for synthetic oil manufacture.

Of even greater scarcity than oil in general was the high-octane aviation fuel used by the Luftwaffe's aircraft. Difficult to produce, the Luftwaffe never had enough, always operating in something of a hand to mouth fashion, building up stocks before any major engagement, which it then rapidly used up. When Albert Speer began to take control of Nazi Germany's industrial infrastructure in 1943, he considered aviation spirit production as a priority, and was dismayed to discover no meaningful reserves had been built up during periods in the war of relative quiet. He set himself to the task with vigour, and by the end of the year the reserve was a respectable 400,000 tons. Four months into the new year and this figure had grown to 580,000 tons, with 195,000 produced that same month, outpacing consumption by some 35,000 tons. Most of that 195,000 tons was produced at just one site, the giant

*IG Farbenindustrie Ammoniawerk Merseburg*, commonly called *Leuna*.

Leuna was a behemoth, the Reich's second largest chemical works. As well as being a synthetic oil manufacturer, it produced one third of Germany's ammonia and other chemicals such as methanol and nitric acid, all needed for explosives production, and even made artificial rubber – *buna* – for the Army's truck tyres. The site boasted 250 separate buildings spread over three square miles, with the diminutive chemist, Heinrich Bütefisch, holding sway over a 35,000-strong workforce that included 10,000 forced labourers, his position as one of Nazi Germany's *Wehrwirtschaftsführer* (war economy leaders), buttressed by his membership of the *Freunde des Reichsführer-SS* (Friends of the *Reichsführer-SS*). Anti-aircraft protection for Leuna was provided by the guns and crews of Rudolf Schulze's 14th Flak Division, which was concentrated around the city of Leipzig some 15 miles to the west.

That defence was set to be severely tested. On the morning of 12 May in a main effort attack, over 880 B-17 and B-24 bombers with 980 fighter escorts took off from their airfields across eastern England and headed for five oil refineries and one aircraft factory in central Germany. Leuna was one of the targets. To reach it, the American bomber crews would have to fly a round trip of almost eight hours, more than half of which was on oxygen, while battling temperatures of 38 degrees below zero. No diversionary raids were made and Luftwaffe ground control was able to concentrate forces from across the Reich.

Among them was Hans Weik, veteran of the 6 March US raid on Berlin. As a group leader, Weik assembled his men in formation and took them into the attack. "I fired on a Boeing Fortress on the right side of the formation and saw hits in the fuselage and the left wing. I then saw explosions and flames in the nose section. The airplane immediately fell away in flames ... I saw several parachutes." Weik went on to score another victory but as he was pulling away from this attack, "an air gunner hit my cockpit and the right side of my fuselage." His oxygen equipment failing, Weik was forced to land. No replacement fighter was available and he made no second sortie. He wasn't alone. The American escort fighters were ferocious, tearing into the Bf 109s detailed to keep them away from the heavier Sturm fighters going for the bombers.

Horst Petzschler was an NCO in JG 3 Udet, recently transferred from the Russian front "to beef up units against the huge Eighth Army Air Force day raids". Petzschler's job "was to fly high-altitude sorties to cover the Sturmstaffel of JG 3 attacking the bombers ... we flew the Bf 109G-6 with the methanol injected supercharger," which provided excellent speed and performance at great height. Assembling in the Magdeburg-Kassel area, Petzschler and his fellow fighter pilots were surprised to see "the big boxes of B-17s splitting up before the target was reached". Then the Germans realised why: "Their escort was obviously delayed and so we were able to hit them hard!" With something approaching glee, the 109s abandoned their role as Sturm escorts and went for the bombers. Diving down towards their targets, Petzschler picked out a B-17 "that was flying on the outer right of the formation and grew very big very fast in my gun sight". Giving it a full burst, the young airman saw it "catch fire in its outer engines and wing tanks. Parts were falling off and parachutes were coming out fast."

Eighteen-year-old Herwig Befeldt was also flying a Bf 109G that day on his first mission, having arrived at his unit a month previously with little flying experience and having never even sat in a Gustav before, let alone flown one. His boss, *Oberleutnant* Koch, had insisted he familiarise himself with his aircraft before being rostered for active duty, and on 12 May that insistence saved his life. One of 22 Bf 109s from his group that went up that day, Befeldt and his comrades hadn't even reached the bombers, when "We were attacked by Lightnings and got entangled in a dogfight." Sticking to his leader, the young airman "felt bullets striking my machine" and very quickly, "my cockpit hood became increasingly smeared with oil." Jettisoning the hood, he then threw away his oil-covered goggles and flew the plane while "wiping my eyes all the time". Seeing an airfield ahead, he lined up the aircraft for a crash landing. Sliding to a halt, he climbed out of his stricken machine, shaken but unhurt. Ground crew ran to him from across the airfield, saying that "it bordered on a miracle that I'd pulled off a belly landing in such a damaged aircraft."

One of the Sturm fighters Befeldt was trying to protect was an Fw 190A-8 flown by the Russian front veteran, *Leutnant* Walter Hagenah. Scrambled from Salzwedel, on reaching the Viermots he saw they were "well protected by Mustangs, so it was of paramount importance to engage the bombers in a swift surprise attack." Turning sharply in towards the bombers, he saw a Mustang latch on to him but felt certain "he would break off his attack so as not to expose himself to the defensive fire of his own bombers." Hagenah pushed home his attack, "firing at the bomber with all my guns", but the Mustang took the risk and "I was suddenly hit from behind ... there was a dull bang and in no time at all the cockpit windows were completely covered in oil." Unable to jettison his canopy cover and bale out, Hagenah managed to make an emergency landing where he was "congratulated on my victory, which I hadn't been able to see myself. Two of my comrades had seen and reported it." This was the third time the young officer had been shot down.

Like Weik and Hagenah's sorties, the majority of German attacks that day were against the bombers on their incoming leg; the Luftwaffe's air defence control system worked superbly, interception conditions were perfect, and they assembled their largest ever fighter force to attack the bombers. A total of 515 single and twin-engine fighters sortied up that day, fighting a ferocious battle through Nazi Germany's skies as tens of thousands of their fellow citizens craned their necks to watch as con trails swirled above them and burning aircraft fell from the sky, parachutes blossoming down – or not. In an almost exact replica of the Schweinfurt raids, the American losses were 55 bombers and 10 escorts.

The price the Germans paid was high. Befeldt, Hagenah and Weik's aircraft were just three of 88 fighters shot up, with 31 of their comrades wounded and 29 killed. On the bombers' homeward leg, only a few improvised attacks were made. The German pilots were exhausted and had taken a battering. It was the American escort fighters who had done the damage, their pilots beginning to show their qualitative superiority – alongside their quantity – against an increasingly inexperienced enemy. Horst Petzschler was one of the lucky ones that day. Having downed his first Viermot, he found himself set upon by a "pearl string of five Mustangs". Somehow, he managed to down one of them. "I saw my adversary explode in a large fireball," but by then "my underwear was already wet" and he found himself "literally fighting for my life as I was chased down to ground level by four P-51s."[19] With some quick thinking he headed to a nearby airfield and drew the Mustangs into the sights of the base's anti-aircraft crews, whose combined fire sent the Americans skywards looking for easier pickings. He crash landed, his undercarriage having been badly shot up, and walked away on legs like rubber.

Many of the Luftwaffe's casualties that day were young pilots who had only flown a handful of sorties. Lack of flight time in the training schools was now leading directly to growing losses in the air for the Luftwaffe. The average 210 hours a Luftwaffe fighter pilot spent in training back in 1942 had been slashed to just 112, with a meagre 20 hours of operational training, and even these numbers were rarely met. The youngsters coming through couldn't even rely on some basic manoeuvres anymore. The most glaring of which was the escape manoeuvre; execute a half roll and dive. It had worked for years, only now it was a death sentence. The Thunderjug and the Mustang were both far faster in the dive than the Bf 109 and Fw 190, with one Thunderbolt pilot remarking on his dogfight with a Bf 109: "The Messerschmitt seemed to crawl as my Thunderbolt fell out of the sky." He pulled out of his dive, lined up his German opponent, fired, and "my second kill vanished in a blinding explosion that tore the fighter to shreds."

The 12 May raid was a disaster for the German fighter arm while providing total affirmation of Tooey Spaatz's assertion that the Luftwaffe would "defend oil to their last fighter plane". The Americans had finally found the Reich's Achilles heel, and from now on would hit it remorselessly. In a double blow to the Germans that day, the Americans flew on anyway and the bombs rained down.

On the ground was 16-year-old Luftwaffe 'flak boy' Albrecht Riedel, serving a 105mm gun guarding Leuna, his battery two kilometres west of the site. "It was a beautiful spring day ... we lay in the sun on the top of our gun revetment. We were at readiness, otherwise we would have had some duties or school lessons." When the first reports came in of incoming bombers Riedel and the other boys leapt to their guns. Looking, up he remembered "never having seen so many aircraft in the sky". Riedel was a gun layer, he had to "operate the elevation control with a wheel, like the steering wheel of a car, following the command pointer with the elevation position pointer". The sun was dazzling the fire controllers, which was a big problem, as Riedel knew. "Effective fire was only possible during the bombers' run into the target as they weren't able to alter direction, height or speed. This time was usually just 20 seconds and that was all we got." Recovering just in time, the entire battery fired as one. The teenaged gunner "thought we'd shot one of the aircraft down, but it was the smoke signal from a pathfinder to commence bombing." He remembered the air being filled with "swishing and roaring sounds" and then "One of the bombs fell beside our gun emplacement, thankfully our surrounding revetment prevented any damage. Only earth from the impact, and perhaps a few splinters, fell into our position." The attack lasted half an hour: "The silhouette of the Leuna Works disappeared behind the fountains of earth thrown up by the bombs."

At the end of the raid, Riedel and his comrades sprawled exhausted on the ground, their ears ringing from the blasts and concussions. They judged success by how many rounds they'd fired, with Riedel's crew "in second place with 53 rounds. All the other guns were behind with 30 to 50 rounds, but one gun had only fired six."[20]

The same clear skies and light winds that helped the German ground controllers assemble their fighters had also aided the American bombardiers. Accuracy was high, and almost a third of bombs dropped on Leuna had actually hit it, badly damaging the site and killing 175 workers. When the call came through to Albert Speer's Berlin office confirming Leuna had been attacked, the alarm bells went off.

The architect-cum-armaments supremo immediately sprang into action. He launched his *Hydriesfestungen* (Hydrogenation

Fortresses) programme, with 7,000 skilled Wehrmacht engineers recalled from frontline service to lead on repairing the damaged refineries and installing new protective measures. Concrete blast walls were built around essential machinery, deep bunkers were constructed to allow workers to shelter and then restart work as soon as the all-clear was sounded, and all non-essential site activity was dispersed to other locations. The Army engineers laid the plans, but the work was done by 350,000 slave labourers specifically drafted in for the task. Speer did not neglect his active defences either, instructing the responsible flak units to make any refineries in their vicinity top priority. As for Leuna, Speer personally told Rudolf Schulze he could have whatever he needed to defend the site. True to his word, the first additional anti-aircraft guns began to arrive shortly after the 12 May raid.

Soon Leuna would become the most heavily defended industrial site in the Third Reich – better protected than even the Krupp works in Essen. Over 500 heavy guns, including huge 120mm cannons, were emplaced around it and the other six main refineries on Eighth Army Air Force's target list. Schulze's 14th Flak Division expanded to accommodate the new weaponry, with 9,000 German auxiliaries – of whom a third were female – joining Albrecht Riedel and his comrades on its ration strength, along with 3,600 ex-Red Army PoWs and 900 Hungarian and Italian 'volunteers' – in reality pressed labourers.

For the latter half of May the main Allied bomber forces focused on attacking transportation targets in support of the planned D-Day landings, but also found time to return to Leuna and the other oil installations. Speer's protective measures were only just getting going and this left Leuna and the other sites to take a pounding. As Albrecht Riedel recalled, "The next attacks came at Whitsun, 24 May, with equal ferocity." The May raids wreaked havoc within the Nazis synthetic fuel production sector, particularly regarding aviation spirit. April's production total of 195,000 tons fell by half in May and then again to just 54,000 tons in June, and the Luftwaffe was forced to use its carefully husbanded reserves to keep its aircraft flying.

Enigma decrypts of Nazi communications made it clear that the bombing was causing near panic among Germany's high command, and the target list was expanded as a result. The Americans instructed the Eighth Army Air Force to cover the seven large synthetic manufacturing plants in central Germany – including Leuna – along with 20 other refineries across northern Germany, while the Fifteenth Air Force would attack Romania and Hungary's oil industries, as well as the refineries and plants in occupied Poland, Austria, and German Silesia. To Harris's annoyance, Whitehall made it crystal clear they expected Bomber Command to join in the effort. Leuna would be attacked on no fewer than 21 additional occasions by the war's end – twice by Bomber Command – with disastrous consequences for the Luftwaffe. Aviation spirit production dropped again in July, this time to 35,000 tons, then 16,000 in August before reaching its nadir in September of barely 7,000 tons. By then the Luftwaffe's reserves had been eaten away to 180,000 tons – one month's supply.

Losses among the American bomber crews were heavy – the Leuna run became gloomily known as *Murderous Merseburg* – but the oil offensive was working. Winter weather would provide some respite for the Germans from the American bombers, and Speer's ruthless exploitation of his slave labour army would help him push aviation spirit production up to 21,000 tons in October and 39,000 tons in November, but it wasn't enough. The Luftwaffe was on borrowed time. A fortnight after the first Leuna raid, German home defence could only muster just over half the fighters it could on 12 May. If it was going to protect the homeland against the American day bombing offensive something had to change.

During the hours of darkness, the Luftwaffe's campaign against Bomber Command was taking a somewhat different path. The cat-and-mouse nature of the nightly conflict between fighter and bomber meant there were no huge, visible, aerial battles and, consequently, nothing like the blood-sapping attrition of the daylight fighting. German technology was far in advance of where it had been at the war's beginning, with a third of the Reich's optical industry and half its electronics sector dedicated to radar development and production by the beginning of 1944. Investment at this level had helped the Nachtjagd to keep pace with the growing strength of Bomber Command, and the Germans were able to cause significant losses to the RAF bomber stream when their night fighters could be inserted into it to hunt. The Nuremburg victory proved that. But Nuremburg was not the norm. More often than not, the majority of night fighters would spend their nights circling their assigned areas in dreary holding patterns, achieving little more than guzzling up precious fuel. Josef Kammhuber's modus operandi of a favoured few pilots being positioned in the most likely interception areas still persisted, and translated into an air defence operation that could damage Bomber Command and kill a lot of RAF airmen, but couldn't do enough to stop them coming.

The upshot was that the spring of 1944 presaged no dramatic shift in the air war at night as there was during the day. Goebbels and his propaganda machine were still able to divert the mass of the population from the misery of nightly raids and the destruction they wrought by demonising Bomber Command's airmen on the one hand and glamorising Germany's night-time Experten on the other. It was a policy with consequences, as Jim Chapman saw for himself. Shot down in a raid over Germany one night, he was captured and marched to the train station for transit to a PoW camp. En route, he "heard the German word for 'murderers' accompanied by spitting. That's what they thought of us ... we had to go through Frankfurt, which was absolutely wrecked by the bombing, and we saw an RAF flight lieutenant in his uniform strung up, dangling on the end of a pole outside an upper window. It was safer to remain in the hands of the Luftwaffe officers and the ordinary servicemen."[21]

As for its poster boys, the Nachtjagd was dealt a significant blow on 12 March 1944 when the second of its princes, Egmont Prinz zur Lippe-Weissenfeld, was killed in an air accident. Credited with 51 victories, a holder of the Knight's Cross with Oak Leaves, and commander of NJG 5 at the age of 25, he set off on a routine flight from Parchim in northern Germany to Athies-sous-Loan in northern France. Bad weather closed in over the Belgian Ardennes and he never arrived. His crashed and burnt-out Bf 110 was found the following day on a mountainside near St Hubert. Killed with him were his crew, *Oberfeldwebel* Josef Renette and *Unteroffizier* Kurt Röber. United in death, Lippe-Weissenfeld was buried alongside Prinz zu Sayn-Wittgenstein in the Dutch cemetery at Ysselsteyn. Eleven days later, the 66-victory Experte Werner Streib was also struck off the poster boy list by virtue of getting promoted to Inspector of Night Fighters, an appointment he would hold to the end of the war. Goebbels needed another hero, and he found one in Heinz-Wolfgang Schnaufer.

Schnaufer was tailor-made for the role. Tall for a pilot, the Württemberger's dark, swept-back hair, immaculate turnout and dashing good looks were a propagandist's dream. His background was ideal, too. His family was wealthy, his father and grandfather having started their very successful wine distribution business in the ashes of Germany's defeat in the First World War. Heinz-Wolfgang himself had opted to join the junior branch of the Hitler Youth in 1933, the *Deutsches Jungvolk* (German Young People), and then attended the élite Nazi leadership academy, the 'National Political Teaching Institute' – the *Nationalpolitische Lehranstalt* or *Napola* for short – in Backnang. On joining the Luftwaffe, he opted for the Nachtjagd in November 1941 and ended up in the ranks of frustrated pilots shunted into secondary roles behind the established Experten. He didn't achieve his first victory until June the following year, and by the end of 1942 his tally was a paltry seven. Finally hitting his stride in mid-1943, he rapidly built up his score, reaching 42 victories by the year's end and becoming ghoulishly nicknamed the 'Ghost of St Trond' (his home air base) by fearful bomber crews. On Prinz Lippe-Weissenfeld's death and Werner Streib's elevation, he was catapulted to stardom by the Nazi propaganda machine and promoted to *hauptmann*.

In the run up to D-Day, Harris was having to send his precious bombers to attack transportation targets across northern France and western Germany, instead of his preferred strategy of 'de-housing' the urban German population. For the likes of Schnaufer, this allowed him to build his score, while providing much of Germany with a brief respite from the bombing. It also meant the night-time campaign went on much as before, although the increasing use by Bomber Command of night fighters to escort the bombers and counter the Nachtjagd had an impact, as Wilhelm Herget described: "I was shot down the night of 14/15 June 1944 by a Mosquito, I was sitting in my burning Ju 88 for three minutes and not able to bale out, it's a horrible feeling."[22]

Despite Goebbels' vitriolic propaganda, there were still echoes of compassion between the hunters and the hunted, and German night fighter pilots could still be found visiting the wounded crewmen of bombers they had shot down, as Norman Jackson discovered. "The pilot who shot us down later came into the hospital to say hello, which I thought was nice of him – the bastard."[23] Jackson had been wounded when the night fighter pilot in question attacked his Lancaster and set the starboard wing on fire. He had then climbed out onto the wing with a fire extinguisher to put the blaze out, before the returning fighter made another pass and shot him off the wing in question – somehow Jackson survived and was awarded the Victoria Cross after the war for his bravery.

Ralph J. Munn, a ball turret gunner in a B-17, did not receive the same treatment as Jackson at the hands of his German captors after being shot down on the 12 May oil raid. Wounded before baling out, he touched down safely "in a lush meadow" and was then buzzed by a couple of German fighters who "made two passes but didn't fire a shot". He was handed over to the the Gestapo, who "bashed my head in, knocked out all my teeth, broke my toes and fingers, and beat me to a pulp at least once a day, sometimes twice or three times. My testicles were the size of indoor baseballs."[24]

Ralph Munn – like so many of his comrades – wasn't abused by the local citizenry he landed among, despite so many of them seeing for themselves the effect of the bombs raining down on them and their being goaded to retribution by Goebbels and his ceaseless propaganda. This forbearance was all the more surprising given the level of involvement in the air war of the German people. By 1944, there were 22 million Germans in the RLB air defence organisation, some 15 million in the social welfare NSV – mostly female volunteers – and service in an air attack *Selbstschutztruppe* (Self-Protection Squad) was now a legal obligation for every German citizen. These units were responsible at a street and community level to prepare for possible raids and to provide a practical response as soon as the bombs stopped falling. Assisting with firefighting, helping the homeless, distributing food and water, and dealing with compensation claims, were all activities that fell to the local teams in conjunction with the RLB and NSV. The whole structure was supported by a comprehensive civil defence education programme that distributed leaflets, made short films for cinemas, and held training programmes where citizens were exposed to fires in a controlled environment in so-called 'air protection exercise houses', so they could learn to overcome their fears and tackle a fire effectively.

Even before the United States entered the war, it had instigated studies into the prevailing nature of Germany's housing stock, with input from several well-known German architectural exiles. The studies concluded that most German houses were susceptible to fire. Washington then commissioned Hollywood movie set designers and engineers from Standard Oil to build two complete replica working-class neighbourhoods in the Utah desert, one German and one Japanese. Authenticity was key, with the same building materials used including roofing, stairs and floorboards, with the interiors kitted out with furniture, bedding, clothing and so on. Experiments were then carried out to see how best to burn them down with incendiaries. A teenaged *Flakhelfer* in Berlin recalled after the war what it was like being underneath them:

> During night raids the pathfinders flew overhead dropping their incendiary devices which we called 'Christmas trees'. For us it was a terrifyingly beautiful sight ... when we watched them it was like watching a fiery umbrella slowly falling to earth ... I couldn't or didn't want to see fireworks anymore, if fireworks were ever let off, for years after I avoided them. All I could see was the incendiary devices and how awful and dreadful they were.

The German civil defence training programme looked to counter the incendiaries and helped the national fire service recruit 1.7 million volunteer firefighters by 1944, although as the Army's need for manpower drained more and more men to the various fronts, the gaps – just as in the flak arm - were increasingly filled with foreign workers from the East, some of whom were forced labourers. Incredible as it may seem, this policy meant, for example, that by the war's end a quarter of Hamburg's fire service was composed of ethnic Ukrainians, many of them marched at gunpoint out of their own villages and shipped to the Reich in cattle trucks.

In like manner, in 1942 the industrial workforce that Harris aimed to de-house had been overwhelmingly German, in 1944 only two-thirds were, and half of those were women. The traditionally patriarchal structure of German society was breaking down under the strains of war, especially the twin scourges of the slaughter in Russia and the bombing of the home front. Goering may have pontificated about German women carrying out war work at home while watching their children, but Albert Speer had no such illusions.

By now, Speer's control of the Nazi economy was as near to absolute as anything could be in the divide-and-rule organizational labyrinth that was the Hitlerian State. The reforms his predecessor Fritz Todt had initiated were in full flow, and combined with his own energy and ruthlessness were producing a miracle in wartime production. The results were astonishing. Despite the attentions of the bombers, almost every major category of armament reached its peak output in 1944; artillery went from 36,000 pieces produced in 1943 to 56,000 in 1944, panzers from 11,000 to 19,000, munitions from 2.5 million tonnes to almost 3.5 million, and aircraft manufacture leapt from 25,000 to 38,000.[25]

Just as with the flak artillery versus fighters debate, there has been much post-war discussion on the topic of the 1944 production upswing; were the likes of Speer and Milch as influential as they later claimed they were, or were the increases more the result of underutilised capacity in the economy than any reforms carried out? Was the emphasis on a few tried and trusted vehicle and aircraft types responsible for much of the bubble that would have burst anyway in 1945, as Allied technological advances leapfrogged the Wehrmacht's earlier edge? All valid issues worthy of debate, but somehow beside the point. In 1943, the combined Anglo-American bomber fleets dropped just under 200,000 tons of bombs on the Nazi empire, in 1944 that more than quadrupled to 887,000 tons, of which Bomber Command was responsible for the lion's share. Yet despite that deluge the German economy didn't break down, in fact it went up at least one gear, if not three or four. True, a sizeable proportion of that growth was delivered on the scarred backs of brutalised forced and slave labour, but the ordinary German citizen must also be given some credit for the achievement.

Some of those new fighters rolling off the production lines were the latest up-armoured and up-gunned Fw 190A-8/R7s. One of the units equipped with the new variant was Sturmgruppe IV/ JG 3 Udet, under the command of *Hauptmann* Wilhelm Moritz. Moritz, the son of working-class parents from the pre-war communist-supporting neighbourhood of Altona in Hamburg, was an intense, driven officer, who wasn't afraid to use his personal charm to get what he wanted. Walter Hagenah was one of his pilots. "Moritz ... used his influence to get his own way." What Moritz wanted in the summer of 1944 was an opportunity to show what his gruppe could do, and on Friday 7 July he was about to get it.

It was a beautiful summer's day across East Anglia, and 1,129 B-17 and B-24 bombers took off from their airfields and climbed to rendezvous with almost 800 fighter escorts as they crossed the North Sea. Making landfall in the Netherlands, the giant armada headed almost straight east, aiming for aircraft production and oil targets across central Germany, including Leuna. Luftwaffe ground controllers scrambled 374 single- and twin-engine fighters to meet them, including Moritz's Sturmgruppe and two accompanying Bf 109 escort groups under Moritz's friend, the cigar-chomping *Major* Walther Dahl. To try and avoid the escorts, who usually flew at the front and rear of the bomber formations, the Germans attempted the difficult manoeuvre of intercepting the bombers from the side, and then turning in to begin their attack run from behind. Walter Hagenah described the plan: "It would be a close formation attack from the rear, at the same level, to very close range ... the gruppe flew in two broad vees, the rear one was 1,500 metres back and higher up." It was a complicated manoeuvre, but it worked.

Getting within striking distance of the armada over the Saxon town of Oschersleben, Dahl's heart skipped a beat; an entire wing of Liberators was out of formation and unescorted. He immediately alerted Moritz, who began the attack. "Tanks were dropped at the last minute. After the turn-in for the approach, the leader [Moritz] assigned targets by staffeln." Now positioned behind the Liberators, the Sturm fighters opened up their throttles, chasing the bombers down like dogs after rabbits. The Germans closed in. "From 1,000 metres out, to within firing range, took about one and a half minutes." This was the worst time for the German pilots. Their weight made them slow, and close formation flying meant they were unable to take evasive action but had to fly straight and true into a hailstorm of lead from the rear-facing guns of the Viermots. It was an incredibly unnerving experience for the German fighter pilots to slowly gain ground on their targets, while at the same time see lines of tracer fizzing towards them at terrific speeds. Moritz, Hagenah et al were also at their most vulnerable to a sudden escort attack; fixated as they were on the bombers, they had no time to scan the sky and had to rely on their Bf 109 comrades and press on regardless. The key to the Sturmtaktik was to close to almost touching distance and then unleash a storm of firepower that would shatter the bombers in one approach, "second passes were very rare."

Moritz led his men in, braving the defensive fire until "the leader ordered 'Pauke, Pauke!'" A torrent of cannon and machine-gun fire engulfed the Liberators, and in moments a dozen of the 18 unescorted machines had either exploded in mid-air or were spiralling earthwards in flames. Hagenah's battle was over as soon as it started: "I made only one pass and was then out of ammo." Not so for his comrades in the escorting Bf 109s, who swung in to attack the main B-24 formation. *Oberleutnant* Kurt Gabler was initially ordered "to ward off P-38s", but on becoming separated he instead led an attack on about 20 B-24s in the Leipzig-Halle-Halberstadt area. Once again, there was no sign of escorts and the Germans attacked from the rear like their Sturm comrades. "We hit the heavies from an empty sky. Their tail gunners opened fire from 200 metres – too late." Gabler pressed home his attack. "In a few seconds we'd reached ramming distance, the [tail] gunners were silenced, and the sky was filled with columns of fire and parachutes." Friedrich Kowalke was a 17-year-old flak observer based just outside the city of Magdeburg. Kowalke and his fellow teenagers witnessed the Sturm attack:

> Suddenly the silence was interrupted by our special broadcasting system reporting on an air battle between Oschersleben and the Harz mountains. We searched the sky with our optical instruments and saw a macabre scene ... Some B-24s were in flames, while others were surrounded again and again by flashing projectiles. What had happened? *Hauptmann* Moritz had started a gruppe attack from six o'clock on the low-flying squadron ... with the result that all were downed.

In the aerial melee that was being fought out in the skies in the Leipzig-Oschersleben area, the Magdeburg gunners had front row seats, including to a remarkable feat of arms by Kurt Gabler:

> In three minutes my target exploded in the air and I was sitting behind another. The defensive fire was very strong but there were still no enemy fighters and our backs were free. By the fifth minute my next target crashed to earth in flames ... My fighter's effective fire left 20-25 parachutes in the air. Since I had ammunition left, I made a second pass with my wingman – *Unteroffizier* Franzel Knoll – and brought down a third bomber – three in less than 11 minutes.

Elated, out of ammo and low on fuel, he turned for home, his "nerves and strength exhausted". Dazed by the combat, Gabler forgot to lower his landing gear, "so my score read three shootdowns for one belly-landed Messerschmitt."

Günther Sinnecker was flying an escort Bf 109 like Gabler, but instead of scoring successes over the bombers he and his staffel "were hit by a heavy flak barrage over Leipzig and split in all directions like a spreading fan. Who wants to be shot down by their own flak?" Communications on the ground had become confused, leading to the gunners – although not Kowalke's battery – opening up on their own aircraft. To add insult to injury for Sinnecker, after his unit reformed "the American escort fighters engaged us in heavy air battles which led to large losses on our part." Sinnecker was one of them. "Baling out proved to be very difficult – the canopy was probably jammed by the shellfire. I pressed against it with all my strength and suddenly it flew away. I tumbled into the air and pulled my ripcord, which didn't let me down. Several swings of the pendulum, then I hit the ground near the crater dug by my aircraft." Utterly drained, Sinnecker collapsed under a "nearby bush that gave me shade. My body was soaking wet with sweat."

The German defence was hailed as a huge success by the Nazi authorities. Hagenah remembered that "The news called it *Blitzluftschlacht von Oschersleben* [the Lightning Air Battle of Oschersleben]." Young Friedrich Kowalke saw it reported the next day in the *Wehrmachtbericht*, the Armed Forces Daily Report, "especially as it was the first Sturmgruppe sortie which had shot down 30 Viermots." But by this stage of the war even a teenager like Kowalke was dismissive of official claims. "Such events were often used by Nazi propaganda to keep up the nation's morale." For once, however, Goebbels' hyperbole had more than an element of truth. In reality, the Sturm attack had only shot down 12 bombers, but the rest of the defending fighters and flak had added another 28 bombers and seven escort fighters to the tally.

A raid on the same by the American Fifteenth Air Force on oil targets in southern Silesia had resulted in another 27 bombers and three fighters lost, for a total of 67 heavies and 10 escorts lost on just one day. Losses on this scale back in late 1943 would have been a major setback for the Americans, but that was then. Now they were more or less shrugged off. German losses, however, of 25 dead aircrew and another 31 wounded, could not be accepted so readily, although the success of Moritz's attack encouraged Galland to order the formation of more Sturmgruppen. His problem now lay in filling the pilots' seats in the Focke-Wulf juggernauts, and to solve it, Galland had to employ more and more drastic measures.

A relatively easy first step was to switch trainee pilots away from the Bf 109 to Focke-Wulfs. *Unteroffizier* Ernst Schröder, for one, was only too willing to make the move.

> I couldn't see behind me in the Bf 109, and the all-round visibility was poor ... The rear-view mirror was near useless due to excessive vibration in flight, it lacked electrical equipment and the cockpit canopy was difficult to jettison ... the aircraft tended to swing on take-off or landing, and although experienced pilots soon grew accustomed to this, novices often found themselves brutally pulled to the left, which caused countless accidents.

Other trainees were pulled off their assigned specialisation and drafted into the day fighter force. Twenty-one-year-old Helmut Rix was one such individual. Having begun his training for the Nachtjagd, he was told that his new options were now either a conversion to day fighters or a transfer to Nazi Germany's famed paratroopers, the *fallschirmjäger*! Not exactly over the moon with either choice, he decided to stay flying, but quickly found that in training, "We were limited to five take-off and landings each day due to fuel shortages and Allied fighter activity."

While the likes of Schröder and Rix were welcome, there still weren't nearly enough pilots to fill the ranks, forcing Galland to issue a notice to the rest of the Luftwaffe:

> The strained manpower situation in units operating in defence of the Reich urgently demands the further bringing up of experienced flying personnel from other arms of the service; in particular for the maintenance of fighter power, tried pilots of the ground-attack and bomber units, especially officers suitable as formation leaders, will now also have to be drawn on.

Galland put his proclamation into action immediately, as the one-time Bf 110 pilot Johannes Kaufmann found out for himself.

By now an instructor training new crews on the Ju 88C-6 night fighter in Illesheim in Bavaria, he was surprised when Dolfo Galland arrived unannounced and "I was ordered to report to him immediately." The fighter general told the mystified Kaufmann to cease all training flights as of now, and recall any aircraft engaged on exercises. "[Galland] then quite bluntly informed me that our Ju 88 staffel was to be disbanded forthwith, and the pilots re-trained on single seaters for daylight fighter operations! This decision was a direct result of the deteriorating war situation ... all available resources had to be channelled into the defence of the homeland." Kaufmann wasn't unhappy about the unexpected news. "At least something was happening."[26] It was a signal, however, that the Nachtjagd was increasingly regarded as something of a Cinderella service, with daylight operations taking a bigger and bigger slice of the shrinking cake in terms of aircraft, crews and fuel. Peter Spoden understood why and was resigned to his fate. "There were far too many [bombers], we were outnumbered ... We couldn't do anything ... Our only aim was to shoot down as many Viermots as possible ... our feeling was to fight to the very end. I was a trained fighter pilot, it was my duty."

August 1944 was a month of beautiful warm sunshine across Europe, and the clear blue skies meant the tempo of American daylight raids did not slacken off. Oil and aircraft industry targets were now being repeatedly hit, with Speer's engineers and slave labourers working round the clock to try and repair them as fast as they were being damaged. German dispersal efforts were working well at mitigating the worst of the impact, although the added strain on the Reich's already overburdened transport system was proving a huge headache. The decision to move as much of Germany's vital industries as possible below ground, however, was not going well. There simply wasn't the labour, materials or necessary expertise to carry out such an ambitious programme, leaving much of the idea's promise unfulfilled.

In the meantime, the Third Reich was still in shock at the attempt on Adolf Hitler's life on 20 July by a coterie of Army officers led by the one-handed Claus von Stauffenberg. The fighter pilot Heinz Knoke was in a convalescent home at the time, recovering from a fractured skull sustained in a dog fight: "Attempt to assassinate the Führer! A wave of indignation sweeps through the German people … the ordinary German soldier regards the unsuccessful revolt as treason of the most infamous kind." Knoke was far from alone in his sentiment. Nazi censorship was indeed something to be feared, but there is no denying the innumerable letters, diaries, journals and notes written at the time that condemned the assassination attempt and denounced the plotters as traitors. The plot having failed, the Nazi authorities were now beginning to take their revenge, hunting down the conspirators and subjecting them to a series of show trials and gruesome executions, some involving slow strangulation.

The effects on Hitler of the July plot were quite marked. His physical health – already poor – deteriorated further, even as his grip on almost every aspect of Germany's war effort tightened. Always a commander who viewed the war overall as overwhelmingly a land battle, he was relentlessly focused on the Army and its daily travails. His interest in the Navy remained limited, and he was content to allow the Kriegsmarine to sail on without too much interference, leaving Admiral Karl Dönitz to direct the shrinking U-boat fleet, confining his interjections to half-hearted exhortations to sink more Allied shipping, and enquiries as to when a new class of 'super-U-boats' would come on stream. But his opinions on the Luftwaffe – already beyond exasperation – took a significant turn for the worse following his brush with death. With the American break-out from the Normandy beach head – codenamed Operation *Cobra* – a stunning success, the Nazi dictator swiftly planned his own counterstrike, believing that an armoured attack at Mortain in western France would cut off George Patton's rampant Third Army and deliver a shattering blow to Allied fortunes in France. He ordered the Luftwaffe to provide vitally needed air cover for Operation *Lüttich*, as it was called, to try and keep the marauding Allied fighter bombers – the *jabos* as the Germans knew them – away from the panzers.

It was a pipe dream. Luftwaffe strength in France had long been broken, and when all attempts to support the spearheads ended in bloody losses, Hitler only saw failure and not more burning wrecks and long casualty lists. The dictator's ire was directed at his deputy and one-time right-hand man, Hermann Goering himself. At one of his more excruciating daily conferences, Hitler rounded on the *Reichsmarschall*, furiously shouting that "The Luftwaffe's doing nothing, it is no longer worthy to be an independent service and that's your fault, you're lazy!" The Nazi 'man of steel' responded by bursting into tears and burying his head in his hands on the conference table. Once he had left the room, Heinz Guderian – the Acting Chief of the General Staff since the 20 July bomb plot – urged Hitler to replace Goering with someone more capable, but Hitler refused, telling the panzer general he couldn't shame his own designated successor in so public a way.

Goering had no such qualms about his own behaviour, however, and called a summit of senior officers from across the fighter arm at the Reich *Luftkriegsakademie* (Air War Academy) at Berlin-Gatow. Goering held these sessions occasionally, and they were known by one and all as *Areopags*, a Luftwaffe version of the ancient Greek *Areopagus* court of justice. Once assembled, Goering proceeded to harangue his subordinates as only he could. "I've spoiled you, I've given you too many decorations, they've made you fat and lazy. All that about the aircraft you've shot down was just one big lie … a pack of lies I tell you! … You didn't make a fraction of the victories you reported." Despite the straitjacket of Teutonic obedience to orders and deference to authority that kept the assembled men in their seats, it isn't difficult to imagine the thoughts of the vast majority of those present. One of the attendees – Macky Steinhoff – was perhaps a little understated: "… for sheer cynicism and arrogance he [Goering] outdid himself."

*Cobra*'s success led to the collapse and near-annihilation of the German Army in France at Falaise, and the subsequent Allied advance into Belgium. In so doing it robbed the Nachtjagd of its early warning systems and frontline defences. With the radar stations lost or abandoned and Allied fighters only a few minutes flying time away from the Luftwaffe's night fighter bases in the Netherlands, Heinz Schnaufer and Peter Spoden et al were all pulled back into Germany itself. From then on, Luftwaffe ground control's ability to track the night bombers and react accordingly was extremely limited.

With the Nachtjagd's ability to intercept the bomber streams severely impaired, Germany's flak arm became ever more important. Horst Hirche was already a teenaged apprentice in the Signals Corps in his home city of Berlin when he was transferred over to the guns. The 16-year-old Hirche was more bemused than afraid at his change in fortune.

In 1944 it wasn't only high school boys who were called up, but boys from technical schools were also enlisted in the anti-aircraft units. We were called up according to our birth year, so those apprentices who were born in 1928 were called up, and so were high school and grammar boys who were born in 1926 and 1927 ... Most of us already had some kind of military training because we'd been in the Hitler Youth. We were still rather surprised we couldn't finish our training or education but that wasn't possible because the regular flak personnel had been sent to the Eastern front.

His main annoyance was the lack of success he and his fellow crews were having: "The attacking bombers did suffer some casualties, and we had some hits, but very few." He was clear morale was still good, although it seemed to stem more from hope in miracles than anything tangible. "We weren't demoralised. We believed what we'd been told about the *Wunderwaffen* [Wonder weapons] that were still to come, that the war wasn't lost and to keep going. "[27]

Flak wasn't a one-way street and the bombers were happy to drop their payloads on the gunners who tormented them, as 16-year-old Heinz Riediger could attest after a night raid on Friedrichshafen in August 1944 hit his own battery.

At 'Berta' [name of one of the guns] the gun lay outside its revetment, the carriage up in the air. No-one survived there I thought. Smoke rose up at 'Cäsar', a bomb had torn open the revetment. A couple of powder-blackened and dirt-smeared figures were just appearing from the confusion. At 'Dora' a demolished barrel stood sadly. Nothing moved ... an almost unbearable smell of powder and blood was everywhere. The *Obergefreiter* stared at us with maddened eyes and kept moaning, 'Oh shit', and 'oh God, I'm sick, I want to die.'

Twenty-three of Riediger's fellow teenaged auxiliaries were killed in the bombing and another 34 wounded.

On 29 August, the American Fifteenth Air Force dispatched 599 bombers and 294 escorts on something of a routine attack on a number of targets in Hungary and occupied Czechoslovakia. On the ground, at the paratroop training school in Pápa in eastern Hungary, was the Danish Waffen-SS volunteer, Eric Brørup. Watching the bomber fleet overhead, he and his comrades were discussing the apparent ease with which the enemy could penetrate Reich air space, when

... a large number – perhaps 30 or 40 – of our own aircraft appeared and went straight into the attack. We could see the spent cartridge cases from all the gunfire glittering in the sun as they came down to earth. In the action three of the bombers were shot down. Then, one of the Messerschmitt 109s that had scored a victory flew over, waggled its wings and landed – it had run out of fuel. We half expected the pilot to be an ace wearing a Knight's Cross, but it turned out to be a 19-year-old private 1st class. Grinning from ear to ear he reported that it was his fourth victory in three weeks which would make his father – a test pilot – very proud. We invited him into the officers' mess and treated him like a prince.

The celebrations were interrupted by the arrival of a Hungarian officer. "Having full bomb loads on board, all the Ami aircraft shot down exploded on impact with the ground, but some crew members baled out and were picked up by the Hungarians." The Magyar officer asked if anyone in the para mess could speak English. Brørup put his hand up and was duly driven to the nearby barracks where the prisoners were being held. On seeing he was a member of the feared SS, the American aircrew were understandably concerned. "The Amis were very nervous when they saw the deaths head insignia on my cap, thinking they were in for it ... but I allayed their fears and said we were just fighting soldiers like them ... I told them they were lucky to have been picked up by regular soldiers, as baled out bomber crews were often torn apart by the inhabitants of the towns and cities they'd bombed if the civilians got to them first. Even our own airmen were issued with armbands saying *Deutsche Luftwaffe* to make sure they weren't killed by irate civilians if they were shot down over their own territory."[28]

Alongside the feted teenager that day, the under-strength Luftwaffe units covering the area benefited from a mix-up between the bombers and their escorting fighters that allowed the Germans to concentrate their attacks and shoot down 15 bombers in total. It was a victory for the day fighters opposing the Fifteenth Air Force, and a last hurrah. In yet another sign of the Luftwaffe's growing weakness, after the 29 August raid all the remaining day fighters facing the Fifteenth were withdrawn back to Germany to face the threat from the English-based Eighth Army Air Force. Czechoslovakia, Austria, Hungary and much of southern Germany were left undefended.

Early September brought a temporary respite for Germany in the ground war, as both the Anglo-Americans in the west and the Red Army in the east outran their logistics and were forced to halt until the necessary supplies could be brought forward. There was no such break in the air war, but the loss of France did free up the remnants of what had once been Goering's '1,000 fighter' host he had promised to deliver to the invasion front. In reality, the Luftwaffe had lost that many aircraft trying in vain to break through the almost impenetrable Allied air umbrella to reach the invasion front, but now the battle was lost Dolfo Galland had a 'big idea' as to what to do with the surviving units. Ever since the success of Walther Dahl and Wilhelm Moritz's Sturm attack on 7 July over Oschersleben, Galland had been ruminating on how to turn that one-off victory into something far more decisive.

His thinking was simple – if Dahl's 100-strong battle group could shoot down 40 bombers, what could a thousand, or two thousand, fighters achieve? He had discussed his ideas with Johannes Kaufmann when he saw him at Illesheim. "The General was planning to create many more new fighter units for the daylight defence of the homeland – a total of 2,000 operational aircraft in all." His reasoning was clear. "The American bomber streams that were now parading almost with impunity into the furthest corners of the Reich had to be stopped to give our forces and industries the necessary breathing space for the next round of the battle." Developing the idea, Galland calculated that a big enough fighter force could shoot down between four and five hundred Viermots in one go – roughly half the attacking force – while losing perhaps four hundred aircraft of their own, and maybe a hundred to 150 pilots killed. For once the losses would be acceptable for the Germans, and catastrophic for the Americans, causing them to suspend their attacks.

Galland christened his idea, *Der Grosse Schlag* – the Big Blow. With Hans Jeschonnek's successor, Günther Korten, dying of the wounds he sustained in Stauffenberg's failed bomb plot, Werner Kreipe was the Acting Chief of Staff of the Luftwaffe, and although he didn't get full-throated backing from the new chief for his idea, Galland got enough to go ahead with assembling and training his *Grosse Schlag* force whilst leaving the defence of the homeland in the hands of a relatively small number of fighters. Those few fighters would endure a torrid month.

On 20 August 1944, the Soviet Red Army invaded Romania, an Axis ally. Three days later, young King Michael, in a desperate attempt to save his kingdom from disaster, deposed Ion Antonescu as Romania's dictator, following which the new Government surrendered and switched sides. At a stroke, the German position in Romania became untenable. The next day Ploieşti fell, its myriad flak units unable to do anything but capitulate. Nazi Germany had now lost her largest source of natural oil. In the west, the Americans responded by stepping up their offensive against Germany's synthetic oil industry, hitting multiple targets at the same time and splitting up the defenders, as Johannes Kaufmann described. "The Americans were regularly sending more than a thousand bombers on raids over Germany, but they were rarely all aiming for the same target. More often than not the bomber stream would split into smaller formations, each with a screen of escort fighters, and attack different targets many kilometres apart."

The American attacks began in earnest on Monday 11 September. The oil plants in Ruhland, Chemnitz, Böhlen and Brüx were attacked by 384 B-17s, those at Misburg and Magdeburg by 396 Liberators, and 'Murderous Merseburg' by another 351 Fortresses. Over 700 escorts went with them. The Luftwaffe ground controllers scrambled every plane they had – 355 fighters. Having now very quickly converted to the single-engine Bf 109 – with exactly 22 hours and 46 minutes flying time in his Gustav – Kaufmann was one of them. "At around 0900hrs we received the first reports of large numbers of enemy bombers assembling over England." Taking off from Alteno field southeast of Berlin, the young officer followed his group commander, *Hauptmann* Friedrich Eberle, into the sky. On reaching altitude, Eberle then radioed Kaufmann: "Take over command, fuel transfer pump malfunctioning, am returning to base." A shocked Kaufmann acknowledged the transmission with the single word 'Viktor' – radio code for 'message received and understood' – and immediately contacted ground control for instructions. Kaufmann was now in charge of the entire group on his very first single-engine sortie.

Rendezvousing with the other groups over Finsterwalde, Kaufmann was relieved that the one-eyed Günther Specht was there to take the lead. The Germans then waited in a holding pattern. "The sun was almost full in our faces, and despite our excellent goggles its glare was extremely troublesome." Keeping a close watch on their fuel and oxygen levels, they scanned the sky for the incoming Americans, "but the minutes were ticking by … time – and our fuel – were getting dangerously short." Increasingly anxious that they had missed the bombers all together, Kaufmann was relieved when he heard the ground controller's voice over the radio "with the message we'd all been desperately waiting to hear; '*Dicke Autos* in front of you heading east.'" The former night fighter pilot still couldn't see them, but then "I gradually became aware of a myriad little pinpoints of light twinkling in the far distance – bright sunlight glinting off glass and metal!" Reporting the sighting to ground control, he "followed this up with a loud '*Pauke, Pauke!*' over the radio, warning the groups' pilots to prepare for imminent action". With the adrenalin building, he led all four staffeln "in a wide sweeping curve to get us into position behind and slightly above the Ami bombers, just as we'd been taught in training."

Now, with the enemy in front of him, all tension left the young flier: "I had my choice of targets from among the gently undulating mass of bombers now growing rapidly larger in our sights." He picked out a "formation of bombers flying a little lower than the main body of enemy machines" and which, crucially, "seemed to be devoid of fighter cover." Kaufmann led his men into the attack, "approaching in a shallow dive, we were closing in fast on the enemy." The Americans were waiting for them. "Muzzle flashes from the tail guns and upper turrets of the B-17s showed that they were already blazing away at us." Kaufmann held his nerve. "I waited until the range was down to about 200 metres before opening fire." The few brief bursts of cannon fire saw his chosen victim "slide away from its fellows trailing a thin banner of smoke". Then all was mayhem. "Bombers exploding in mid-air, others rearing up almost vertically before tumbling helplessly earthwards, torn-off wings spinning through the air, thick clouds of black smoke, stabbing jets of flame … blossoming parachutes – an absolute inferno!" The assault had spent Kaufmann's group, and there was no hope of reforming for a second attack, especially as now "we were under attack ourselves from a horde of American Mustangs that had suddenly appeared out of nowhere."

Low on fuel and ammunition, Kaufmann escaped from the melee and headed for home. Safely landing back at Alteno, Kaufmann was sure that "We'd succeeded in delivering the devastating blow to the enemy we'd hoped for," and that his own staffel "had reaped the lion's share, being credited with eight of the bombers during our opening pass". His group had indeed done well, and in total the Americans lost 46 bombers and 25 escorts on the day, but German losses were even worse. A third of the German fighter force was shot down and 79 pilots killed or wounded. Kaufmann admitted "We paid a high price for our success. Our group alone lost nine pilots killed and five wounded, and with many others having to bale out or crash-land, our losses in aircraft were even higher; 27 Bf 109s lost or written-off and another four damaged … our baptism of fire had cost us very nearly half our strength!"

As if to reinforce the point as to the differing regenerative powers of the Eighth Army Air Force versus the Luftwaffe day fighter force, the next day the Americans came again with 888 bombers and 662 escorts. The Germans could reply with fewer than two hundred fighters. Johannes Kaufmann's group went into action for their second ever mission. "Despite our catastrophic losses in men and machines we were sent up again less than 24 hours later." They were accompanied again by the Fw 190s of II.(Sturm)/JG 4, "but today we could barely muster 40 machines between us." Over Magdeburg, "We manoeuvred into an attacking position behind one of the bomber boxes." Unfortunately for Kaufmann and his comrades, "This time the escorting Mustangs were ready and waiting for us." The Germans attacked anyway, with Kaufmann's staffel having "just enough time for two quick passes, which netted us three *herausschüsse*" – shoot-outs, where a bomber was so badly damaged it dropped out of formation but wasn't yet destroyed. Kaufmann himself claimed one and "a young *Unteroffizier* claimed the other two." The cost was high once more, "Eight pilots killed, two wounded and 10 aircraft lost". The other German units lost an additional 34 pilots killed, among them the "the officer widely acknowledged as the 'father of the Sturm attack'", *Oberstleutnant* Hans-Günther von Kornatzki. Hit by fire from the B-17s he was attacking, he attempted an emergency landing in open country but hit some power lines and died in the resulting crash.

The Americans had also been hit hard – almost as hard as the previous day – but it was obvious to Kaufmann and his comrades that they could replace their losses and carry on regardless. Kaufmann was stunned: "For the second day in a row we had suffered 50 per cent casualties. How long could we go on like this?" A mathematics degree is not necessary to answer that.

Kaufmann wasn't the only one asking himself that question. Princess Margaret of Hesse and the Rhine – 'Peg' as she was known on account of her being British by birth – had married Prince Ludwig before the war, and she now lived in some splendour in the Schloss Wolfsgarten a few miles from the beautiful medieval city of Darmstadt in Hesse. The night before the 12 September US raids she had watched in horror as Darmstadt was "bombed and burnt to pieces ... we were in our dugout, the very earth shaking and plane after plane roaring over our heads. In about three quarters of an hour it was over, leaving between 6,000 and 8,000 dead (some say 20,000 but I don't believe that) and nine-tenths of the town burnt to the ground."[29] Bomber Command had used a new technique during the raid; the 226 Lancasters flew in several parallel streams across the city rather than just one, aiming to spread the bombing and increase the destruction rather than simply incinerate the centre. It was a success, and as the fires blazed some 220 fire engines with 3,000 firefighters were ordered in from across the region to try and check the conflagration. An eyewitness saw "burning people race past like living torches", while a survivor wrote that they "saw a man dragging a sack with five or six bulges in it as if he was carrying cabbage heads, it was the heads of his family - a whole family – that he'd found in the cellar." Bodies were fused together by the heat and had to be prised apart for burial using machine tools.[30]

After two consecutive days of American main effort raids on central Germany's synthetic fuel industry, the exhausted Luftwaffe day fighter force was desperate for a respite – they would be disappointed. If anything, the attack on Wednesday 13 September was even bigger, with 1,026 bombers and 603 escorts heading once more for Nazi Germany's vital oil installations. After two days of bloody losses, the Luftwaffe could call on just 137 fighters – not much over one third of what it had on the Monday. With a sense of dread, Johannes Kaufmann and the remnants of his unit were put on readiness. "For the third time in as many days, we received orders to take off and intercept the enemy." Looking across at the taxiways on his airfield, he could see that "The Group was only able to put seven aircraft into the air – a tenth of the number that had scrambled just 48 hours earlier." Luckily for Kaufmann and his comrades they failed to make contact with the raiders – less than half the Luftwaffe fighters did – and they returned to base unscathed.

*Unteroffizier* Robert Jung was one of the few who did make contact. Lifting off from Esperstedt "on a beautiful, cloudless autumn day", his unit took up position as top cover for the Sturm flights. Spotting the bombers and their escorts 1,000 metres above them, "we were seen well before we could make an attack." As the Mustangs dived down, Jung realised, "There were no clouds into which we could escape." His *Schwarm* was attacked by 11 P-51s, and he saw the Messerschmitt of one of his comrades explode. Desperately weaving and ducking over the sky, he "fought alone with four Mustangs for about 30 minutes. I shot one down but was eventually forced to crash-land in my Yellow 3 [his Gustav's callsign], which overturned." Badly wounded, Jung would remain in hospital until the following February. Of his group's 26 aircraft, only nine returned to base, with eight of his fellow pilots killed or wounded. The Americans lost another 48 bombers and 12 fighters – a tremendous victory for the Germans considering how few fighters actually made contact – but it was clear the Luftwaffe day fighter force was teetering on the edge. *Oberleutnant* Werner Vorberg had claimed his first and second victories, both Viermots, on 12 September, but saw little to celebrate. "The missions of 11 to 13 September cost us 38 pilots, including our *Gruppenkommandeur* [Kornatzki], and our 6th and 8th Staffeln had to be grounded."

For Johannes Kaufmann, the three-day battle over the oil sites "marked the end of Galland's ambitious scheme to bring a halt to the American daylight bombing offensive by delivering a series of knock-out blows from massed fighters". As far as he was concerned, "The Luftwaffe's overall loss rate was unsustainable. The task was beyond us. The dream was over." A clearly emotionally and physically drained Kaufmann can be forgiven for sounding somewhat apocalyptic, and the numbers were indeed gloomy to say the least. In three days, the American Eighth Army Air Force had lost 187 aircraft, three-quarters of them bombers, losses as great if not larger than the first and second Schweinfurt battles. Those battles had caused a pause to American attacks, but this time the bombers kept on flying and the armada on the last day was bigger than the first, whereas the Luftwaffe had dropped from a defensive effort of 355 fighters on day one to 137 on day three.

German aircraft losses were bad, but they were transitory to a degree. September would turn out to be the zenith of German aircraft production in the war, with 4,103 fighters built and 3,013 accepted by the Luftwaffe as meeting requirement. The bigger issue was pilots. A staggering 110 had been killed and another 47 wounded. Many, like Robert Jung, would be out of action for months, if indeed they were fit to return at all. The American training schools may have been turning out tens of thousands of pilots, Germany's were not.

The homeland did get a respite however – a whole fortnight – as Bernard Montgomery's 'A Bridge Too Far' Arnhem operation was launched in a blaze of glory, only to fall at the final hurdle. The American aerial response was to return to western Germany in force. Some 1,192 bombers and 678 escorts took off from eastern England on 27 September, with the B-17s aiming for oil and industrial targets in Cologne, Ludwigshafen and Mainz, while 262 Liberators headed for the Henschel motor transport plant at Kassel. The Luftwaffe ground controllers latched onto the latter force as their best chance of scoring a success and concentrated 111 aircraft in a single battle group to intercept the Liberators. As they began to vector the fighters in, they noticed one of the bomber groups was unescorted and out of formation. They immediately radioed the discovery to the gathering fighters, as Werner Vorberg remembered: "Twenty aircraft flew the mission in two attack wedges, with *Oberleutnant* Othmar Zehart – the day's formation leader – in the middle." Climbing rapidly, "the controller ordered us to make numerous course changes to avoid the escorts and finally led us to an unescorted Pulk of Liberators." The unit in question had become separated from its home formation by cloud and had mistaken the university city of Göttingen for Kassel. Opening their bomb bay doors, the lost fliers had dropped their payloads near the main railway station, causing minor damage and killing a handful of residents.

Vorberg's unit wasn't the only one in the sky. Having successfully converted from Bf 109s, Cologne-born Ernst Schröder was now flying "a standard Fw 190A-8 ... I'd nicknamed it *Kölle alaaf!* [Cologne lives!] in my local dialect." He and 29 of his comrades had scrambled from Finsterwalde where "we had an overcast sky and had to climb through a relatively thin cloud layer at about 1,500 to 2,000 metres to get at the Americans ... around 11am we were flying further and further west and the ground commander became more and more agitated and said we had to see the enemy planes in front of us. Indeed we did. We saw a large Pulk of B-24 Liberators at our altitude like a swarm of mosquitoes, flying right in front of us, going in the same direction." It was a target not to be missed – 37 unescorted Liberators – and Schröder's unit went after them, when "suddenly several of the Dicke Autos began to burn and plunge down in fire and smoke – even before we'd fired a single shot – a group ahead of us had already begun the attack. Immediately the sky was full of parachutes and wreckage and we were flying right into it."

It was Werner Vorberg and his comrades. "We flew from behind into the stream and split up to attack individual bombers. Whoever wasn't shot down had to be rammed. Flying from the back of the formation to the front we shot down planes, and crews from Viermots flying further ahead were baling out. Ten or 12 bombers exploded in the air, although they'd already dropped their bombs." Vorberg himself – an experienced *oberleutnant* – had led his rookie pilots all the way into the bombers and picked his target before pressing his own triggers. "Within minutes the bomber stood in bright flame, ablaze, burning, bursting apart, losing wings, debris and entire engines with which some of our fighters collided." The young officer's tactics ensured maximum damage to the bombers but weren't without risk. "We had collision losses due to the closeness when opening fire."

In the meantime, Schröder's unit had caught up with the bombers. "My *Staffelkapitän* and I had installed a new aiming device that included very rapid running gyros ... you could shoot precisely and accurately from a greater distance than before." Picking out a bomber, "Short bursts from my six guns chewed into its left wing, and even before I'd reached it both its engines on the left wing were already in flames. The bomber lurched downwards." He immediately spotted another opportunity. "I set my sights on a nearby bomber that was already smoking. My fire caused it to erupt in bright flames, which streamed to the rear as I hurtled past. I saw the bomber roll over on its back and plunge downwards."

Oskar Romm was a member of Wilhelm Moritz's group that day and was determined to make an impression. "I was in a good tactical position and attacked a flight of Liberators. Just like during my first victory over a Viermot over Oschersleben on 7 July, my approach was divided into three swift actions: I first fired at the fuselage to hit the gun positions and the cockpit, and then tried to set two engines on fire on one side. With these two engines burning, control was lost almost immediately, an aircraft hit in this way lost its flight stability and dove in a spiral over the burning wing." Romm didn't confine himself to a single bomber, instead "I first attacked the bomber on the left, then the one on the right, and lastly the leading B-24 of the flight. I then pulled up in a steep turn and watched all three B-24s descending in spirals, with pieces of their burning wings breaking off."

It was a massacre. In just five minutes 25 Liberators were shot down, another five were badly damaged and didn't make it, either crash landing in France or back in England. Only seven made it home, and most of those were damaged. Ernst Schröder had followed his two victories earthwards – "I wanted to confirm both their crashes" – although he was "forced to dodge parachutes and falling wreckage, shutting my eyes at times". Breaking through the cloud and flying as low as 100 metres above the ground, he saw "airmen running in all directions, some raising their hands in an apparent attempt to surrender to me". Elsewhere on the ground, Walter Hassenpflug heard

> ... the sound of the alarm sirens [which] meant the children were sent home from school ... we were outside and suddenly heard the sound of cannon fire. Seconds later the debris of an exploding aircraft dropped through the clouds into a wooded

area. Because it had a double rudder assembly we knew it was a B-24. Several airmen were floating to the ground ... four bodies were rescued from the front section of the wreckage.

Hassenpflug was 12 years old and already an expert at aircraft recognition. His hometown of Bad Hersfeld would itself escape the bombing, but his parents would both be killed in an air raid two months later while visiting relatives.

The almost complete annihilation of an entire Liberator bomber group was a major success for the Luftwaffe, and possible proof of the Big Blow concept, but even as the B-24s were falling in flames a cloud of escort fighters were racing towards them to provide cover. Arriving too late to save the bombers, they were nevertheless able to wreak revenge on the German fighters, as Werner Vorberg saw: "We attempted to escape in split-S manoeuvres, but the Mustangs arrived and hit us hard." Vorberg was raked by fire but managed to make a getaway. On returning to base "a wheel and its support fell off when I lowered my landing gear and I had to make a belly landing." Ernst Schröder was hit, too. "My Focke-Wulf took hits in the tail and my rudder pedals decreased in effectiveness. I then ran out of ammunition and had to evade by skidding and yawing." Romm, Vorberg and Schröder were, at least, experienced fliers, which was more than can be said for many of the other German pilots, as Johannes Kaufmann admitted. "Our fighter groups contained far too many inadequately trained youngsters who were ill-prepared for frontline service."

The upshot of this lack of proper preparation for combat was a clustering of the new boys around a small number of experienced pilots, which worked well in concentrating attacks on unescorted bombers, but when the Mustangs and Thunderbolts appeared it made for easy pickings for the qualitatively superior American fighter pilots, as one of them recognised that day. "When he [the German pilot] found out his attacker could stay on his tail, most of them baled out." The results for the Germans were serious. Vorberg's group had started with 20 aircraft that day. "Eleven machines failed to return, seven pilots including Zehart [the acting commander] were killed, and three more were injured."[31] Losses among the other groups were just as bad. For the other American bomber wings their only enemy that day was flak, meaning they could bomb their targets relatively unmolested, as a woman from Ludwigshafen told her husband at the front in a letter. "I'll describe to you how our hometown looks. The middle of Ludwigshafen is flat ... each successive attack is more terrible than the last. Horror and fear run through every street."

To add insult to injury, the following day's raids included the dropping of propaganda leaflets over Kassel and its surrounding area decrying the Nazi regime and its inability to protect its own citizens. Walter Hassenpflug remembered that "All local youngsters in the Hitler Youth, including me, were hastily called together to pick up the leaflets and burn them immediately."

Johannes Kaufmann's doom-laden prediction after the September oil raids had been disproved by the Göttingen battle, and Galland's Big Blow dream was still alive – but only just. The likes of Werner Vorberg, Oskar Romm and Ernst Schröder would have to hold the line a while longer while Dolfo built up his reserve fighter wings and filled their cockpits with fresh pilots. Pilots like Fritz Wiener.

When I joined JG 11 at the beginning of October 1944, I'd never flown the Bf 109 with the additional 300-litre belly tank, never practised take-offs and landings in formation, and I'd never fired the MK 108 cannon and MG 151 machine-guns with which my Bf 109G was equipped. Combat tactics, combat formation flying and combat manoeuvring in formation were entirely new tasks to be learned. All of this had to be done with severe restrictions on flying time because the gasoline supply was already very limited – even at combat units.

As Wiener struggled to master the techniques that would help keep him alive in the air, he suffered not one but two flying accidents that could have killed him. The first happened at altitude, when "The oil pressure went to zero and the cockpit filled with smoke." Forced to make a belly landing, he forgot the additional fuel tank was still attached and was lucky a barbed wire fence tore it off just before he hit the ground. Trees he hadn't seen sheared off his wings and the aircraft was a complete write-off. Miraculously, he walked away unscathed. The second mishap was again due to a loss of oil pressure, only this time the young flyer was able to carry out a wheels-down landing on a nearby airfield.

By that stage of the war half of all German aircraft losses were from accidents rather than enemy action. The vast majority of those accidents were the result of pilot error, with youngsters pitching up at their units with a couple of dozen flying hours at most – one-tenth of their opponents' average. Lack of fuel for training was the predominant issue, but almost as pressing was the simple lack of numbers. Between January 1941 and the D-Day landings, the Luftwaffe lost 31,000 aircrew to all causes, after D-Day that casualty rate dramatically increased, with another 13,000 lost up to the beginning of October. One German pilot wrote that "every time I close the canopy before take-off I feel I am closing the lid of my coffin." The American decision to free up their fighters from a close escort role, so they could range across Europe and actively hunt their enemy, was decisive. The Germans would end up losing 3,706 aircraft over Germany in daylight operations during 1944, and it was those well-trained, fit and fresh American fighter pilots who would be responsible for the lion's share. Little wonder that Fritz Wiener described how he and the other young pilots, "who had only a limited chance to survive in air combat, were massed as cannon-fodder".

As summer slipped into autumn and the nights grew longer, the Nachtjagd found itself with its back to the wall. Overall, it had never been stronger, with the number of night fighters now exceeding 1,300 – a number which would have been astonishing even a year earlier. But the figures were deceiving. There simply wasn't enough fuel for the whole service, and the loss of the early warning system across liberated France and Belgium was crippling. Aces like Helmut Lent, Martin Drewes and Heinz Schnaufer were still taking a toll on the bombers, but that toll was becoming smaller and smaller each month. In January 1944, Bomber Command lost 314 aircraft, in September that was down to 96, and fell again to 75 in October, when the number of sorties flown was at its highest in the war so far, at over 10,000. At the same time, Harris didn't let up for a moment, and city after city was relentlessly pounded. A teenaged flakhelfer recalled how the attacks terrorised the civilian population:

> We had to witness so many houses, not barracks or military targets, deliberately targeted. We saw how entire residential areas were bombed to the ground or were destroyed by fire or bombs. When we were called up, we felt it was our duty to do our utmost to protect civilians – women, children and older people. We were told it was our duty to shoot down as many enemy planes as possible. We had to fight against this bombing terror.

For Peter Spoden it was hugely demoralising. "We had battle fatigue and Germany was devastated, the cities in flames. We didn't regard this as a victory anymore, but as a necessity. To the very end we wanted to show the RAF that we were there and we were protecting our wives and children ... we just wanted to show them we weren't going to let them shoot everything to bits."[32] Increasingly – to conserve scarce fuel – only the Experten were sent up after the bombers, a decision which put those crews at even more risk. It seemed to suit some, with Schnaufer continuing to prove how deadly a night hunter he was, reaching the 100-victory mark on 9 October. His closest rival was the exceptional Helmut Lent, who had reached 110 victories – with 102 of those being nocturnal – almost a month earlier on 11 September. However, the pastor's son wouldn't add any more victims to his tally, accidentally flying into an overhead power cable on 5 October as he attempted to land on a temporary airstrip at Paderborn on the way to meet with his friend, Hans-Joachim Jabs. The ensuing crash killed all three other crew members on board, and Lent himself was severely injured, both his legs being badly broken. Rushed to hospital, the doctors refrained from amputation only to be forced into the operation two days later when gangrene set in. It was too late. Lent died on the operating table, too weak to survive the trauma. Posthumously promoted to *Oberst*, he was given a State funeral at the Reich Chancellery in Berlin on 11 October.

In an attempt to help redress the balance in the night war, Lent's comrade and former Wilde Sau pilot *Leutnant* Kurt Welter was carrying out experimental flights in a Me 262 to assess its suitability as a night fighter. In fact, trials of the new jet fighter had been going on since April, when *Erprobungskommando* ('test squad') 262 was formed at Lechfeld under the leadership of *Hauptmann* Werner Thierfelder to prepare the Me 262 for large-scale deployment across the day fighter force. After Thierfelder's death in July, Dolfo Galland appointed the Austrian ace *Major* Walter Nowotny to command the 40-strong group, moved it to Osnabrück and renamed it *Kommando Nowotny*. 'Nowy', as he was known, had achieved stellar success on the Russian front, becoming the first ever pilot to reach 250 victories back in October 1943, after which he was banned from operational flying to avoid the propaganda disaster that would have occurred had he been killed in combat. A friend of Paul Galland – Dolfo's younger brother – Nowotny was an exceptional fighter pilot, but there were some doubts as to his ability to carry out such a monumentally important task. Under his direction, trials progressed sluggishly, and it wasn't until August 1944 that the first operational missions were flown against the Allies.

This delay was important, given that the Me 262 may not have been a war winner – almost nothing could have been that late in the conflict – but it had the potential to be a game changer in the aerial battle over Nazi Germany. Its speed and performance at altitude were superior to any other aircraft, including the Mustang, and just as importantly the firepower it could bring to bear was phenomenal. The weaponry needed to destroy the colossi that were the Fortress and Liberator Viermots had turned the previously sleek and streamlined Bf 109 and Fw 190 into musclebound thugs, weighed down by cannon and gun gondolas that made them easy prey for the faster and more manoeuvrable American escorts. The 262 changed all that. A three second burst from a Gustav delivered 35lb weight of fire (almost twice the 18lb of the 1940 super trim Emil version), while for the Focke-Wulf it was slightly more at 37lb. The 262's figure was an incredible 96lb. A single burst from its Rheinmetall-Borsig cannons could rip a bomber apart, without sacrificing the speed and performance to take on the Mustangs. As one of the 262 fliers exclaimed with real satisfaction, "Flying this jet gave us young pilots the feeling that we were finally sitting in a superior aircraft."[33]

The former bomber pilot and Wilde Sau originator, Hajo Herrmann, believed the jet fighter was the answer to the Luftwaffe's prayers.

> The number of aircraft didn't matter anymore, what mattered was the genius of the inventors and the constructors. A thousand Ami fighters were no match for 10 jet fighters which dived straight for the bombers ... if all our fighter wings were equipped with the Me 262 it would mean the end of the American bomber attacks on Germany; its cities, its oil installations, its communications, and the factories that made its panzers.

However, even an optimist like Herrmann had to admit that due to a lack of fuel, "Our Me 262s had been towed by teams of oxen to their take-off positions, being switched on only when they got there." It wasn't just the operational trials that were slow either, so was production, with Speer's dispersed industrial system providing an element of protection for its assembly but hampering a move to mass manufacture. By the end of October 1944, only 265 jets had been built, and 30 of those had been destroyed by bombing as they sat in factory parks waiting to be transported to their flight units. The Luftwaffe hoped that a another 130 could be built in November and then 200 in December, but the programme was continually stalling as German industry suffered under the rain of bombs.

That deluge grew ever greater during October 1944. Raids on 3 and 5 October went largely unmolested by German fighters, but when the Americans returned to oil targets on 6 October, the Luftwaffe met them in force. Johannes Kaufmann was in action that day. "On the morning of 6 October came the by now all too familiar reports of enemy bomber activity. We were the first flight to cockpit readiness and then scrambled shortly after 1030hrs."

Rendezvousing with a Sturm group, Kaufmann's unit was "to provide top cover for the Focke-Wulfs ... but the escorting fighters were a little slow off the mark on this occasion, which allowed us to simply follow the Fw 190s down in the usual wide sweeping curve that put us into the ideal position for a stern attack." Speeding into the rear of the bombers, "The results were devastating. In the space of just five minutes the pilots claimed no fewer than 22 B-17s! ... our group added a further five bombers and two P-51s at the cost of two of our own killed." In reality, 20 bombers and six escorts were destroyed. Kaufmann's initial elation did not last long. "It was one of the last major successes we would score in defence of the Reich operations." The former Bf 110 pilot could be forgiven his pessimism – the American armada that day outnumbered the German fighters by an astonishing 16 to one.

Just over a week later, on 14 October, RAF fighters escorted almost a thousand aircraft from RAF Bomber Command on a raid over the city of Duisburg. A hub of industry in the Ruhr valley, replete with important centres for chemical, iron and steel production, Duisburg had already been extensively bombed in 1943 during the Battle of the Ruhr, and its old town was still a pile of ruins. Now, the RAF would widen out the bombing to encompass the city's residential areas as well as its industrial sites. Over 4,000 tons of high explosives and incendiaries were dropped, casualties were high and the damage significant. What really made the raid different though, was that it was carried out in daylight. The attack was codenamed Operation *Hurricane* and was designed to "demonstrate to the enemy in Germany generally the overwhelming superiority of the Allied Air Forces in this theatre". A German woman described her ordeal during the attack:

We had an early alarm about 6am, but no planes came. I stayed up and did my housework. At 9am a preliminary alarm came and then a full alarm almost immediately thereafter. My baby, who was only a few weeks old, was in his pram. I snatched him up and rushed to the cellar. The other people in the house were also in the cellar and there was much crying and praying because almost immediately large bombs began to fall directly on our part of the city.

In the makeshift shelter the men had to brace the timbers to hold up the walls and ceiling, and then knocked holes into the neighbouring cellars and "called out to see if the people in there were still alive". She recounted people's collective anger at the Nazi hierarchy for what they were having to endure. "They said we had to thank our Führer for this, the Party leaders had their safe bunkers and most of them were in Berlin."

The Duisburg raid was followed by almost two thousand American bombers and escorts hitting rail marshalling yards near Cologne, before Bomber Command went back to Duisburg that same night. Having stayed in the house all day and tried to get some sleep after the morning's nightmare, the hausfrau and her fellow residents heard the alarm go off again.

It came at about 2am, but it was too late to go to the bunker. We went to the cellar where again there was a fearful scene of crying and praying. After about 15 or 20 minutes there was a pause, my sister and I put our babies in our prams and ran to the bunker with our father. Phosphorus bombs were dropping and everywhere was in flames, while our father was shouting at us to hurry. Finally, I took my baby out of the pram and ran with him in my arms. By the time we reached the bunker, bombs were again falling everywhere ... I was completely exhausted and said I could never go through this again.

After the bombing finally stopped, they "got some soap from the NSV and also some food for eight days afterwards".

At the same time another 240 aircraft from Bomber Command were releasing their payloads on the ancient city of Braunschweig. Using the fan bombing technique pioneered over Darmstadt in September, and helped by diversionary raids that completely fooled the German ground controllers, Bomber Command had a clear run in and were able to cause immense damage. Hundreds of fires merged into one mighty conflagration that threatened to suffocate 23,000 Braunschweigers who had taken shelter in eight overcrowded bunkers in the city centre. Rudolf Prescher, a junior officer in the city's fire brigade, realised the danger and improvised a 'water alley' by cutting holes in multiple hoses that created an overlapping mist in the air. Keeping the water pressure constant this mist kept the worst of the fire at bay long enough for the fire teams to reach the shelters and get the civilians out. Their rescue was the only piece of good news to come out of *Hurricane* for the Germans. The operation's stated aim 'to apply within the shortest practical period the maximum effort of RAF Bomber Command and the 8th United States Bomber Command against objectives in the densely populated Ruhr', was achieved. Some 10,050 tons of bombs were dropped on Germany during *Hurricane*, the highest total for any 24-hour period in the war. Duisburg was shattered. Braunschweig burned for two days after it was attacked and was so badly damaged the RAF never bothered to go back. Total Allied losses amounted to just 29 aircraft.

While Braunschweig burned, Dolfo Galland's Big Blow idea continued to take shape. Large numbers of new aircraft were arriving at the fighter wings and there was even some fuel for training, albeit only a fraction of what was needed. Even the perpetually gloomy Johannes Kaufmann admitted Galland's plan "enabled my group to rebuild its strength" so that it once again "had an establishment of over 50 fighters; a mixture of the latest Bf 109G variants plus a handful of new Bf 109Ks". Although, true to form, Kaufmann also saw the downside. "But this was on paper. The reality in terms of serviceability was somewhat different." Nevertheless, Galland planned a major training exercise for his Big Blow units, and the date he picked was Thursday 2 November.

What Galland didn't know was that the Americans had decided to make November the zenith of their offensive against Nazi Germany's battered synthetic oil production sector. In fact, Leuna hadn't been attacked since 7 October, with Albert Speer believing his decision to mass huge numbers of flak guns around the mega-site the key factor in deterring the Americans. He would be resoundingly disabused of such a notion that self-same Thursday. That morning, 1,174 bombers and a staggering 968 escorts took off from their bases across eastern England and headed east for 'Murderous Merseburg' and several other oil plants. A teenaged German flak gunner saw them fly overhead. "We could see the trail of condensation and their silver tails shimmering in the sunlight ... we might as well have given up on the war there and then." With the bomber fleet flying a straight-line course, the Luftwaffe ground controllers quickly identified the central German oil sites as their targets. Galland had no option but to cancel his planned exercise and scramble 490 of his carefully husbanded Big Blow force.

Johannes Kaufman's unit was one of those chosen to fight that day, but serviceability issues meant "We were hard pressed to put more than half our 50 fighters in the air." Oskar Bösch's group would also fight that day, and the young *Unteroffizier* prepared to take off as his *Staffelkapitän*'s wingman. "We were told we would be defending the Leuna synthetic oil plant. It was a cold morning with dark clouds on the horizon."[34] Climbing away alongside seven of his comrades, Bösch sighted the bomber stream and, at 1230hours, "we were directed to a B-17 Pulk near Halle that had no visible escort." Hardly daring to believe their luck, the JG 3 group "turned in 1,000 metres behind it" even as they came under heavy fire as soon as the tail gunners saw them. In line abreast, the German fighters pressed on, relying on their bulky front armour to absorb the punishment. Flying alongside his leader, Bösch held his fire "until we were only 400 metres away", whereupon they released a devastating salvo that caused havoc among the bombers. "*Oberleutnant* Gerth [Bösch's leader] and I each downed a bomber." Flashing through the shattered formation, Bösch flew right, as previously detailed, to reassemble en masse for another attack. Then "the cry came, 'Indianer!' Red-nosed Mustangs were diving on us. We were outnumbered and abandoned any thought of a second attack." Throwing his Focke-Wulf into a "maximum speed spiral dive", Bösch managed to escape his pursuers, but had lost so much height that as he came out under the cloud deck he only "narrowly missed chimneys and roofs as I levelled off".

By now the guns around Leuna were throwing a torrent of steel and high explosive up at the bombers. A young flakhelfer saw a B-17 blown apart by a direct hit. "An aircraft door fell on the field in between our gun emplacements. Inside we found blood spatter and small scraps of meat. We laughed about it then. We were so callous as 16-year-olds." Bösch could see the refinery site from his cockpit and remembered "the area around the refinery looked like a battlefield, with numerous explosions and B-17s crashing all over." Frank Farr was a navigator in one of the B-17s that day, and he baled out of his burning aircraft before it exploded. After landing he was surrounded by curious but not unfriendly locals and was taken to a *Volkssturm* post, the Nazi Home Guard, where "a sympathetic soldier, several years older than me, took a cookie from his footlocker and gave it to me. He told me his mother, who lived in Hamburg, made it."

The battle that day over central Germany was one of the largest in the war to date. Losses among the bombers were high, one US flyer reported seeing "eleven out of 12 B-17s [in one wing] knocked out in one pass". In total, 42 bombers were destroyed along with 16 escorts, with as many as 500 bombers damaged to varying degrees by Speer's massed guns. But German losses were eye-watering. Seventy-one pilots were killed and another 31 wounded. The Luftwaffe lost 133 aircraft in the battle, including four new Me 163 Komet rocket fighters and one Me 262. Johannes Kaufmann's group suffered "three killed and two wounded, without achieving a single victory". The veteran pilot was thoroughly despondent. "Given the enemy's overwhelming numerical superiority it was almost immaterial whether we sent up 25 or 50 of our fighters in opposition." Galland's Big Blow force had taken a hammering, but the fighter general still believed it was Germany's last best hope.

Unfortunately for him, the 2 November raid had not had the sobering effect on the Americans that it had on the Luftwaffe's day fighter arm. Indeed, the bombers hit oil targets again on 4 November, the Vienna-Florisdorf refinery on 5 November, and Leuna once more on 6 November. Only 26 bombers and escorts were downed over the three days, most by flak. When Hitler heard of the Luftwaffe's losses at his daily situation conference on 6 November he went off on one of his by now frequent rants. Denouncing the Luftwaffe, he told those present that he had lost all confidence in the day fighter force in particular, and it was, therefore, "insanity to go on producing aircraft … [when] the hope of decimating the enemy with a mass deployment is not realistic." The Nazi dictator had never believed in the Big Blow idea, and his rage that day effectively killed Galland's plan, even though the Luftwaffe general didn't know it yet.

Murderous Merseburg was raided again on 8 November, and this time Walter Nowotny was determined not to follow orders and remain earthbound, but instead take to the skies. The Austrian Experte lined up with his wingman, Günther Wegmann, on the Achmer airfield and prepared for take-off, only to find his turbines refused to start. With Wegmann already airborne, Nowotny finally managed to start his engines and head off, opening the throttle to try and catch up. Two other Me 262s from Nowotny's unit had also been scrambled, but only one, flown by Franz Schall, had made it up, with Erich Büttner's suffering a punctured tyre during taxiing and left on the ground. All three airborne jet fighters were pounced on by escort fighters – of which there were 890 – and Schall and Wegmann were forced to break off after suffering battle damage. Nowotny pressed on alone, radioing in that he'd downed a Mustang and possibly a Liberator, before saying he had engine failure. One of his fellow 262 pilots, *Feldwebel* Helmut Lennartz, was back at base at the time and "*Feldwebel* Gossler, a radio operator with our unit, had set up a radio on the airfield. Over this set, I and many others listened to the radio communications with Nowotny's aircraft. His last words were, 'I'm on fire' or 'it's on fire'. The words were slightly garbled." Witnesses on the ground saw his 'White 8' fighter dive vertically out of the clouds and crash near Hesepe in Lower Saxony. After his State funeral in Vienna, Nowotny's jet unit was withdrawn from combat and expanded into a full wing.

Leuna then had a brief reprieve and wasn't bombed again until 21 November. Sheeting rain hampered the Luftwaffe response but did little to deter the Americans. As one German fighter pilot recalled, "The weather was not at all 'fighter friendly.'" Willi Reschke was flying a Focke-Wulf Sturm fighter that day, but like most of his comrades his unit was ordered to scramble too late to catch the incoming American bomber stream and instead "wound up trailing it". Flying in JG 301 – one of Galland's Big Blow wings – it was their first mission after three months off operations to rebuild. The escorts at the rear of the bombers spotted the Focke-Wulfs and attacked. "Casualties were high, especially among the inexperienced new pilots." Having trained for a tail approach, Reschke was dumbfounded when "*Hauptmann* Fulda attempted to lead the formation in a head-on attack." Needless to say, the skill required to attack head-on was way beyond the mass of German pilots by that stage of the campaign, and more than a few "broke away from the group and made a more familiar rear attack from slightly above". Reschke was one such pilot and recalled with quiet satisfaction that "my heavy armament did the job, and both inner engines of my target quickly burst into flames; the bomber dropped from the formation trailing thick smoke."

Reschke's victory was one of 33 bombers brought down, along with 15 escorts, but once again the story was about the Luftwaffe's losses and not the Americans'. Gerhard Hanf was a Fw 190 Staffelkapitän in JG 1 and was "hit in a dogfight with the Mustangs, but was fortunately able to make a smooth belly landing near Gotha." On returning to his group, he found that "of the 57 aircraft to take off, 26 were shot down and 15 pilots lost their lives. The 4. Staffel suffered the worst. Eight of its 14 aircraft were shot down and four pilots killed." In utter despair he wrote that "For many of our young pilots, some only 19 years old, their first mission proved to be their last. They were nothing but cannon fodder, as was the rest of the fighter force."

The damage done to Leuna that day was major, and even Speer's ruthlessness couldn't make miracles happen. Post-raid reconnaissance convinced the Americans there was little more they could do against the former synthetic giant, and it was only attacked twice more in the first half of December. By then, under significant pressure from the Air Ministry, Arthur Harris had taken over much of the responsibility for hitting the site, even while declaring it was a distraction. Bomber Command's reluctance to fully engage in the oil offensive was partly down to Harris's natural obduracy, but also partly due to the lack of information he was getting from the Air Ministry. Farcically, the Ministry was receiving regular reports from the top-secret Ultra code breakers at Bletchley telling them how dire the German fuel situation was, but they never thought to pass that information to Harris, hence why he thought the bombing of oil targets was an unnecessary diversion of effort.

Bomber Command's first foray to Leuna was launched on the night of 6 December and was primarily opposed by the installation's multiple flak batteries rather than the Nachtjagd, which had taken a beating in the previous couple of months, especially as more and more Mosquitoes accompanied the bombers as escorts. Frustration among the anti-aircraft crews was rife: "The American attacks had caused a shortage of shells, which meant not every flak gun could be used." Sent to collect more ammunition, one teenager "shouldered two shells and took this load back to our guns ... while the flames in the Merseburg-Leuna works blazed in the sky ... after this raid the Leuna works were so destroyed that – as we were later told – full production couldn't be resumed before the war ended."

Leuna was far from alone in having been reduced to a sea of craters and half-shattered buildings. Across the Reich, particularly in western and central Germany, city after city had been devastated. Heilbronn in northern Baden-Württemburg was typical; attacked some 20 times from 1940 onwards, most of the raids were small-scale and did little damage, but on the night of 4 December over 200 aircraft from Bomber Command appeared over the city and in 12 minutes dropped 1,254 tons of bombs. Over 80 per cent of Heilbronn's built-up area was destroyed and 7,000 of its residents were killed. The Nachtjagd tried to intervene, but "the order for take-off came very late." Helmut Bunje and his Ju 88 crew managed to scramble as the "the British markers lit up the sky." Opening the throttles to try and catch the bombers before they dropped their payloads, Bunje latched onto a Lancaster's tail. "The distance was still far too great, some 600 metres – but it had to be now." More in hope than expectation, he opened fire, only to see his first burst go low. "A corrected second burst appeared to show hits. Now, after a longer third burst – carefully aimed at the wing tank – its contents burst into flames! It burned!" Bunje's victory was one of a bare handful that night, the Nachtjagd increasingly unable to land blows of any significance on the bomber streams.

With the frontlines contracting back to the borders of the Reich itself, more and more German soldiers were brought face to face with the reality of their bombed-out homeland. The *SS-Leibstandarte* officer, Jochen Peiper, was ordered to help the clean-up of Cologne with his men after yet another raid. "A good number of them had lost their parents, their sisters and brothers during the bombing. They had seen for themselves thousands of mangled corpses after a terror raid had passed. Their hatred for the enemy was such, I swear it, that I couldn't always keep it under control." Peiper was not exaggerating. His men would infamously massacre unarmed American prisoners at Malmédy a few weeks later. Utilised as a clear-up crew once more – this time in Düren on the banks of the River Rur – Peiper's horror at the scene made him want to "castrate the swine who did this with a broken glass bottle".

Peiper and his men were not in western Germany at the time by accident. The elite SS panzer division was refitting to play a key role in Hitler's last gamble of the war in the West – Operation *Wacht am Rhein* (Watch on the Rhine), known as the Battle of the Bulge. The only major Wehrmacht winter offensive of the war, Hitler threw in his last reserves in an attempt to break through the heavily wooded Ardennes, recapture the port city of Antwerp, divide the British and American field armies, and score a victory that would even now turn the tables in Germany's favour. Every man, gun and panzer the Wehrmacht could muster was committed, and the Luftwaffe had to play its part. Dolfo Galland still harboured a faint hope his Big Blow could yet be landed on the American bombers, only to receive the order to send every fighter he had to support the new offensive. Demoralised, the Luftwaffe general wrote despairingly: "The Luftwaffe received its death blow in the Ardennes."

Gustav Rödel would no doubt have agreed with his fellow fighter pilot had he spoken to him at the time. Instead, he was in the air giving combat training to a few young pilots when they were jumped by roaming American fighters. "I wanted to give them a fight, but my young pilots didn't stay with me and broke formation. The Americans could see how inexperienced they were and zoomed in to pick them off one by one." In an act of almost suicidal bravery, Rödel tried to save his terrified charges by attacking the Americans to draw their fire. "It worked! Soon I had their full attention and they beat the hell out of me." Somehow, he survived what he described as "a game of cat and mouse" and when they abandoned the chase he made it back to base. After landing he "tried to conceal just how terrified I was, but my knees began to shake as soon as I climbed out of the plane."

Rödel's youngsters were the lucky ones, as Helmut Rix explained of his own first time under fire. "My introduction to frontline flying wasn't good, my fellow pilots and I hardly had time to meet before the 'scramble' order came through – eight out of my 10 comrades didn't return! Things were getting very bad, with shortages of everything. We newly trained pilots were supposed to get some flying experience before being sent into action, but that didn't happen. We were just thrown straight into combat."

The Nachtjagd, still home to some of the most specialised and highly trained aircrew in the Luftwaffe, were beginning to come apart at the seams too. In response to Hitler's demands to support the Ardennes offensive, 140 of its aircraft, Ju 88s and Bf 110s, were diverted to carry out night ground attack missions in the region. Albert Spelthahn was a radio operator in one of the Junkers, and he and his crew spent several fruitless nights flying up and down the frontlines trying to find a worthwhile target to engage. One night, after being fired on by enemy ground troops, "Franz [the pilot] pushed the machine down and returned the fire, letting go with tracer from our four guns." Everything seemed fine until "Franz shouted 'Jump!' I thought I hadn't heard him right, is he joking?" In seconds all three crewmen were out of the apparently undamaged aircraft and floating down towards the snow-covered countryside. Spelthahn landed safely and headed east to try and find German ground forces, only to run into an American anti-aircraft unit instead. Made a prisoner, he was reunited with his fellow crewmen, whereupon "Franz was able to tell me what had happened. Our elevator control lines had been shot through, and Franz had been left with no control pressure on his stick ... in no time at all we would have bored into the ground." Spelthahn was overcome with relief. "Franz had given the best order of his life."

Two German pilots who survived the Ardennes battle were Erich Sommer and Norbert Hannig. Both experienced veterans, Sommer was flying reconnaissance missions in December 1944 in the Luftwaffe's latest technological breakthrough, the Arado Ar 234 *Blitz*. The world's first jet bomber, the Blitz was a magnificent feat of engineering; fast, manoeuvrable, with a long range and able to carry a useful payload at height, it was developed far too late in the war to make any difference to Germany's fortunes, but on 21 December 1944 it saved Erich Sommer's life. Coming across "B-17 Fortresses with their massive contrails over my target area ... I turned for home and saw, high above me, four Mustangs diving towards my Arado. The first one made a half roll, followed by the second, then the third. The fourth hesitated. I pushed my throttle to full power and dipped the nose to pick up speed." By now this tactic had been abandoned by the Luftwaffe as the American fighter's superior speed in the dive had led to the deaths of literally hundreds of German fighter pilots. But the Blitz was a different beast from the Bf 109 and Fw 190. "I knew that the first three would have no chance of catching up, but the fourth was in a critical position ... I saw him levelling off behind me from his dive at about a thousand metres, but by then I was at full speed and he had no chance of catching me." Having lived to fight another day, Sommer arrived over his home airfield to a vista of destruction. "The previously pure white snow-covered field had been transformed into a dirty mass of craters."[35] Trying to find an alternate landing site, he ended up being shot down by German ground fire.

As for Hannig, he had served most of the war in Russia and was now tasked with "converting twin engine Me 410 pilots onto the Fw 190A-8" to fight the American bomber streams. On arriving "in Grossenhain on 18 December, we presented ourselves to *Hauptmann* Schlossstein as instructed." Hannig was horrified to discover that on their last mission, the *hauptmann* and his men had been attacked by "swarms of American Mustangs ... the twin-engine Messerschmitts didn't stand a chance. Fifteen of their number were hacked down, and only three crews – including his – returned from the mission unscathed." Hannig and his fellow instructor "could hardly get a word out of the other surviving pilots, and these were the people we were supposed to convert to Fw 190s so they could be returned to operations as quickly as possible." His verdict was sobering. "Such were the depths the German Luftwaffe had been reduced to by the end of 1944."[36]

Even Joseph Goebbels could no longer sustain the delusion of final victory – at least to himself. Writing in his diary, "We find ourselves in a situation of helpless inferiority and have to receive the blows of the English and Americans with dogged fury."

Meanwhile, in the continental United States 70 per cent of new pilot training programmes were cancelled. Washington no longer believed it needed another one hundred thousand pilots for the Air Force.

# 8

# 1945

# THE ENDGAME

"I was drafted into the anti-aircraft service as an auxiliary. I can still remember being in my father's study when he told me I'd been drafted. I remember my mother's despair and the clear realisation that this event had ended my childhood ... I had just turned 16." Wolfgang Kasak joined tens of thousands of other youngsters among the mass of batteries that were still trying to defend the Third Reich as the start of 1945. Another teenager trying to do his best was Horst Hirche. "None of the comrades I fought with were afraid. We had been trained to do our duty – it had been drummed into us in the Hitler Youth ... at the age of 16 we were all far too young and completely unaware of the danger we were in." Hirche and his comrades may not have been afraid, but they were still human, and to help keep their nerves under control the auxiliaries focused on doing their jobs to the best of their abilities.

On the guns every single person had to carry out a certain function, and this was checked and that was checked, and then reported to the anti-aircraft commander that we were ready to fire. He then had to report this up to the battery chief. At first the defences were covered with tarpaulin, but it was very heavy and hard to remove, especially if it was wet, so it was dispensed with as it wasted too much time ... we'd receive the first electronic and optical values from the main tower, we'd calculate the co-ordinates, the altitude, their timeframe and the guns were adjusted accordingly.

Before he saw them, Hirche could hear them. "As the bombers came closer there was an almighty humming noise in the heavens, the sound of a thousand aircraft ... We shot group fire, and if it was a large-scale attack we'd employ continuous fire ... we were covered in gunpowder smoke and steam, sometimes it was very difficult to breathe. When we had to fire continuously the empty shell casings lay all over the place."[1]

Hirche, Kasak, and the like, were now not complimentary to the Luftwaffe fighter force in defending the homeland but were instead the mainstay of the defensive effort. The losses among the fighter groups during the November oil raids had been compounded by the attempted support of the Ardennes attack, and if that wasn't enough the Luftwaffe launched Operation *Bodenplatte* (Baseplate) on New Year's Day 1945. Dreamt up by Goering, Bodenplatte's concept was simple; destroy the enemy's air forces on the ground in one mass attack when they were at their most vulnerable, with luck after the previous night's celebrations. Fritz Wiener remembered that "It was hoped the Allied aircraft would all be on the ground, nicely lined up, and present excellent targets for strafing attacks, and that the alcohol consumption during the News Year's Eve celebrations would have affected their defensive capabilities." *Oberst* Hanns Trübenbach recalled his feelings on hearing of the proposed mission. "At the turn of the year 1944/1945 the crazy order was given for all available German fighter units to attack the enemy air force on their European airfields and to destroy them in a single blow."

By now, Goering had lost faith in Dolfo Galland, and instead turned to *Generalmajor* Dietrich Peltz to execute the operation. Peltz, a bomber pilot, was a highly controversial figure in the Luftwaffe, and his close working relationship with Hajo Herrmann – another bomber pilot – was viewed with suspicion by the senior fighter leaders. Cast adrift, Galland spelt out his concerns about Bodenplatte to his long-time comrade and friend Johann Kogler: "He poured out his troubles to me, it was pretty grim." Regardless of Galland's misgivings, with the sky still dark, on the morning of 1 January 1945 over a thousand aircraft from 34 fighter groups took off from bases in western Germany heading for airfields across northern France, Belgium and the Netherlands. In an understandable but misconstrued attempt to maintain secrecy for the attack, the majority of pilots had not been briefed in the run-up to the operation, and with only a few minutes to prepare, were heavily dependent on their leaders to ensure they found their targets, which, with tragic irony, had all been former Luftwaffe airfields until liberated by the Allies. Even worse for the aerial armada, the planners had blundered by directing most of the fighters on a flightpath over the V2 rocket launch sites clustered around the Dutch city of The Hague – an area with the heaviest concentration of anti-aircraft guns on the Continent. Some batteries had been pre-warned the Luftwaffe was coming, some weren't, and some that were warned were not kept updated on changes to timings and so on. The result was a storm of flak and a quarter of the units taking part lost aircraft to friendly fire.

Otto Theisen was flying towards Melsbroek airfield near Brussels, when "our formation was met by heavy flak. Heinrich Wiese's machine received a direct hit. I saw a ball of flame on my left and knew our staffel commander had been killed." After enduring the massed anti-aircraft fire, several groups became disorientated, and while some hit their designated targets, others did not. At the Allied airfields, the German pilots found a mixed picture; at Eindhoven twenty-six RAF Typhoons were lined up on the airstrip like sitting ducks and smashed, while other bases had alarm flights in the air that thoroughly disrupted the German attacks. The Germans hope of undefended airfields was, as Fritz Wiener, realised, "wishful thinking".

By midday it was all over. The Allies had lost three hundred aircraft destroyed and an additional 190 damaged – even Montgomery's personal plane was a burning wreck. This was no small loss but given production numbers it would be a couple of weeks at most before these aircraft could be replaced. For the German fighters involved in the operation it was a different story. Bodenplatte was a disaster. Almost one in three of the aircraft that took off were shot down, but it was pilot losses that hurt the most; 214 were killed or missing, including a host of senior flight leaders, and dozens more were wounded. Hanns Trübenbach was left bitter by the debacle: "The greater part of the remaining German fighters and their outstanding leaders were sacrificed. As it was thought that a surprise attack could be carried out at low level, many of our fighter pilots were killed by our own flak!" Johannes Kaufmann – spared having to take part in the attack due to his attendance on a formation leaders course – was equally despairing. "Galland's carefully husbanded force was squandered on a costly low-level attack for no lasting gain and would never again pose any serious threat to the enemy … Bodenplatte sounded the death-knell for our fighter arm." As for Galland, he was clear that in going ahead with Bodenplatte, "We sacrificed our last substance." Perhaps he knew his days as commander of the Luftwaffe fighter force were coming to an end.

On hearing of Bodenplatte's failure, Hitler flew into one of his rages and told Galland that "the whole fighter force was good for nothing, that from now on we were only going to produce anti-aircraft guns and that all fighter production would be stopped." Goering sacked Galland on 13 January. That same day Macky Steinhoff and Günther Lützow – both friends and supporters of Dolfo – flew to meet with the one remaining senior Luftwaffe leader they believed they could trust, Robert Ritter von Greim. Greim was a fighter ace in the First World War and had further distinguished himself in various command appointments throughout the Second. Now, it was to him that the two desperate Experten appealed for help to remove Goering and try and save the Luftwaffe. 'Papa' Greim heard them out before turning them down.

I have served the *Reichsmarschall* faithfully all these many years. I believe in the Führer – and damn it I still believe in him, at least I try to … No, gentlemen, you're asking too much of me. I can't become a traitor, I just can't. Least of all against Hermann Goering. Do you understand that? I can't!

Crestfallen, the two fighter commanders departed, with Greim's warning that Goering was bound to hear of the meeting ringing in their ears. Steinhoff and Lützow weren't the only Experten determined to force some sort of showdown, with anger and despair at the situation – and especially at what they saw as Goering's culpability – rife among their peers. Discontent now became conspiracy, as Steinhoff explained. "For most of us the step to insubordination was quite literally appalling, but we had to take it; subordination had become more than we could bear." Four days later, in what became known as 'the Fighter Pilots Revolt', almost a dozen of the Luftwaffe's most highly decorated fighter leaders confronted Goering and demanded he resign. They further insisted that Galland be reinstated and the Luftwaffe's entire effort be turned to protecting the homeland from the relentless bombing. Goering was outraged. Shouting down their demands, he threatened them with court-martial and charges of high treason. The gamble was lost. Early that same morning, the teenaged flakhelfer Friedrich Kowalke was in Tangerhütte in Lower Saxony with his family. "We watched an RAF raid ... when we saw the illuminating cascades in the south we knew the city of Magdeburg was the target. The bombers left a wasteland of ruins."

In the aftermath of the failed mutiny, Goering posted most of the conspirators to various non-jobs across the crumbling Reich, ensuring they could not threaten his position. As for Galland, he took no part in the revolt, being under virtual house arrest at a retreat in the Harz mountains at the time. Nevertheless, Goering wanted his pound of flesh from the man he considered the inspiration for the mutiny. Dissuaded from his revenge by Hitler's fondness for the dashing airman, Goering instead offered him command of a new unit of Me 262 jet fighters – Dolfo accepted. His post as fighter general was taken by an old enemy, Gordon Gollob, while Dietrich Peltz – he of the Bodenplatte debacle – took day-to-day control of all homeland fighter defence.

In Italy meanwhile, the Fifteenth Air Force stood at a strength of 1,170 bombers and 630 escorts, and in England the 'Mighty Eighth' could muster 2,700 bombers and 1,200 fighter escorts.

Harris's Bomber Command was over a thousand strong. On Sunday 14 January, the Luftwaffe day fighter force reported it had 225 aircraft ready for operations.

As if to underline their superiority, the Americans chose that same Sunday to launch their first sortie in a fortnight. Some 348 Liberators bombed synthetic oil plants around Braunschweig, while 187 Fortresses went for the road bridges over the Rhine at Cologne. The main attack, however, was aimed at the Brabag synthetic oil refinery and Derben oil storage works near Magdeburg. The Luftwaffe ground controllers correctly assumed the Braunschweig and Rhine bridge attacks were large-scale diversions and concentrated their fighters on the 370 B-17s heading for Lower Saxony. The first Sturm attack was a success, downing nine bombers in quick succession, but then the escorts appeared and in a little over 10 minutes massacred the German fighters. The German fighter pilots were totally outclassed by the Americans, with a single Mustang group shooting down a staggering 56 Luftwaffe fighters. In one of the worst days of the war for the German day fighter force, 106 pilots were killed in all and dozens more wounded. By then, Norbert Hannig had returned to his unit in the East, and was sharing a billet with an old friend; Helmut Wettstein. Wettstein asked his roommate, "When do you think the war will be lost?"

By now, large numbers of Germans just wanted the horror to be over, but not enough, and they kept on fighting, killing Allied soldiers, sailors and airmen in great numbers. Bomber Command would lose 711 bombers in the first four months of 1945, and the American Eighth Army Air Force a gruesome 1,123. In the face of such bitter resistance the Allies had no choice but to go all-out to defeat the Nazis and end the war – to end the killing there would be a lot more killing. In fact, Harris's men would launch 24 night and 12 daylight raids and drop 181,740 tons of bombs in those four months, and the Americans even more at 188,573 tons, half as much again as in the whole of 1944.

American raids continued against oil targets and transport hubs, the latter now increasingly viewed as vital in paralysing German defensive operations. On Saturday 3 February 1945, the Eighth Army Air Force once more hit Magdeburg's synthetic fuel sites and also launched its largest raid yet on Berlin. Aiming for the city centre and the Government quarter, the Reich Air Ministry was badly hit, as was the Chancellery, Goebbels's Propaganda Ministry and the much-feared Gestapo headquarters on Prinz-Albrecht Strasse. A bomb also brought down much of the People's Court, killing Roland Freisler. Freisler was a rabid Nazi jurist who had sentenced members of the anti-Nazi student White Rose peace movement to be guillotined in 1943 and had presided over the show trials of the 20 July bomb plot conspirators. He was not mourned. Fires raged over two square miles of the city centre, and the teenaged flak gunner Horst Hirche saw two American aircrew land near him after baling out. "The people really hated the Allied bombers, they were very angry, they'd lost everything." The two airmen were frogmarched into one of the capital's flak towers, where "about 10 soldiers had to protect them from the people."[2]

In the tower at the same time was the Danish correspondent of Sweden's *Svenska Dagbladet* newspaper, Jacob Kronika. Kronika was sheltering from the bombing like everyone else and was astonished to hear Berlin housewives sitting alongside him loudly disparaging the Nazis for bringing this calamity upon them. Thirty-two bombers and 10 escorts were shot down – none by Luftwaffe fighters. Josef Goebbels initially claimed that up to 25,000 civilians had been killed, but the real figure was just under 3,000, with another 20,000 injured and 80,000 made homeless.

The Russians were now only 50 miles or so from the outskirts of Berlin, and with typical black humour Berliners were now calling their *Luftschutzräume* (LSR) air raid shelters *Lernt schnell Russisch* (Learn Russian quick). The young Waffen-SS officer – and son of Nazi Germany's Foreign Minister – Rudolf von Ribbentrop was in the capital visiting Kristina Söderbaum, an actress friend, at the UFA film studio in Grunewald where she was filming *Kolberg*, a Napoleonic war movie, with her co-star Heinrich George. The "weird situation turned into absurdity when the air raid sirens sounded ... as we watched hundreds and hundreds of Viermots as they flew above us to sow death and destruction somewhere."

Fierce fighting was still going on in parts of East Prussia and Pomerania, and an entire German army group were cut off in Latvia's Courland peninsula. Most of the cities and larger towns of the Ruhr valley and western Germany were little more than heaps of rubble; Arthur Harris was running out of places to bomb. One city that was still relatively unscathed was the capital of Saxony, Dresden. Described by the 19th-century German philosopher Johann Gottfried Herder as the 'German Florence' on account of its beautiful baroque architecture, high culture and artistic treasures, Dresden had already been bombed. On Saturday 7 October the previous year, 30 American B-17s dropped 70 tons of high explosives on the rail marshalling yards to the west of the Old City, killing 270 people. The Americans had come again just over four months later on 16 January 1945, targeting the rail yards near the Friedrichsstadt hospital, but both attacks were small-scale and shrugged off. One young resident went so far as saying that "before 13 February 1945 there hadn't been any air activity over Dresden, we had warning exercises but that was all." But the city's transport links – and primarily its rail yards and junctions – were clearly a draw for Allied bombing and they were to prove fatal for 'Florence on the River Elbe'.

The Red Army was taking enormous casualties as it pushed ever closer to the Nazi capital, and to aid its advance Moscow requested the Anglo-American bomber fleets prioritise hitting the Reich's remaining transport system to stop the flow of reinforcements and supplies to the east. It was a request that was readily accepted by both London and Washington, with neither expressing doubts as to the need for it. Dresden was regarded as an important link in the transport chain.

The city wasn't just a nexus for the west to east railway network via Prague, it also had a sizeable industrial base, including the large Zeiss Ikon plant in the city's southeast near the Great Garden Park, which had switched from making cameras to weapons sights. Nearby was the Seidel und Naumann factory, a pre-war manufacturer of typewriters and household goods that now employed almost 3,000 workers – mostly women and forced labourers – to churn out fuses for shells and ignitors for depth charges.

Nevertheless, Dresdners believed themselves safe from large-scale bombing, a belief in part based upon the beauty of their city. Karin Busch was a schoolgirl in the Saxon capital at the time and considered Dresden "a safe city, as we believed that culture loving people would never destroy a jewel like Dresden." Most residents thought the British and Americans were fond of the city – it was a popular tourist destination before the war – and there was even a widely believed rumour that Winston Churchill himself would personally spare the city because his American grandmother – Clara Jerome – had visited it and fallen in love with the place, imbuing her grandson with the same feelings. Some, like Liselotte Klemich, even speculated that "Perhaps Churchill had relatives in Dresden and that was the reason it hadn't been attacked." None of this was true.

What was true was that the city was ill-prepared for an attack of any size. Martin Mutschmann was the city's Gauleiter; an early convert to Nazism, he had joined the Party in 1922 and was rewarded for his loyalty with control of all Saxony. Nicknamed 'King Mu' by one and all, he was habitually seen in his brown Nazi Party uniform sporting all manner of decorations and gold braid, and perfectly represented the ordinary citizens disparaging term for all such party apparatchiks – *Goldene Fasane* (Golden Pheasants). An extremely keen hunter, he had been appointed the *Gaujägermeister* (Regional Hunting Master) before the war, and now lived in the opulent splendour of a luxurious villa stolen from its former German Jewish owners. He had personally overseen the persecution of Dresden's 6,000 Jewish citizens, and by early February 1945 there were fewer than 200 left in the city, almost all in hiding. Responsible for the city's air defences, he considered substantial, purpose-built shelters an unnecessary expense and instead encouraged cheaper alternatives.

The Dresden hausfrau Liselotte Klemich remembered her shelter was "very primitive, the exterior protection was a large box filled with gravel that stood directly in front of the window." Elsewhere, cellars in the Old City had been fitted out with old bits of furniture and bare light bulbs strung up on hooks in the walls, passed as fit for purpose. One Dresden schoolgirl remembered that "No proper shelters had been built. The only defence measures were buckets of sand." King Mu clearly believed – like most of his fellow Dresdners – that the city was almost immune from mass attack. However, that didn't stop him from ordering the construction of a specially built concrete bunker for himself and his family in the grounds of his stolen villa. He had tried to convince the city's parents to evacuate their children away from the city to supposedly safer rural locations, but just as in the rest of Germany, the evacuation drive was half-hearted, and most had drifted back. Now, with the Red Army not far away, there was no chance Dresdners would send their offspring east into imminent danger, or west when they saw for themselves a flood of refugees arriving constantly from the bombed-out cities of the Ruhr. Those refugees had helped swell the city's pre-war population of about 650,000 to close on a million by February, with thousands taking shelter with relatives or friends, or housed in temporary accommodation across the city.

Harris gave the order for a maximum effort raid on Dresden at his daily conference on the morning of Tuesday 13 February 1945. There was nothing unusual about the conference, the order, or the target selection. On Bomber Command's bases the crews went through their normal routine, received their briefings and were trucked out to their waiting aircraft, which had been fuelled and bombed up, and were sitting waiting to go. It was already dark when the first Lancasters taxied for take-off at 6pm. All together there would be 796 bombers on the raid, accompanied by a number of Mosquitoes, some as markers and others as escorts. The plan was to hit the city with two waves, the first composed of 244 bombers, followed by the remaining 552 a short time later. The bomber stream would be 120 miles from front to rear and would be over the city for 20 minutes or so.

At 9.40pm the city's air raid sirens, *die Fleigeralarme*, began to blare out, the sound an octave lower than the British alarm and sounding more like the end of a working shift than the British banshee. Dresden – like so many other German cities – had had false air raid warnings night after night for months, and as the weary citizenry trudged disconsolately down to whatever shelters they had for yet another wretched night's sleep, they half-expected to hear the all-clear of another false alarm at any moment. A teenaged member of the Hitler Youth busy directing refugees to their assigned temporary accommodation as they arrived at the city's main train station from the east remembered that "The sound of aircraft engines became audible." Finishing up their duty, he and a friend left the station and began to jog home. Looking up from the near deserted streets the two boys saw the Christmas tree target markers start to fall; the first ones were green and silver for illumination, and then came the red ones – these were bombing indicators. In another part of the city, a resident recalled, "You could hear the muffled hum of aircraft engines ... and then the first detonation of bombs."[3]

Twenty-three minutes after the alarm had sounded, at 10.03pm the first wave began to drop their payloads. As usual, those payloads were mixed. Most of the leading bombers dropped high explosives; the so-called 'blockbuster' or 'cookie' bombs, each around 4,000lbs in weight and about the same size as three grown men standing together in a huddle. Primed to detonate on contact, they could demolish entire blocks of flats with astounding shock waves. After them came incendiaries, dropped in clumps to fall among the damaged buildings and start multiple fires that would spread, link up and burn out of control. Karin Busch was sitting sewing a bag for a friend when she "heard a roaring noise. I didn't know what it was ... then all hell broke loose. It was terrible, absolutely terrible. We ran into the cellar, my mother grabbed two Japanese lacquer boxes, one had food in it and the other all our documents – and we ran down, my father and brother [home on leave] were both in uniform and began organising people."[4] Karin's nightmare had only just begun.

It was very hot and we heard all this noise, when suddenly a bomb fell into the cellar. It didn't go off but total pandemonium broke out and we tried to climb out. I tried to help my mother ... I lost my grip on her and she disappeared. Outside I was hit by an inferno of wind and firestorm. It was like looking into a huge burning oven.

There was drizzle that night coming in off the Elbe, but it was simply evaporated by the fires. Finding one of her brothers amidst the confusion, Karin and her sibling ran to the river, only to see people burn to death after throwing themselves in – wrecked boats on the river had spilled oil into the water. "There were bodies everywhere and the gasmasks that people were wearing [to protect from smoke inhalation] were melting into their faces." Brother and sister tried to find a cellar to hide in, but they were all full of corpses, suffocated by a lack of oxygen. "I looked around and saw the whole city in ruins. Everything, all the beautiful churches, everything was destroyed ... my brother had lost his sight from the heat, one eye recovered but the other didn't."

By now the second wave were overhead. One Lancaster crewman looked down in sick fascination and saw "blazing streets ... from east to west, from north to south, in a gigantic saturation of flame". Twice the size of the first wave, the second added hugely to the destruction. One Dresdner lucky enough to be in a shelter recalled how "The fire was so strong it blew open a steel door ... the walls trembled, even the ground under our feet seemed to tremble."[5] Ursula Gray, a young woman at the time, said "The only idea we had was to get out into an open space ... you had to make your way over stones and rubble and dead people and you just didn't care – you stepped on whatever you could just to get out and away from it all."

Then, it was over. "After the raid the city was just an ocean of fire, thousands and thousands of people killed, killed right beside us, around us, screams and smells. The most gruesome picture was the nakedness of the people killed by the bombing; the tornado or the air pressure of the bombs had apparently torn their clothes to shreds."[6] In the aftermath, Karin Busch and her sibling found their father and elder brother and went back to the cellar where they had first taken shelter. "Inside I saw a pile of ashes in the shape of a person ... I didn't know who it was, but then I saw a pair of earrings in the ashes. I recognised them. It was my mother." Lothar Lumm, a serving soldier home on leave, had fought in Normandy and seen the carnage Allied air power had wrought there, but thought that had "not been as bad" as what he saw in the shattered city.

The following morning, Dresden was shrouded in smoke and fires were still burning. The city's emergency services, drained after hours of frantic firefighting, were still struggling to deal with the effects of the raid. The zoo had been badly hit and many of the animals killed or injured. A few had found themselves momentarily free after their cages had been blasted open, and amidst the rubble a young giraffe was seen picking its way through the wrecked streets.

Just after noon, the drone of massed aircraft engines was heard once more. It was the Americans. The Eighth Army Air Force had dispatched 1,377 bombers to hit oil and transport targets across the Reich – Dresden was on the list. The Luftwaffe tried to respond, but in what the Americans described as a "strikingly weak and almost entirely ineffective" riposte, they could only put some 140 aircraft into the skies, and they were easily brushed aside by the 962 escort fighters. In truth, the Americans had originally been scheduled to attack the city the previous day, with Bomber Command then following on that same night, but bad weather had meant it was Bomber Command who hit first. As it was, the smoke and remaining cloud cover proved a real challenge for the bombers, and a quarter of them missed the city all together, accidentally bombing Prague instead. In the end, 311 actually found Dresden, and most of those bombed through the cloud with little accuracy. A nose gunner on the raid was somewhat mystified by the fact that "at the briefing we were told we were going after railroad yards, but my plane was loaded with firebombs."

The Jewish diarist and Dresden resident Victor Klemperer had somehow survived Nazi persecution and "heard the ugly hum of an aircraft above me coming rapidly closer and diving. I ran towards the wall around the Jewish quarter, threw myself to the ground, my head against the wall, my arm over my face ... I thought, 'Just don't get killed now!' There were a few more distant explosions then there was silence."

In something of a reprieve, Bomber Command didn't return that night. The next morning – Thursday 15 February – the glorious

*Frauenkirche* church, its beautiful 200-foot-high dome dominating Dresden's skyline since the 18th century, was obviously unstable; some of it glowing hot, while other pillars were cool to the touch – it was too much, and with a roaring crash it imploded. Around it, 75,000 apartments and houses in the Old City were gone.

Berlin sent Theodor Ellgering to take charge of the recovery. Ellgering was a close associate of Joseph Goebbels and had done similar jobs in Cologne, Hamburg and Kassel. On arrival he set out his top three priorities: providing food and clean water for the survivors, shooting looters and defeatists, and identifying and disposing of the dead. SS troops from as far away as Berlin appeared in the streets, and gangs of forced labourers were used for the worst jobs, earning themselves the nickname 'corpse miners'. If bodies couldn't be dug out, flamethrowers were used to cremate them in situ. Some 10,000 dead were identified and taken by truck to Dresden Heath, where they were buried in vast communal graves in the woods. Many others were stacked on metal shutters recovered from the shattered Renner department store and then burnt in tranches; once one layer had turned to ash, more bodies were added and the fire started again. The official German report on the attack – the *Tagesbefehl* (Order of the Day) No. 47 – wasn't issued until 22 March, and it stated that the dead numbered 20,204. Goebbels thought this too low for propaganda purposes, and simply put a zero on the end, claiming that the real total was actually 202,040. The reaction in Britain and the rest of the world was one of horror, and the bombing of Dresden was transformed into a controversy that has raged ever since.

At the time, the reaction was more muted. The war was still going on, and men were still being killed and maimed at the front. Bomber Command continued its offensive, as did the Americans. Joseph Goebbels despaired, pouring out his innermost thoughts in the pages of his diary. "The situation grows daily more intolerable and we have no means of defending ourselves against this catastrophe."

By now the Germans were desperate for some sort of respite – any respite at all. To try and stop the bombers Galland noted they had experimented with "dive bombing [the bombers], towing bombs on cables, parachute bombs, steel nets, hand grenades, very heavy cannon and other unusual methods of attack … but none were practical or effective … air to air bombing and rearward firing rockets were promising but came too late." *Feldwebel* Otto Schmid thought that such approaches were "the dreams of our higher command", and eventually "these things were put back in the mothball cupboard of our Mr 'Meier' [Goering]". Schmid and Galland were right, but there was one type of attack that hadn't yet been tried, and it was now an idea whose time had come. Back in August 1943, the much-lauded female test pilot and Nazi poster girl Hanna Reitsch met two friends of hers at Berlin's Aero Club, *Hauptmann* Heinrich Lange – a fellow test pilot – and Dr Theodor Benziger, head of the Aviation Medical Institute at the Rechlin Test Centre.

Talking over lunch, all three agreed the war was lost and Germany had little choice but to negotiate with the Allies to avoid annihilation, but they also agreed that any such talks could only be held when Germany was in a position of strength. The three believed the best way for Germany to achieve such a position was to cause mass casualties among the Allies, particularly their maritime forces. Lange and Benziger were so enthused by the idea that they authored a memorandum outlining the concept and circulated it to the Nazi hierarchy. "The military situation justifies and demands that naval targets be fought with extreme means like manned missiles whose pilot voluntarily sacrifices his life." Reitsch half-jokingly suggested calling it Operation *Suicide*. Nothing came of it, although Reitsch later claimed that there was significant interest in the proposal from a host of pilots who were only too eager to lay down their lives for the Fatherland.

Somewhat counter-intuitively, the naysayer for the idea of Germany's own kamikaze was Hitler himself. Content to preside over the murder of millions of innocents and the slaughter of millions more in combat, he was against German pilots committing suicide as a battle tactic. For the Führer to sanction the idea, the pilot had to have at least a chance of survival. Now, with their backs to the wall, planners in the Air Ministry revisited the Aero Club three's idea. At first, they looked at using specially built, lightweight aircraft which would be packed with explosives and flown into the daylight bomber boxes. The pilot would set a timer, and then have a few seconds to bale out before it exploded. An alternative idea was for a glider filled with explosives to be towed to a point above a bomber formation and then released. The glider pilot would then dive his flying bomb into the heart of the box and deliberately ram a bomber – after somehow baling out of course. Both ideas were designed to break up the bomber formation, allowing 'normal' Luftwaffe fighters to then attack and destroy the now-isolated aircraft. Albert Speer was alerted to the ideas doing the rounds of the Ministry and thought them preposterous. He went so far as to issue his own memo based on the Luftwaffe's manpower returns, which suggested that to achieve the required level of attrition each and every German pilot taking part would have to ram and destroy three American bombers – downing one each simply wasn't enough.

Nevertheless, in a sign of just how far the Luftwaffe had sunk, on 8 March 1945 Goering himself issued a written call up asking for volunteers to undergo "immediate flight training" for "an operation from which there is little possibility of returning". Several hundred candidates put their hands up and were given no more than 10 days training, before being assembled at Stendal airfield west of Berlin and formed into *Sonderkommando Elbe* (Special Commando Elbe). Once there, they were instructed that to bring down a Viermot they needed to ram any one of three specific areas: the tail section with its relatively delicate control surfaces, the engines, which were directly connected to the fuel supply, or the cockpit itself. They were also bombarded with exhortations from a host of speakers; Nazi Party officials spoke of the glories of the Reich and the virtue of Nazi race theory, Russian front veterans told them of the brutality of the Red Army and what awaited Germany if the Communist hordes took over, while other officials and witnesses described the destruction of Germany's cities by American bombers. In short, everything was done to fire up the volunteers to make the ultimate sacrifice.

On Thursday 5 April 1945, Luftwaffe high command gave the order to initiate Operation *Werwolf* as the suicide mission was christened. Some 188 Bf 109s were allocated to the barely trained pilots. Due to the dire fuel situation, and the requirement to put just enough aviation spirit in their tanks for a one-way trip, fuelling the 109s was going to be deliberately left to the last possible minute so the target bomber formation could be identified and marked.

On the morning of Friday 6 April, everything was ready. The Sonderkommando pilots were dispersed from Stendal to seven separate airfields where the Bf 109s were sitting, stripped of all guns bar one, and any other superfluous equipment. At the airfields, the ground crews and other pilots had not been told of the mission and were bemused to watch the arrival of the unbloodied youngsters, in their new uniforms, with hardly a decoration among them. Why were scarce Bf 109s being given to these boys?

Saturday 7 April dawned bright and sunny over the Reich, as predicted by the Luftwaffe's weather forecasters. In eastern England, however, bad weather delayed take-off for the Eighth Army Air Force, and it wasn't until 10.20am that the bombers began to lift off and head for a number of targets across northern Germany. These included an underground oil storage site at Buchen, a munitions factory at Geesthacht near Hamburg, and an Army ordnance depot at Güstrow. Across its airfields the Sonderkommando pilots were told that "after our daily routine of washing and shaving we were all to assemble in the breakfast room for a special last meal and a further surprise." *Unteroffizier* Werner Zell had spent a sleepless night thinking of what the day would bring. He had completed his elementary flight training back in June 1944, but due to a lack of fuel he'd never received enough fighter training to be posted to an operational unit. Now, alongside his friend *Obergefreiter* Horst Seidel, he would fly his first and last *Rammjäger* (Pile Driver) mission, as they were called. Zell, Seidel and the rest, were given one last pep talk by "some highly decorated officers in gala uniforms with Knight's Crosses around their necks", although Zell noticed that "none of them climbed into a crate later to go with us."

Incredibly, Zell thought that ramming an enemy bomber wasn't a death sentence: "We weren't kamikazes and had no thoughts of suicide." Indeed, even as he contemplated possible scenarios – "would our machines wedge into a bomber and take us to a deadly crash? Or, since the bomber would surely perform violent defensive movements, would we explode in a fireball with it?" – he believed it entirely possible, even probable, that they would either "escape our aircraft and land with our parachutes", or "make emergency landings in our disabled machines". This level of optimism is astonishing, especially when one considers that Zell intended to down a bomber by using his propeller as "a circular saw with many sharp teeth" to cut through "the right side of my target's tail assembly". Finally given the go order, Zell and Seidel took off. "The assembly point for the ram fighters was to be Magdeburg, from there we would be guided to the bomber stream."

The Elbe pilots had been told they would be escorted to their target by the 59 Me 262 jets of JGs 7 and 54. Given the jet's superior speed, they would take off 30 minutes after their charges and meet them in the air. It would seem this was a lie. The jet fighters would indeed be scrambled, but were seemingly not instructed to act as escorts, or even told anything at all about Operation *Werwolf*. The Sonderkommando would be on their own.

With their radios set to receive only, ground control played stirring patriotic music through the air waves, the Horst Wessel lied, the Deutschland lied and the Badenweiler Marsch. Perhaps more inspiring, given their objective, they also had a female announcer proclaiming them to be "werewolves of the air" and exhorting them "to think of Dresden and the other bombed cities, and the civilians dead in the carpet bombings".

Flying as a pair away from the main formation, Zell and Seidel managed to approach the bombers without being spotted by the escorts. When his first target took evasive action, Zell "left it alone, it had probably already jettisoned its bombs and was trailing a smoke plume." He then spotted a second and approached its tail with the sun behind him. "No defensive reaction, no defensive fire, it flew straight and level through the skies." Opening the throttle to maximum, Zell's 109 leapt towards the doomed bomber. At the very last second, "the tail gunner must have seen the approaching disaster ... he dropped his guns and put his hands over his face."

Hitting the tail assembly, "the impact was of such violence that I immediately lost consciousness." Zell came round still sitting in the cockpit and falling through the air. Unable to see how high he was, he tried to jettison the canopy and bale out, only to find the mechanism was jammed, no doubt from the ramming. Panicking, Zell was saved by an attacking American escort fighter. "Suddenly there was a rattle of bullets hitting the left side of the canopy and cockpit. The shattered canopy flew away and I was sucked from the cockpit." Badly wounded, he managed to pull the ripcord before passing out again.

There were other successful rammings that day. One Bf 109 downed Bill Howard's B-17, six crew managing to escape. Another 109 hit Arthur Calder's Fortress – both machines exploded and there were no survivors. In all, some 117 bombers were downed or damaged beyond repair that day, the worst losses since 3 February, but the cost was high. Forty-five of Sonderkommando Elbe's 109s were shot down or destroyed in the act of ramming, but amazingly, only 24 pilots were confirmed as killed, with five more wounded. Werner Zell was one of the latter, suffering a dislocated shoulder, broken collarbone, and multiple shrapnel wounds. Found by a local farmer and taken to a nearby hospital, he was still there two days later when the advancing British arrived and took him prisoner. Zell's friend was not so fortunate. "The body of my friend and wingman, Horst Seidel, was discovered some weeks after the end of the war on the southern edge of the Ostenholzer Moor. His parachute was unopened."[7]

According to the official American report into the day's operations, no-one thought the higher-than-normal number of aerial crashes was anything but the result of poor flying skills on the part of inexperienced Luftwaffe pilots. Without official recognition of the ramming attacks, there was no damage done to Allied morale, and given the high rate of loss and the imminent ending of the war, the Sonderkommando Elbe was disbanded and the whole idea shelved.

The Third Reich was now visibly shrinking day by day, with potential targets captured before the Allies' bomber fleets could take to the skies to attack them. On 17 April, Dresden was bombed once more, to ensure its use as a transport hub was curtailed. Two days later the Luftwaffe's day fighter force flew its last mission in any strength, with 42 fighters going up against 609 bombers and 584 escorts. The last US attack was launched on 25 April as American soldiers met and shook hands with their Red Army compatriots at Torgau on the River Elbe. Thereafter, Tooey Spaatz ended American strategic bombing missions across Europe.

For the Nachtjagd, March 1945 was a busy month. Heinz Schnaufer shot down two more Lancasters to take his tally to 121 and make him officially the highest scoring night fighter pilot in history, while Martin Becker destroyed an incredible nine bombers on the night of 14/15 March as they attacked a synthetic oil refinery. April saw large numbers of Nachtjagd bases overrun by the advancing Allies and by the month's end almost all of Germany's night fighter units had surrendered. In co-ordination with Spaatz, Arthur Harris suspended Bomber Command's strategic offensive on 25 April 1945. Only a few small-scale operations were flown after that. The last recorded German night fighter victory was claimed by Fritz Brandt on the night of 2/3 May – a Halifax brought down north of Hamburg.

The air war over Nazi Germany ended with the Third Reich's collapse.

# 9

# AFTERMATH

The campaign fought out over the skies of the Third Reich was a battle lost by the Germans. The cost of fighting it was huge. Precise figures for those killed, injured or made homeless vary, but the Federal Statistical Office in Wiesbaden calculated that 635,000 people within the boundaries of the Greater German Reich as was, were killed in the air and on the ground. The vast majority, some 570,000, were German civilians, but thousands more were foreign workers, forced labourers, and some were PoWs. For comparison, the Soviet Union suffered 250,000 civilian dead in German bombing raids, and Great Britain 60,000. In Germany, Berlin lost the most, 49,000, with Hamburg not far behind. The list goes on: Cologne 21,000, Magdeburg 15,000, Kassel 13,000, Munich 6,300, Bremen 3,500, perhaps the biggest surprise being Essen where only 6,500 died in one of the Reich's most heavily bombed metropolises. In all, 131 German cities and towns were attacked, with damage so great that 7 million people were made homeless in a country that was suffering a housing shortage even before the war. Almost every historical Old Town in Europe's largest country was erased.

After the war, a poll was conducted as to what the civilian German population thought the hardest part of the conflict to deal with was, and 91 per cent said it was the bombing. The Hungarian Jewish slave labourer, Agnes Erdös, was part of the clear-up in Bremen in November 1944 after one air raid: "A nice little boy, about three years old, came carrying a toy shovel in his hand. He was completely uninjured. He started digging in the cold pile of ruins. 'What are you doing I asked?' He replied quietly, 'I have to dig up my mother.' It had been four days since the bombing."[1]

Unsurprisingly, it was the Luftwaffe that almost exclusively fought the battle. They were Germany's youngest military service, and as such an entirely Nazi creation. The new kid on the block when the war started, they swiftly and ruthlessly became the most powerful tactical air force in the world. Thereafter, under-resourced, appallingly led from the top, and atrociously mismanaged, they were drawn into a battle of attrition that ground them to dust. In the 22 months from September 1939, when the war began, through the invasions of Denmark, Norway, Belgium, the Netherlands, France, Yugoslavia and Greece, plus the fighting in North Africa, right up to the invasion of Soviet Russia in June 1941, the Luftwaffe lost 18,533 aircrew killed, missing or wounded. In the 12 months of 1944 it lost 29,830, the majority of whom were in operational units, although 3,384 were killed in training accidents. Overall, Luftwaffe fighter pilot mortality rates hovered around the 90 per cent mark. After the war, when the celebrated RAF fighter ace Douglas Bader was invited to a Luftwaffe fighter pilot reunion in Munich by his old adversary Dolfo Galland, the famously acerbic Bader remarked: "My God, I didn't think we left this many of you bastards alive." Galland replied, "You didn't, most of these bastards were on the Russian Front. Come, I'll introduce you." Galland would break off a business trip to California to attend Bader's funeral service in September 1982.

Mistreated and mishandled by its own side, the Luftwaffe's day and night fighters were still a force to be reckoned with. Credited with destroying 70,000 enemy aircraft during the war – some 45,000 of which were Soviet – they, and their comrades in the anti-aircraft arm, caused immense damage among the Anglo-American forces ranged against them. Their most enduring enemy was RAF Bomber Command. Entirely staffed by volunteers, with recruits from dozens of nations, Bomber Command lost 55,573 aircrew killed – with 5,327 of those dying in training accidents – along with 1,570 ground staff, of which 91 were female. Another 22,000 were wounded and 11,000 taken prisoner. For comparison, RAF Fighter Command, who sacrificed so much in the Battle of Britain, lost 5,506 killed, wounded and missing during the war. Forty per cent of all Bomber Command aircrew didn't live to complete their first operational tour – half of those didn't survive their first 10 missions – a casualty rate far higher than for British infantrymen in the trenches during the First World War.

The Mighty Eighth lost 26,000 aircrew killed. Daylight bombing had cost them dearly – albeit their fighter escorts had butchered the Luftwaffe – and the average life expectancy of a bomber crewman in the first half of 1944 was just 15 sorties, not even close to a full tour that was initially 25 missions, then 30, and then finally 35 as the war ground on. The worst time was the first half of 1944, when for every 1,000 American bomber crew serving six months in combat, 712 were killed or missing and 175 wounded, a loss rate of 89 per cent.[2]

The air war over Nazi Germany may have ended in 1945, but the controversy surrounding it continues. For some, it was little more than a mass assault on innocent civilians, which at the same time destroyed a huge part of central Europe's artistic and cultural history. The one-time West German Chancellor, Helmut Schmidt, who lost his parents, grandparents and parents-in-law to the bombing, called the campaign "inexcusable". For those of a similar view, the attack on Dresden in particular has come to symbolise the inhumanity of the entire offensive. The *Daily Telegraph* reported on 17 February 1945 that 'The Allies have turned Dresden ... to ashes.' What the British newspaper didn't reveal to its readers at the time was that they were repeating a phrase the Nazis' Overseas News Agency had used in its own report on Dresden. One other interesting point of note from the *Telegraph* report was the German focus on the *Allies'* destruction of Dresden, and not just the British. Bomber Command had indeed played the major role in the attack, but the Americans had also joined in – indeed, only bad weather stopped their bombers from being first over the target. But it has been the men and women of

Britain's Bomber Command who have shouldered the burden of responsibility since the war's end.

The campaign's detractors also maintain the offensive was of limited military value to the war effort and point out that by mid-February 1945 the war was effectively over, and the destruction of any city, let alone an architectural jewel like Dresden, packed to the gunnels with fleeing refugees, was unnecessary and, for a few, akin to a war crime. There is though, one counter argument that is difficult to dismiss. The war may have been *effectively* over in February 1945, but it wasn't *actually* over. Hitler and the Nazi machine were still in power and being obeyed by the mass of the population and the armed forces; German soldiers were still fighting and killing British, American, Canadian, French and Soviet soldiers, as well as others from a host of allied countries.

Erich Dressler was a soldier in the German Army's elite *Grossdeutschland* Division and fought all over Europe and Russia. His parents were killed in the bombing.

> I reached our house in Steglitz [southwestern Berlin] and found only a heap of rubble. The neighbours told me my parents were still underneath ... after six days digging we found the unrecognisable shape of the body of an elderly woman. On the eighth day we found my father, I knew his clothes, and his spectacles were still grotesquely perched where his nose must have been. The woman may have been my mother. Anyway, I buried them in the corner of the park.[3]

Dressler fought on, supporting a regime whose Minister for Propaganda had earlier invented the word *Koventrieren*, meaning 'to devastate by aerial bombing'. It wasn't over until it was over.

Adolf Hitler – the architect of all the misery – consistently tried to avoid seeing the horror for himself. On the rare occasions he left the capital in his personal train, he would insist he returned at night when the blackout meant he couldn't see anything, or that the blinds be tightly closed. "[The bombing] actually works in our favour, because it is creating a body of people with nothing to lose – people who will therefore fight on with utter fanaticism."

In retrospect, the bombing of Dresden may look disproportionate, but context is all, and at the time it was simply another target, and one that an allied government – albeit a totalitarian one – had requested be attacked to help them advance into Germany and beat the Nazis. To prove the point, one week after Dresden Harris ordered an attack on the city of Pforzheim. Known as the 'Gateway to the Black Forest', pre-war Pforzheim had been a centre for the manufacture of ornate clocks and fine jewellery, resplendent with baroque architecture. It thrived in the 1920s because of the new enthusiasm for wristwatches. It was known as *die Goldstadt* (the Golden City). The industrial base now produced ammunition shell fuses and precision ordnance. Pforzheim's burghers believed they had escaped the worst ravages of the war, the city only having been bombed on a limited number of occasions, and never on a large scale.

On the night of 23 February Bomber Command hit the city with a main force strike. Just as in Dresden, a firestorm began that raged through the city centre and surrounding districts. Over 80 per cent of the city's buildings were destroyed and 17,600 people killed, one in four of the population. The Old Town and Market Square areas were particularly badly hit, the State authorities recording that the 1939 residency figures of 5,109 and 4,112 respectively had dropped to three and none after the bombing. Bomber Command itself assessed the attack as one that had "probably the greatest proportion [of destroyed built-up area] in one raid during the war." The Germans themselves glossed over the raid, merely describing it in an official Army report as "a forceful British attack".

A teenaged member of the Hitler Youth in Cologne during the war, Hugo Stehkämper grew up to become director of the city archives, and recalled how the bombing affected him. "A deathly fear, fear for your life, a fear that still haunts me today. Even after 40 years I cannot bring myself to watch a film about the bombings, it would rob me of at least three nights sleep. Those memories are still very real."[4]

# MAPS

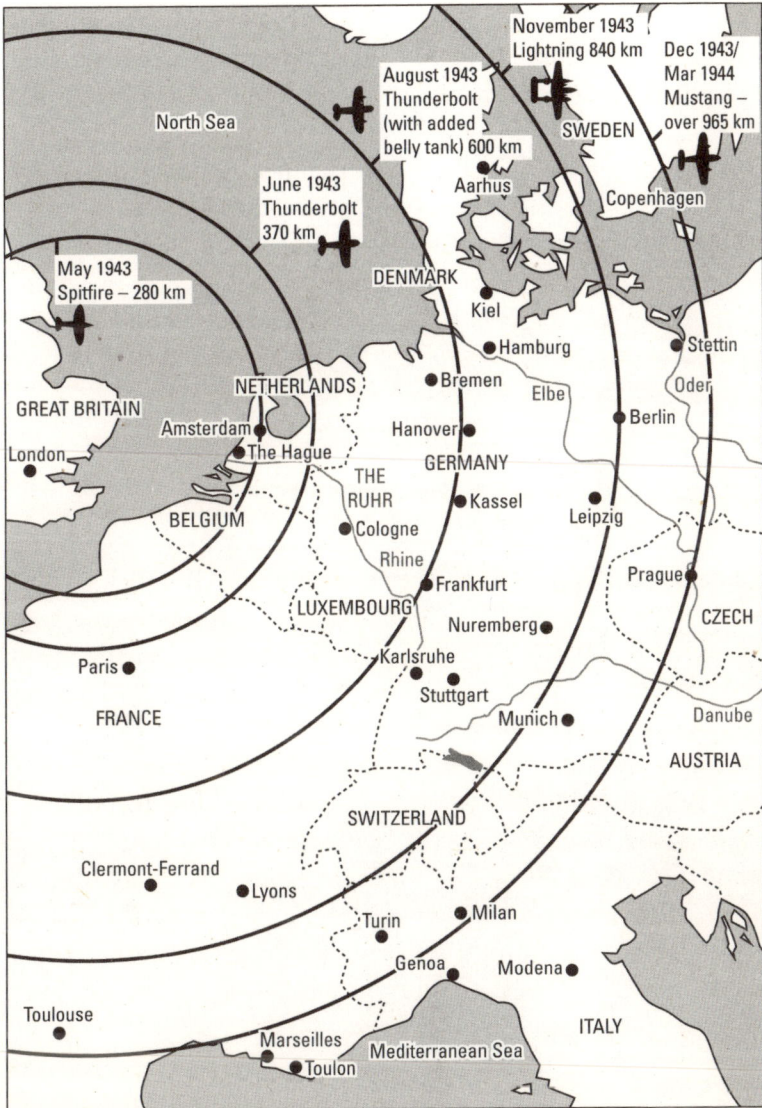

The ranges of Allied fighters during the Battle of Germany over time.

*Left*: The Kammhuber line was initially an effective night air defensive system employing a series of control sectors, or boxes. First, acoustic detectors and searchlights and then radar and searchlights would direct the night fighter allocated to the sector into visual range of the bombers. But the concentration of bombers flying through a few of the boxes – the bomber stream – resulted in those defences being (temporarily) overwhelmed by spring 1942.

*Below*: The bear approaches Berlin. *Time* magazine, 12 February 1945. Despite the bombing, he didn't just walk in. Nearly 80,000 Russian soldiers would die in the final push to take the city.

# Appendix A

# RANK EQUIVALENCES

| Luftwaffe | RAF | USAAF |
|---|---|---|
| Generalfeldmarschall | Marshal of the RAF | General (5 star) |
| Generaloberst | Air Chief Marshal | General (4 star) |
| General der Flieger | Air Marshal | Lieutenant-General |
| Generalleutnant | Air Vice-Marshal | Major-General |
| Generalmajor | Air Commodore | Brigadier-General |
| Oberst | Group Captain | Colonel |
| Oberstleutnant | Wing Commander | Lieutenant-Colonel |
| Major | Squadron Leader | Major |
| Hauptmann | Flight Lieutenant | Captain |
| Oberleutnant | Flying Officer | First Lieutenant |
| Leutnant | Pilot Officer | Second Lieutenant |
| Oberfeldwebel | Flight Sergeant | Master Sergeant |
| Feldwebel | Staff Sergeant | Staff Sergeant |
| Unteroffizier | Sergeant | Sergeant |
| Obergefreiter | Corporal | Corporal |
| Flieger | Aircraftsman | Private |

Hermann Goering held the rank of *Reichsmarschall*, a rank created solely for him by Adolf Hitler.

# Appendix B

# LUFTWAFFE TACTICAL UNIT SIZES

| | |
|---|---|
| Rotte | two aircraft |
| Schwarm | 4-6 aircraft |
| Staffel | 9-12 aircraft, usually commanded by either a Hauptmann or Oberleutnant |
| Gruppe | 40-50 aircraft, usually commanded by either a Major or Hauptmann |
| Geschwader | 90-120 aircraft, usually commanded either by an Oberst, Oberstleutnant or Major |

Unit sizes were not set in stone and could fluctuate significantly, for example a fighter Gruppe could comprise between 20 and 70 aircraft and a fighter geschwader between 50 and 150. It depended on their role and task at the time, overall Luftwaffe strength and ongoing casualties.

# ENDNOTES

## 1 *1939-1940: Round One to Germany*

1. Taylor, James & Davidson, Martin, *Bomber Crew*, p127.
2. Ibid, p52.
3. Ibid, p51.
4. Ibid, p56.
5. Steinhoff, Johannes, Pechel, Peter & Showalter, Dennis, *Voices From the Third Reich*, p80.
6. Walter Knickmeier would go on to become the most successful Luftwaffe night fighter controller of the war, taking part in the shooting down of eighty-eight bombers.
7. Carruthers, Bob, *Voices from the Luftwaffe*, p104. Heinz Philip, gunner on a Junkers Ju 88 night fighter.

## 2 *1941: Stalemate*

1. Galland, Adolf et al (edited by Isby, David, C.), *The Luftwaffe Fighter Force: The View from the Cockpit*, p171. Post-war interrogation of Adolf Galland, Heinz Bär and Walther Dahl, Kaufbeuren, Germany 20-23 September 1945.
2. Boiten, Theo, *Night War: Personal Recollections of the conflict over Europe, 1939-45*, p29.
3. Taylor, James & Davidson, Martin, *Bomber Crew*, p134.

4. Gordon, Iain, *The Night Hunter's Prey: The Lives and Deaths of an RAF Gunner and a Luftwaffe Pilot*, p174. Kreutz's article was entitled *Victory in the Night Sky*.
5. Ibid, p127.

## 3 1942: *The Tide Turns*

1. Evans, Richard J., *The Third Reich at War*, p329.
2. Bowman, Martin W., *Nachtjagd: Defenders of the Reich 1940-1943*, p62.
3. Taylor, James & Davidson, Martin, *Bomber Crew*, p177.
4. Holmes, Richard, *The World at War*, p299, interview with Frau Chantrain.
5. Ibid, p297.
6. Bowman, Martin W., *Nachtjagd: Defenders of the Reich 1940-1943*, p75.
7. Ibid p85. Hans-Heinrich 'Skittle' König lost the sight in his right eye and was taken off night fighters, but somehow persuaded his superiors to allow him to switch to day fighting. He fought the American bombers and shot down 28 of them before being Killed in Action during a bomber raid on 24 May 1944. He was posthumously decorated with the Knight's Cross.
8. Sweetman, John, *Schweinfurt: Disaster in the Skies*, p47.
9. Bowman, Martin W., *Clash of Eagles: USAAF Eighth Army Air Force Bombers versus The Luftwaffe in World War*, p13.
10. Holmes, Richard, *The World at War*, p301, interview with Albert Speer.
11. B Taylor, James & Davidson, Martin, *Bomber Crew*, p319.
12. Holmes, Richard, *The World at War*, p297, interview with Wilhelm Herget.
13. Galland, Adolf et al (edited by Isby, David, C.), *The Luftwaffe Fighter Force: The View from the Cockpit*, p171. Post-war interrogation of Adolf Galland, Heinz Bär and Walther Dahl, Kaufbeuren, Germany 20-23 September 1945.

## 4 1943: *Eighth USAAF and Bomber Command's Battle of the Ruhr*

1. Boiten, Theo, *Night War: Personal Recollections of the Conflict over Europe, 1939-45*, p71. Sergeant Angus Robb.
2. Stargardt, Nicholas, *The German War*, p345. Karl Damm was in the middle of his flight training in April 1945, when he and the rest of his course were marched to the front outside Berlin and used as cannon fodder to try and halt the advance of the Red Army.
3. Ibid, p348.
4. Atkinson, Rick, *The Guns at Last Light*, p360.
5. Cawthorne, Nigel, *Reaping the Whirlwind*, p57.
6. Holmes, Richard, *The World at War*, p304, interview with Albert Speer.
7. Cooper, Alan, *Air Battle of the Ruhr*, p112.
8. Williams, David P., *Nachtjäger*, p86.

## 5 1943: *Gomorrah*

1. Middlebrook, Martin, *The Battle of Hamburg*, p146.
2. Ibid, p147.
3. Hagen, Louis, *Ein Volk, Ein Reich*, p231.
4. Middlebrook, Martin, *The Battle of Hamburg*, p169.
5. Ibid, p205.
6. Taylor, James and Davidson, Martin, *Bomber Crew*, p295.
7. Holmes, Richard, *The World at War*, p303 – Ben Witter, Hamburg journalist.
8. Middlebrook, Martin, *The Battle of Hamburg*, p288.
9. Boyd, Julia, *Travellers in the Third Reich*, p394.
10. Middlebrook, Martin, *The Battle of Hamburg*, p380.

## 6 1943: *Battle of Berlin and Schweinfurt*

1. RAF Air Commodore Sidney Bufton.
2. Galland, Adolf et al (edited by Isby, David, C.), *The Luftwaffe Fighter Force: The View from the Cockpit*, p182. Post-war interrogation of Adolf Galland, Heinz Bär and Walther Dahl, Kaufbeuren, Germany 20-23 September 1945.

3. Mayer, Max, *Voices from the Third Reich*, p73.
4. Taylor, James and Davidson, Martin, *Bomber Crew*, p298.
5. Holmes, Richard, *The World at War*, p304. Interview with Albert Speer.
6. Cawthorne, Nigel, *Reaping the Whirlwind*, p51.
7. Carruthers, Bob, *Voices from the Luftwaffe*, p111.
8. Taylor, James and Davidson, Martin, *Bomber Crew*, p331.
9. Ibid, p209.
10. Hagen, Louis, *Ein Volk, Ein Reich*, p76.
11. Holmes, Richard, *The World at War*, p297 onwards – interview with *Major* Wilhelm Herget.
12. Bowman, Martin W., *Clash of Eagles: USAAF Eighth Army Air Force Bombers versus The Luftwaffe in World War 2*, p46.
13. Hagen, Louis, *Ein Volk, Ein Reich*, p267.

## 7 1944: *D-Day and Oil*

1. Cawthorne, Nigel, *Reaping the Whirlwind*, p58.
2. Johnen, Wilhelm, *Duel Under the Stars*, p110.
3. Taylor, James & Davidson, Martin, *Bomber Crew*, p21.
4. Boiten, Theo, *Night Airwar*, p129.
5. Hofmann, Willi, *Voices from the Third Reich*, p221.
6. Cawthorne, Nigel, *Reaping the Whirlwind*, p125.
7. Carruthers, Bob, *Voices from the Luftwaffe*, p104, Hannau Rittau.
8. Atkinson, Rick, *The Guns at Last Light*, p350 onwards – German flak was credited with destroying 6,400 Anglo-American aircraft in 1944 and damaging 27,000 others.
9. Eriksson, Patrick G., *Alarmstart*, p197. It is estimated that half of all American aircraft lost in combat over Europe were brought down by flak, and in total some 66,000 four-engine US bombers were damaged by flak.
10. McLachlan, Ian, *Eighth Air Force Bomber Stories*, p6.
11. Caldwell, Donald, *Day Fighters in Defence of the Reich*, p227.
12. Bowman, Martin W., *Clash of Eagles: USAAF Eighth Army Air Force Bombers versus The Luftwaffe in World War 2*, p128.

13. Boyd, Julia, *Travellers in the Third Reich*, p398.
14. Taylor, James & Davidson, Martin, *Bomber Crew*, p287.
15. Wilson, Kevin, *Blood and Fears*, p147.
16. Galland, Adolf et al, *The Luftwaffe Fighter Force: The View from the Cockpit*, p171.
17. Holmes, Richard, *The World at War*, p304 – interview with *Major* Wilhelm Herget.
18. Hermann, Hauptmann, *The Rise and Fall of the Luftwaffe*, p83.
19. Boiten, Theo and Bowman, Martin, *Battles with the Luftwaffe*, p138.
20. Ibid , p133.
21. Taylor, James & Davidson, Martin, *Bomber Crew*, p366.
22. Holmes, Richard, *The World at War*, p303 – the pilot who shot him down was RAF ace Branse Burbridge.
23. Arthur, Max, *Forgotten Voices of the Second World War*, p277. Flight Sergeant Norman Jackson of the RAF's 106 Squadron was part of a crew shot down over Schweinfurt on 26 April 1944.
24. Bowman, Martin W., *Clash of Eagles: USAAF Eighth Army Air Force Bombers versus The Luftwaffe in World War 2*, p174.
25. IWM, S363, Saur papers, *Auszug aus dem Leistungsbericht von Minister Speer, 27.1.1945*.
26. Kaufmann, Johannes, *An Eagle's Odyssey*, p192.
27. Taylor, James & Davidson, Martin, *Bomber Crew*, p417.
28. Williamson, Gordon, *Loyalty is my Honour*, p171.
29. Boyd, Julia, *Travellers in the Third Reich*, p402.
30. Atkinson, Rick, *The Guns at Last Light*, p360.
31. Caldwell, Donald, *Day Fighters in Defence of the Reich*, p374.
32. Taylor, James & Davidson, Martin, *Bomber Crew*, p363.
33. Fährmann, Gottfried, *Voices from the Third Reich*, p427.
34. Caldwell, Donald, *Day Fighters in Defence of the Reich*, p392.
35. Sommer, Erich, *Luftwaffe Eagle*, p164.
36. Hannig, Norbert, *Luftwaffe Fighter Ace*, p142.

## 8 *1945 – The Endgame*

1. Taylor, James & Davidson, Martin, *Bomber Crew*, p285.
2. Ibid, p368.
3. McKay, Sinclair, *Dresden*, p170.
4. Arthur, Max, *Forgotten Voices of the Second World War*, p403 – Karin Busch.
5. McKay, Sinclair, *Dresden*, p211.
6. Holmes, Richard, *The World at War*, p311 – interview with Ursula Gray.
7. Caldwell, Donald, *Day Fighters in Defence of the Reich*, p440.

## 9 *Aftermath*

1. Palm, Hakan O,. *Surviving Hitler*, p86.
2. Atkinson, Rick, *The Guns At Last Light*, p351.
3. Hagen, Louis, *Ein Volk, Ein Reich*, p76.
4. Stehkämper, Hugo, *Voices from the Third Reich*, p219.

# SELECT BIBLIOGRAPHY

Arthur, Max, *Forgotten Voices of the Second World War*, Ebury 2004

Atkinson, Rick, *The Guns at Last Light: The War in Western Europe, 1944-1945*, Abacus 2013

Baumbach, Werner (translated by Frederick Holt), *Broken Swastika, The Defeat of the Luftwaffe*, Robert Hale 1986

Beevor, Antony, *Ardennes 1944 – Hitler's Last Gamble*, Viking 2015

Beevor, Antony, *The Second World War*, Weidenfeld & Nicolson 2012

Beevor, Antony, *Berlin – The Downfall 1945*, Viking 2002

Bekker, Cajus (translated by Frank Ziegler), *The Luftwaffe War Diaries*, MacDonald 1966

Boiten, Theo, *Night Airwar: Personal Recollections of the Conflict over Europe, 1939-45*, Crowood Press 1999

Boiten, Theo & Bowman, Martin W., *Battles with the Luftwaffe: The Bomber Campaign against Germany 1942-45*, HarperCollins 2001

Boiten, Theo & Bowman, Martin W., *Raiders of the Reich: Air Battle Western Europe 1942-45*, Airlife 1996

Bowman, Martin W., *Clash of Eagles: USAAF Eighth Army Air Force Bombers versus the Luftwaffe in World War 2*, Pen & Sword 2006

Bowman, Martin W., *Nachtjagd: Defenders of the Reich 1940-43*, Pen & Sword 2016

Boyd, Julia, *Travellers in the Third Reich*, Elliot & Thompson 2018

Bullock, Alan, *Hitler: A Study in Tyranny*, Penguin 1962

Caidin, Martin, *Me 109*, Pan/Ballantine 1973

Carruthers, Bob (ed.) *Luftwaffe Combat Reports*, Pen & Sword 2013

Carruthers, Bob, *Voices from the Luftwaffe*, Pen & Sword 2012

Cawthorne, Nigel, *Reaping the Whirlwind: The German and Japanese Experience of World War II*, David & Charles 2007

Cooper, Alan, *Air Battle of the Ruhr*, Airlife 1992

Davies, Norman, *Europe a War 1939-1945: No Simple Victory*, Macmillan 2006

Eriksson, Patrick G., *Alarmstart: The German Fighter Pilot's Experience in Northwestern Europe*, Amberley 2017

Eriksson, Patrick G., *Alarmstart East: The German Fighter Pilot's Experience on the Eastern Front*, Amberley 2018

Ethell, Jeffrey L. & Price, Alfred, *Target Berlin*, Jane's Publishing 1981

Evans, Richard J., *The Third Reich at War*, Allen Lane 2008

Faber, Harold (ed.), *Luftwaffe – An analysis by former Luftwaffe generals*, Sidgwick & Jackson 1979

Fischer, Wolfgang (edited and translated by John Weal), *Luftwaffe Fighter Pilot – Defending the Reich*, Grub 2010

Galland, Adolf, *The First and the Last*, Blurb 2018

Galland, Adolf, Kammhuber, Josef and Messerschmitt, Willi et al, *Fighting the Bombers*, Greenhill 2003

Galland, Adolf et al, *The Luftwaffe Fighter Force: The View from the Cockpit*, Skyhorse 2016

Gordon, Iain, *The Night Hunter's Prey: The Lives and Deaths of an RAF Gunner and a Luftwaffe Pilot*, Pen & Sword 2016

Hagen, Louis, *Ein Volk, Ein Reich – Nine Lives Under the Nazis*, Spellmount 2011

Hannig, Norbert, translated and edited by Weal, John, *Luftwaffe Fighter Ace – From the Eastern Front to the Defence of the Homeland*, Bounty Books 2015

Hargreaves, Richard, *The Germans in Normandy*, Pen & Sword 2006

Harwood, Jeremy, *Hitler's War*, Quantum 2014

Hastings, Max, *Bomber Command*, Michael Joseph 1979

Hastings, Max, *Warriors*, HarperCollins 2005

Herrmann, Hajo (translated by Peter Hinchliffe OBE), *Eagle's Wings: The Autobiography of a Luftwaffe Pilot*, Guild 1991

Hermann, Hauptmann, *The Rise and Fall of the Luftwaffe*, Fonthill Media, 2012 (originally published in 1943)

Holland, James, *Big Week*, Corgi 2019

Holmes, Richard, *The World at War*, Ebury 2007

Holmes, Richard, *Battlefields of the Second World War*, BBC 2001

Holmes, Tony (ed.), *Dogfight – the Greatest Air Duels of World War II*, Osprey 2011

Hooton, E.R., *Eagle in Flames – The Fall of the Luftwaffe*, Arms & Armour 1997

Hozzel, Paul-Werner, *Conversations with a Stuka Pilot*, Verdun Press 2014

Jacobs, Peter, *Night Duel over Germany: Bomber Command's Battle over the Reich During WWII*, Pen & Sword 2017

Johnen, Wilhelm, *Duel Under the Stars: The Memoir of a Luftwaffe Night Pilot in World War II*, Greenhill 2018

Johnson, J.E. 'Johnnie' and Lucas, P. B. 'Laddie', *Courage in the Skies*, Limited Editions 1994

Kaufmann, Johannes (translated by John Weal), *An Eagle's Odyssey; My Decade as a Pilot in Hitler's Luftwaffe*, Greenhill 2019

Knappe, Siegfried (translated by Ted Brusaw), *Soldat: Reflections of a German Soldier, 1936-1949*, Bantam Doubleday Dell 1999

Knoke, Heinz (translated by John Ewing), *I Flew for the Führer*, Evans Brothers 1953

Lucas, James, *Kommando – German Special Forces in World War II*, Cassell 1985

Macksey, Kenneth, *Kesselring – The Making of the Luftwaffe*, Greenhill 2000

Mahlke, Helmut, *Memoirs of a Stuka Pilot*, Frontline 2013

McLachlan, Ian, *Eighth Air Force Bomber Stories*, Sutton 2004

McNab, Chris, *Hitler's Armies: A History of the German War Machine 1939-45*, Osprey 2015

McNab, Chris, *The Luftwaffe 1933-45, Hitler's Eagles*, Osprey 2012

Middlebrook, Martin, *The Battle of Hamburg: Allied Bomber Forces Against a German City in 1943*, Allen Lane 1980

Mitcham, Samuel W. Jr, *Eagles of the Third Reich*, Stackpole 1988

Mitcham, Samuel W., *Hitler's Field Marshals and their Battles*, Guild 1988

Murray, Williamson, *Strategy for Defeat – The Luftwaffe 1933-1945*, Chartwell 1986

Neitzel, Sönke and Welzer, Harald, *Soldaten*, Simon & Schuster 2012

Newdick, Thomas, *German Aircraft of World War II*, Amber 2020

Nowarra, Heinz, *Heinkel He 111 – A Documentary History*, Jane's Publishing 1980

Overy, Richard, *The Bombing War – Europe 1939-1945*, Penguin 2014

Price, Alfred, *Battle over the Reich*, Charles Schribner 1973

Price, Alfred, *Luftwaffe*, Macdonald & Co 1970

Ribbentrop, Rudolf von, *My father Joachim von Ribbentrop*, self-published 2015

Ries, Karl, *The Luftwaffe – A Photographic Record 1919-1945*, B. T. Batsford, 1987

Searby, John, *The Bomber Battle for Berlin*, Guild 1991

Sommer, Erich, *Luftwaffe Eagle: A WWII German Airman's Story*, Grub Street 2018

Spick, Mike, *Aces of the Reich – The Making of a Luftwaffe Fighter Pilot*, Greenhill 2006

Spoden, Peter (translated by Peter Hinchliffe OBE), *Enemy in the Dark: The Story of a Night-Fighter Pilot*, Cerberus 2003

Stargardt, Nicholas, *The German War: A Nation Under Arms, 1939-45*, Vintage 2015

Steinhoff, Johannes, Pechel, Peter & Showalter, Denis, *Voices from the Third Reich: An Oral History*, Da Capo 1994

Sweetman, John, *Schweinfurt: Disaster in the Skies*, Cox & Wyman 1971

Taylor, James and Davidson, Martin, *Bomber Crew*, Hodder & Stoughton 2004

Tucker-Jones, Anthony, *Hitler's Winter*, Osprey 2022

Westermann, Edward B., *Flak: German Anti-Aircraft Defenses, 1914-1945*, University Press of Kansas 2001

Williamson, Gordon, *Loyalty is my Honor*, Motorbooks 1997

# Other books by Jonathan Trigg

*Hitler's Legions series*

*Hitler's Gauls – The History of the French Waffen-SS*
*Hitler's Flemish Lions – The History of the Flemish Waffen-SS*
*Hitler's Jihadis – The History of the Muslim Waffen-SS*
*Hitler's Vikings – The History of the Scandinavian Waffen-SS*

*Hastings 1066*

*Death on the Don - The Destruction of Germany's Allies on the Eastern
   Front 1941-44* (nominated for the Pushkin Prize for Russian history)
*The Defeat of the Luftwaffe – The Eastern Front 1941-45; Strategy
   for Disaster*
*Vlaamse Jongens, Duits Front* [*Flemish Boys, German Front*]
   published by Davidsfonds (Netherlands & Belgium)

*Voices series*

*Voices of the Flemish Waffen-SS: The Last Testament of the
   Oostfronters*
*Voices of the Scandinavian Waffen-SS: The Last Testament of
   Hitler's Vikings*

*Through German Eyes series*

*D-Day Through German Eyes: How the Wehrmacht Lost France*
*VE-Day Through German Eyes: The Final Defeat of Nazi Germany*
*Barbarossa Through German Eyes: The Biggest Invasion in History*
*The Battle of Stalingrad Through German Eyes: The Death of the
   Sixth Army*

*The Provisional IRA series*

*Death in the Fields: The IRA and East Tyrone*

For more information on the author visit www.jonathantrigg.co.uk

# INDEX